Main Street Mystics

Main Street Mystics

The Toronto Blessing and Reviving Pentecostalism

MARGARET M. POLOMA

ALTAMIRA
PRESS

A Division of
ROWMAN & LITTLEFIELD PUBLISHERS, INC.
Walnut Creek · *Lanham* · *New York* · *Oxford*

ALTAMIRA PRESS
A Division of Rowman & Littlefield Publishers, Inc.
1630 North Main Street, #367
Walnut Creek, CA 94596
www.altamirapress.com

Rowman & Littlefield Publishers, Inc.
A Member of the Rowman & Littlefield Publishing Group
4501 Forbes Boulevard, Suite 200
Lanham, MD 20706

PO Box 317
Oxford
OX2 9RU, UK

British Library Cataloguing in Publication Information Available

Library of Congress Cataloging-in-Publication Data
Poloma, Margaret M.
  Main street mystics : the Toronto blessing and reviving Pentecostalism
/ Margaret M. Poloma.
     p. cm.
Includes bibliographical references and index.
  ISBN 0-7591-0353-4 (alk. paper) — ISBN 0-7591-0354-2 (pbk. : alk. paper)
  1. Toronto blessing. 2. Toronto Airport Vineyard (Church) 3.
Pentecostalism. I. Title.
  BR1644.7.P65 2003
  277.3'0829—dc21

                                                    2003007341

Printed in the United States of America

∞™ The paper used in this publication meets the minimum requirements of American
National Standard for Information Sciences—Permanence of Paper for Printed Library
Materials, ANSI/NISO Z39.48-1992.

For Kim
loving friend and faithful companion on life's journey

Contents

Prelude

Walking past the hotdog vendors stationed at the intersection of Attwell Drive and the church entrance a short distance from Toronto's international airport, I quickened my pace to catch up with the middle-aged couple walking ahead of me. After greeting them and commenting on the cold, snowy day, I asked them where they were from. "California," came the reply. The man quickly volunteered, "We arrived yesterday with a group of 25, including our pastor, from central California." From the friendly but brief exchange, I learned that theirs was a nondenominational fellowship of approximately 125 persons, and this was their first visit to the Toronto Airport Christian Fellowship (TACF). Moreover, the pastor had come to Toronto less than a month ago to check out the services, and on the Sunday of his return, a revival had broken out in their church. Nearly a quarter of their small congregation decided to make the pilgrimage across the continent to "soak" in the Toronto Blessing.

The couple and I parted as we entered the door to the entrance area just outside the main auditorium. I followed the sound of the worship band and entered the large room that once served as an exhibition hall. Most of the three thousand souls already gathered were sitting, but others clustered in small groups chatting or praying. Still others could be seen making last minute purchases in the bookstore at the entrance of the auditorium.

The auditorium was covered with worn carpet that fit well with its simple decor. On the wall over the balcony that lined the back of the room was a printed banner, "To Walk in God's Love and Then Give It Away"—the church's motto even before the onset of the renewal that revitalized the worldwide Pentecostal/Charismatic (P/C) movement. Filling much of the large platform at the front of the auditorium were the musicians, various musical instruments, and large amplifiers. A Plexiglas pulpit centered on the front of this platform completed the furnishings. A few ferns and artificial flower arrangements set on the floor of the platform added a bit of color to an otherwise colorless stage.

I stepped over a man who lay prostrate in the middle of the aisle as I made my way to the third row where a seat had been reserved for me. I noticed several other people scattered on the auditorium floor in what earlier revivals referred to as the "sacred swoon," but here in Toronto it had come to be known casually as carpet time. Just as I reached my seat, the music increased in both tempo and volume and brought a celebrative response from the congregation. Most rose to their feet and began to sing, sway, and dance to a familiar renewal song. Without a formal call to order, other pilgrims continued to talk, while others casually walked up and down the aisles looking for friends or a seat.

The music continued uninterrupted for nearly an hour as latecomers streamed in and joined the celebration. After about fifteen minutes, the celebrative sound of light metal gave way to softer and slower love songs to the divine. A few worshipers sat down, others knelt by their chairs, and still others gave way to the sacred swoon. The majority remained standing, most with eyes closed, enjoying what seemed to be a divine embrace. In time the music's tempo and volume increased to prepare worshipers for the next act of revival ritual.

An unnamed master of ceremonies (almost always one of the TACF pastors) ascended the platform and took his place behind the Plexiglas pulpit. As the musicians put away their instruments and worshipers sat down, the voice proclaimed over the microphone, "God is drawing us to fall in love with him again," to which the audience responded with shouts and applause. The impromptu welcome was followed by a query about the origins of the pilgrims, beginning with country and (in the case of Americans who usually made up at least one-half of the audience and Canadians who comprised one-quarter or more) the state or province. During the early years of renewal, generally twenty or thirty countries were represented (sometimes coming in planeloads from a single destination). This evening's count was twenty-six nations. The MC then went on to check the denominational composition of the audience. Although all major Christian denominations were represented, a slight majority of the pilgrims came from Pentecostal and neo-Pentecostal nondenominational churches. Approximately 30 percent of the congregation stood in response to a query about being a first-time visitor, a figure that has remained fairly constant over the nine years of renewal services and conferences.

After making a few pertinent announcements, the MC moved the service toward personal testimonies. He called out, "Is there a Bob here? I understand something happened to you outside." Bob, with the encouragement of his friends, approached the platform. "I injured my back in an accident years ago. Ordinarily I can't stand for any length of time, but I stood outside for an hour and a half. I don't know if my back has been healed, but I feel great! I didn't come . . ." His voice was silenced as he succumbed to the sacred swoon. Two members of the prayer team immediately sat down next to him on the platform, quietly praying over the prone man for the next half hour as the service moved on. The MC explained for the uninitiated, "When someone falls under the power of the Spirit, we like to keep praying for them and soak them in prayer."

The MC then called Wendy and Ron to the platform. Wendy began by sharing how she had always feared intimacy, but now, because of prayer at TACF, there was a new feeling of love for God and for her husband. Ron continued, "Wendy and I didn't know how to love each other. As we drew closer to the Lord, I got a new love for my wife. I had put my job before my family. I now have a new love for God that I never had before." The MC asked for a couple of "prayers" to join him on the platform to pray for Wendy and Ron. As soon as hands were gently laid on the couple, both fell into the arms of catchers standing behind them to guide their limp bodies to the floor where prayer continued.

The third person to give a testimony, a woman in her early fifties, came to the stage mildly shaking and jerking as she said, "I saw it all—I was slain in the Spirit, drunk in the Spirit, spoke in tongues." Her physical manifestations increased as she proclaimed, "God has touched me through this movement. He has taken away the fear that has haunted me for most of my life. All things pass away; all things become new. I have a fresh new love for the Lord." She fell to the floor before anyone was able to respond or pray with her.

Ken, a man in his mid-thirties, was then asked to give the final testimony of the evening. "Hi, Ken. I hear you just got blasted last night." Ken jovially responded, "I just took off my glasses. I know what's going to happen." Before he could say any more, he began shaking and laughing uncontrollably—and then "hit the deck."

Throughout the testimonies, some members of the audience were having their own experiences of jerking, shaking, and laughing while a few lay prone in the aisles. As a close to this section of the service, the MC explained how laughter and playfulness was a sign of the inner joy that was being given to people. He concluded by saying, "We don't want to focus on how you shook or how you fell down. The real issue is what the Lord is doing in your life."

The musicians were now in place to play another renewal song as plastic collection buckets were passed without fanfare through the congregation. By the time the collection taking was completed, most people were on their feet, singing and dancing in celebrative worship. Nearly two hours had passed, but hardly anyone seemed to be noting the time. Most would stay for another two hours or more before leaving for the night

John Arnott, the pastor of TACF, was out of town ministering to a conference being held in England. Jan and Byron Mote, copastors from Eagle Mount, Texas, were scheduled to preach this evening. As commonly done by speakers, Byron began with a narrative that would remind the congregation of the blessed time in which they were living. This account was focused on healing through laughter, involving a pastor and his mother from Dallas, Texas. The pastor's mother had been scheduled for triple bypass surgery and went into a deep depression for three days before the scheduled surgery. During this time, the pastor flipped on a television program in which evangelist Rodney Howard-Browne (often dubbed "God's bartender" because of the spiritual intoxication occurring at his services) was speaking. Both the pastor and his wife were overcome with "holy laughter" and prayed for the spirit of laughter to fill his mother. The next morning before the scheduled surgery, they entered his mother's hospital room to find that her deep depression had lifted. Another miracle was yet to come. During the surgery, the doctors found her to "have the heart of an 18-year-old." The prayer for the "spirit of laughter" was also answered. The pastor's mother started laughing while still in the recovery room. "She was totally healed," proclaimed Mote.

Mote then began to speak about how God is romancing the church during the renewal: "My church had been in a dating relationship with God for years. God is saying to us, 'I want to get out of the dating relationship. I want a bride.'" Jan Mote approached the center of the platform and opened her Bible to read from the first chapter of the Song of Songs: "My lover is mine and I am his; he browses among the lilies." As she continued to read, laughter began to break out in pockets of the gathering, gathering momentum until it filled the auditorium.

I had been watching the couple in front of me throughout the service. The wife had been engaged in holy laughter earlier in the service, while the husband sat stone-faced, frequently looking around the room. Now both were clinging to each other and laughing uncontrollably. The elderly couple sitting next to me was also laughing heartily while Jan continued to read: "I will search for the one my heart loves. So I looked for him but I did not find him. The watchmen found me as they made their rounds in the city. 'Have you seen the one my heart loves?'"

Eventually Jan and Byron began to bless the laughter. As they did so, Byron got a "word" about a healing God was doing. "Three pastors are here who are desperate—coming to TACF was the last stop before throwing in the towel of ministry." The congregation joined the Motes in prayer for these unnamed pastors.

The outbreaks of laughter continued to gather momentum. Mote proclaimed, "God is throwing one major party." He then opened to the first chapter of Luke, seeming to begin a sermon about Mary, the mother of Jesus. As people continued laughing throughout the auditorium, Mote's speech became slurred. "The Virgin had no attachments to the world," he said haltingly, "when she was betrothed to a man from the house of David." He sat down trying to gain composure, looking like a drunk struggling to keep from falling off the bar stool. Mote soon fell to the floor "drunk in the Spirit," as people laughed and applauded. Jan Mote then sought to fill her husband's place as speaker for the meeting, by returning to a passage from the Song of Solomon: "Let him kiss me with the kisses of his mouth." Although Jan Mote, too, was struggling to retain her composure (having to sit down at one point because her "knees were weak"), she spoke about how laughter was opening people up to receive the love of God. Those in the congregation not spiritually drunk, laying on the floor, or laughing out of control then followed her in singing, "My Jesus I love you."

Jan Mote managed to move the meeting from seeming chaos (in which many different things were happening simultaneously in the audience, and the main speaker was struggling to come out of his state of spirit drunkenness) into a ritually designated altar call, "If you could not sing that song and really mean it—if you don't know that Jesus loves you and you love Him—you need to come forward." Byron Mote was on his feet now, leading the congregation in "Amazing Grace." Some twenty-five people came forward to pray a version of the sinner's prayer, asking for forgiveness and giving their lives over to Jesus. A second call was given for those who wanted to be baptized in the Holy Spirit, during which one hundred persons came forward.

The altar call closed the formal part of the service, as the music team took their positions for the time of individual soaking prayer. With music playing in the background, hundreds of people came forward to stand on red lines in the front of the auditorium, behind the platform, and in the back of the auditorium as designated pray-ers (identified with a first name on a TACF badge), and their catchers went from person to person blessing what God was already doing. After sitting quietly and observing the prayer time, I went forward to stand in one of the lines in the back of the auditorium.

To this composite description of a nightly prayer gathering at TACF, I add a note from my journal (February 1995) regarding my experience during one such meeting:

> I had a mildly difficult time with the service last night. The music was ok, but it didn't seem to flow as I thought it should. Moreover, drunks—even spiritual drunks—unnerve me. Byron and Jan, however, were able to convey a message of substance about the call to intimacy with God despite their condition.
>
> I sat for a while in my seat as others were being prayed for, praying quietly in an attempt to "tune in" to God. Then I wandered to the front of the auditorium to the back, observing the varying states and positions of people. I didn't even know if I wanted to be prayed with. There were so many people waiting for prayer as well as others who were "soaking" on the carpet. Finally I returned to the front of the auditorium and found a place to stand. I tried to pray in the midst of the roaring and laughing, sounds of thrashing and pounding, and the po-go-ing (jumping up and down) that were going on around me. I managed to still my spirit when a woman came up to me and asked if I had been prayed for. She gently laid her hands on my shoulder and I immediately felt the power of the divine presence. I did floor time—in the midst of the roaring, laughing, groaning, and weeping sounds that filled the air. My soul was at peace.
>
> What happened to me, I am not sure. I am constantly switching modes from researcher to pilgrim and back to researcher again. I struggle to provide a chronicle of what I see while still being open to grace. It's not easy to be doing both. "Lord, I turn to you. Please speak to my heart about what you would have me do. In the midst of the struggle, help me to stay focused on you."

What is presented in the chapters that follow is a story of revival—the kind found in past Western church history and still witnessed in "primitive" contemporary religion. It is a story framed in the context of a form of religious mysticism that has been commonly experienced within the social context of the P/C movement. It is a narrative that reports individual experiences as well as some of the social consequences of personal encounters with the divine.

This book is about P/C revitalization told by an American insider to the movement—an insider who has studied the movement as a sociologist and who has been refreshed by its spirituality for over two decades. Although dressed in the theories and methods of social science, the narrative reflects an ongoing dialectical dance between a scholar and a pilgrim—one who has sought to make "scientific sense" out of what she has seen and heard. Although much of the content for this analysis comes from one stream of the revival known as the "Toronto Blessing," the Blessing joins other tributaries and streams of the revitalization process that has ebbed and flowed throughout the one hundred year history of the P/C movement.

OVERVIEW OF BOOK

This book is divided into two parts: the first part deals with what I have called the "mystical self," and the second part, the "mystical body." Part I, The Mystical Self, uses social psychological theories to frame the P/C revivals. The focus of these five chapters (including this introduction) is on the actors, especially the participants of the Toronto Blessing. Taken together, they provide a description of their mystical experiences, the meanings they attach to them, and the effects the Blessing is reported to have had on their lives. This introductory chapter provides a discussion of mysticism and some preliminary illustrations of charismatic experiences. It provides the base on which the other five chapters rest.

The second chapter, "Faces of God in Revival: Music, Mysticism, and Metaphor," explores the process of creating a revival reality out of the original amorphous experiences. It illustrates some of the different metaphors and corresponding myths that have been used to frame and legitimate the renewal, placing them within the social context of the larger P/C movement. Particular attention is given to renewal/revival music and its role in the social construction, dissemination, and revitalization of revival metaphor. Using the lenses of musicology, the chapter explores the relationship between music and revival experiences.

The following chapter, "The Spirit at Play: The Body and the Mystical Self," describes the controversial bodily manifestations—laughing, falling to the floor, spiritual drunkenness, and various somatic responses (jerking, shaking, trembling)—that attracted the attention of both seekers and skeptics. The manifestations will be presented first through phenomenological lenses that allow sensitivity to the struggle of leaders and followers alike as they sought to "make sense" out of the strange physiological behavior they were experiencing. After noting similarities to experiences reported by early American revivalists, the discussion will then shift to insights gleaned from scientific studies on the role of the brain in mystical and religious experiences. The chapter introduces the work of the late anthropologist Victor Turner (1993), linking "culturology" and neurology, to shed light on the physical and emotional manifestations that have frequently been part of American revivals.

Chapter 4 on "Divine Healing: Healing of Memories, Relationships, and Physical Ailments" continues to build on the work of Turner and others in relating the P/C subculture to the mystical self. For P/C Christians, healing is holistic—an experience that integrates mind and emotions with somatic responses. It is centered on experiences of the divine that often attenuates emotional hurts and, sometimes, physical pain. Reported experiences of oneness with God, reconciliation with significant (and not so significant) others, and self-integration of mind, body, and spirit are reflected in the survey data collected by me as well as in testimonials found in videos and books about the Blessing.

The last chapter of this section, "Hearing the Voice of God: Prophecy and the Mystical Self" reviews the role that prophecy has historically played in the P/C movement. Particular attention is devoted to how prophecy is personally experienced and defined in contemporary revival circles. An understanding of prophecy is central to any description of the P/C worldview and its mystical spirituality. Prophecy, however, is more than a personal religious experience. It often serves as a linchpin tying the mystical self to its more corporate and institutional expressions. The role that mysticism (especially prophecy) plays in revitalizing P/C institutions is the focus of part II, The Mystical Body.

The metaphor of a "mystical body" has its biblical roots in the apostle Paul's discussion in 1 Cor. 1:12–15, which includes a discussion of the "spiritual gifts," including glossolalia, healing, and prophecy (among others). Paul states in 1 Cor. 12:12–13: "For Christ is like a single body with its many limbs and organs, which, many as they are, together make up one body. For indeed we were all brought into one body by baptism, in the one Spirit, whether we are Jews or Greeks, whether slaves or free men, and that one Holy Spirit was poured out for all of us to drink." Within these chapters and verses, Paul instructs members of this body to put love first, but to also seek prophecy (1 Cor. 14:1). Case studies and survey data provide the materials to describe the process through which personal mystical experiences (especially prophecy) take on corporate flesh in new churches and ministries.

If scholars who posit a central role for religious or peak experiences in the emergence of religious institutions are correct (cf. James [1902] 1961; Maslow 1970), a relationship between revival experiences and institutional revitalization should be no surprise. The interlude suggests the use of Turner's concept of a collective "overbrain" in relation to the alternate ways of knowing that are integral to the P/C worldview. Resting on the foundation laid by the theories and data already presented, part II provides narrative histories to demonstrate how TACF revival experiences have shaped the river of revival and how they continue to influence sectors of the P/C movement.

Chapter 6 of part II, "Water, Wind, and Fire: Prophetic Narrative and Revival," explores the rise of the prophetic during the 1980s beginning with the so-called Kansas City prophets and its attendant controversies. Although experiencing difficulties with varying degrees of acceptance, the prophetic increased in importance as a spiritual gift during the present stage of the P/C movement. Prophecies, particularly those believed to foretell the coming of the revivals of the 1990s, are discussed in relation to recent P/C history. Prophetic voices lay the foundation for discussions found in subsequent chapters on how prophecy and the emerging role of the prophet have been used to launch new P/C institutions and to revitalize old ones.

The next three chapters focus on selected cases to demonstrate how the mystical self acts in ways that influence the mystical body. The gifts of the Spirit, particularly prophecy, are phenomena having an influence that goes beyond the individual actor. Chapter 7, "Digging the Local Wells of Revival: The Los Angeles Story," uses an account of the Harvest Rock Church in Pasadena, California, to demonstrate the role prophecy has played in the founding of new churches and revival networks, including The Call that focuses on youth. Whatever else it is, prophecy is a source of empowerment, resulting in an uneasy relationship between the prophetic and established institutions. Chapter 8, "One in the Spirit: The Rise of the City Church," continues to use the narrative of prophecy to describe another institutional matrix arising from the glowing embers of the 1990s revival. The focus is on the development and functioning of a city church in northeastern Ohio and its attempt to "break dividing walls" that have existed between denominations and congregations and to ready the local community for revival. City churches with their regional focus provide an institutional complement to the neodenominational networks described in the previous chapters.

Chapter 9, "Mysticism in Service: Taking the Renewal to the Streets," provides one key to unlocking the globalization process at work within the P/C movement. It presents the case studies of an inner-city revival congregation and a missionary outreach organization with descriptions of their respective uses of and display of "power evangelism." Power evangelism attempts to harness the mystical power commonly found in revivals to "spread the kingdom of God," especially among the poor and oppressed.

Chapter 10, "Narrative and Reflexive Ethnography: A Concluding Account," is a narrative within a narrative that contains both self-reflections and a synopsis of "America's longest revival." This exercise in reflective ethnography explores the roles played by me with a focus on the interactive dance between pilgrim and researcher. Using a polyphony of voices—mine and other reflexive voices—a concluding narrative history is provided to demonstrate where the revival has been and where it may be going.

There are countless people who have assisted me with this project, especially those who allowed me the privilege of studying them. The reader will come to know many of them by name as this narrative of the 1990s revival unfolds. While I have observed almost all the players in the renewal narrative described in these pages, I have also used many of them to serve as informant interviewees and to read sections of the manuscript or other papers on the revival that I have written over the years of my ongoing research. Although I am unable to list all their names here, may they know that I am grateful to each and every one of them for giving so freely of their prayers, encouragement, and time.

Two leaders, however, warrant special acknowledgement, for without them this study of the Toronto Blessing and the revitalization of American Pentecostalism would not have happened! I wish to thank Father Roger Ames whose willingness to embrace the renewal for St. Luke's Episcopal Church (Akron, Ohio) provided an incentive for a somewhat jaded and skeptical P/C scholar to check out the Toronto revival in 1994. Roger afforded me the opportunity to conduct preliminary research at his congregation and has been a frequent partner in fruitful dialogue about the emerging research findings. John Arnott joins Roger in providing encouragement and support from my earliest request to investigate the renewal in early 1995 through the nearly eight years of ongoing research that has followed. Although perhaps not always understanding the ways of an involved participant observer who writes for the academic community, John has continued to provide assistance and support through the years of this project. I am sure there were times that the significance of my sociological analysis eluded him, but John has always demonstrated a godly patience for my seemingly endless and esoteric efforts to produce a social scientific thesis on the revival.

I wish also to acknowledge my "California family"—Tim and Sue, Elizabeth, Isaac, Naomi, and Josiah Sun—who provided me a "home away from home" where I could spend time observing the effects of the revival at the birthplace of American Pentecostalism. Their loving and gracious hospitality over the years of this project continues to be a priceless gift.

Finally, I want to offer a special word of thanks to Jeff and Beth Metzger who have faithfully pastored the church where I have found both renewal refreshing and spiritual refuge for the past six years. Birthed directly out of the Toronto Blessing, Shiloh Church in North Canton, Ohio, is an ongoing embodiment of the renewal as described in the chapters that follow. On his first visit to TACF, Jeff Metzger had a mystical experience that he has described as "being pinned to the carpet and filled with liquid love." This "liquid love" continues to fill the gatherings at Shiloh (which could be succinctly described as "old silent Quaker meetings with CD music playing in the background"). Having no order of service, no scheduled sermon, and no set prayers for most gatherings, the power and the presence of the divine (often complete with Toronto-like physical manifestations) seem to flow freely. Shiloh's ongoing story could easily have been included in this narrative of the 1990s revival, but instead it became a personal haven—a place of respite where I could step back from my role as a researcher and enjoy the blessings of this contemporary revival.

There are others whose lives intersected with mine and who played important roles at different stages of this long research project, but whose names do not appear in the revival narrative. Some read papers, others served as knowledgeable informants; still others offered words of encouragement or helpful critique. They include Bonnie and Les Barker, Michael Brown, Stacey and Wesley Campbell,

Sharen Cook, Earl Creps, Murray Dempster, David DiSabatino, Daina Doucet, Mark Ford, Paul Grabill, Robin Greene, Ralph Hood, Ralph Kucera, Kimberly Kwon, John Lai, Lisa Murray, José Ortega-Betancourt, Cecil M. Robeck, Betty Richards, David Roozen, Gray Temple, Michael Thompson, and Scott Thumma.

I wish also to acknowledge the collegiality and encouragement that I have received from the Sociology Department of the University of Akron—support that continues even after my official "retirement." I am much indebted to John Zipp, Frank Falk, and Richard Gigliotti for their assistance as present and past department chairs in providing a departmental office and academic covering for my ongoing research.

Acknowledgements and thanks are also extended to all for the editorial assistance and to the reviewers, especially Erik Hanson, Hedi Hong, and Bonnie Fredman.

I

The Mystical Self

1

The "Toronto Blessing," Mysticism, and Pentecostal/ Charismatic Revitalization: An Introduction

On January 20, 1994, a contemporary revival broke out in a church located in an industrial strip mall just outside the runway of Toronto's Lester B. Pearson International Airport. The church, then known as the Toronto Airport Vineyard (TAV), was part of a larger network of churches (the Association of Vineyard Churches [AVC]) established by a former rock musician, John Wimber. Founded during the last quarter of the twentieth century, the Vineyard enjoyed an influence on sectors of Protestantism disproportionate to its size and status as a new religious movement. The Vineyard's trendy worship and music, emphasis on spirituality rather than religious institutions, and programs appealing to the boomer generation and its prodigy had already played a major role in what sociologist Donald Miller describes as "reinventing American Protestantism" (Miller 1997).[1]

Ever since the famous Azusa Street Revival (1906–1909) in Los Angeles (often regarded as a birthplace of global Pentecostalism), the Pentecostal/Charismatic (P/C) movement has battled the forces of modernity with revival fires. More often termed "renewal" or "refreshing" by neo-Pentecostals of the second half of the twentieth century, revivals have birthed and remain the lifeblood of the P/C movement. As I have described elsewhere (Poloma 1982, 1989, n.d.), the democratized charisma in which all believers can enjoy the "gifts of the Holy Spirit," including glossolalia, healing, prophecy, and miracles, is difficult to keep molten. The petrification or "routinization of charisma" can be seen in the rise of new doctrinal proclamations, fixed rituals, and bureaucratic institutions, thus threatening the very experiences that originally launched the movement. Given the centrality of religious experience for the P/C doctrine and practice, however, a minor (or even a major) revival is never far away (Riss and Riss 1997; Hyatt 2002b).

The first wave of the Azusa Street Revival during the first decade of the twentieth century left in its wake scores of emerging denominations, sects, and independent churches. Many adherents of the new movement soon sought fresh experiences of Pentecost, and new revivalists and revivals regularly arose to meet this need. Successful Pentecostal organizations, however, were often hostile toward the newer groups with their renewed and sometimes new Pentecostal experiences and expressions. Perhaps nowhere is this better evidenced in the first half of the twentieth century than in the widespread opposition to the 1948 Latter Rain movement during which criticisms from established Pentecostal churches were reminiscent of those made against the founders of the Pentecostal movement a few decades earlier (Riss 1987; DeArteaga 1992). Despite an unwillingness or inability to form a central organization (not a single denomination came from the Latter Rain), this new revival with its emphasis on healing, prophecy, and revitalized ritual is believed to have influenced the next two waves of the larger movement.

The second wave, during which Pentecostal beliefs, practices, and experiences rolled into mainline Christian denominations, began in the 1950s, especially through Pentecostal parachurch ministries of healing evangelists (including Kathryn Kuhlman and Oral Roberts) and through the Full Gospel Business Fellowship established by California dairy farmer Demos Shakarian (Quebedeaux 1983; Poloma 1982; Synan 1987). After washing over all major Protestant denominations, Roman Catholicism, and (to a lesser extent) Eastern Orthodoxy, the wave crested at the Kansas City Conference of 1977. Over fifty thousand people from all streams of the P/C movement and some of their top leaders filled the Kansas City football stadium to overflowing (Synan 1984). Followers soon retreated to denominational conferences in subsequent years while others made their way to newly emerging independent charismatic churches, sapping the visibility and vitality of the P/C movement of the 1970s. By the early 1980s, it became increasingly apparent that the P/C movement was in need of still another revival wave.

The third wave was already in the making at the time of the Kansas City Conference, fermented by the social unrest of the late 1960s and the Jesus People movement. The Jesus People movement, which began amidst the social chaos of the late 1960s in California, contributed to the development of the three "new paradigm" churches discussed at length by Miller (1997) in *Reinventing American Protestantism*, all of which have ties to the third wave. Beginning in San Francisco's Haight-Ashbury District in 1967 and carried to Southern California by Lonnie Frisbee in 1968, the Jesus People movement attracted young hippies and beach bums who gave up their drugs to get high on Jesus.

Thousands of new countercultural Christians joined visionary Christian churches through the ministry of Frisbee, a street preacher often called the "John the Baptist of Southern California" (DiSabatino 1999). One of the beneficiaries of Frisbee's charisma was Wimber, founder of the AVC, who himself had given up drugs and the life of a rock musician for the Christian ministry. Wimber was soon to become the leading spokesperson for what has come to be called the third wave (Wagner [1988] 2002).

The third wave with its casual California style, its downplaying of glossolalia as the litmus test for Spirit-filled activity, its use of the corporate body of believers rather than special star evangelists for healing, and its demonstration of the ready availability of "signs and wonders" became a new source of refreshing in the 1980s for many who were spiritually dry. These P/C adherents of the third wave remained convinced that there was yet more available to Spirit-filled believers than what they were experiencing.

The revival-like happenings at TAV in January 1994 were not new experiences to third-wave adherents, particularly those affiliated with Wimber and the AVC. Many Vineyard pastors and adherents could attest to having similar experiences at some time or another. The repeated success of the nightly meetings that followed at the Toronto church (nightly meetings that are still being held at the time of this writing) and the transporting of the unusual phenomena to other sites outside the AVC by Toronto pilgrims is what made the so-called Toronto Blessing distinctive. The seeming pandemonium brought about by fresh revival experiences, which first broke out in Wimber's Vineyard church through the ministry of Frisbee, occurred with some regularity in the AVC congregations throughout the 1980s and early 1990s. Wimber's popularity as a conference speaker was catalytic for further revival-like experiences in many non-AVC churches and ministries. Not unlike that which happened to earlier moves of refreshing within the P/C movement, including the Latter Rain, the Charismatic, and the Jesus People movements, opposition to the Toronto Blessing was quick in coming from sectors of the P/C movement—and eventually from Wimber himself (Hilborn 2001).

Despite TAV's dismissal from the AVC in late 1995 (and its subsequent re-naming as the Toronto Airport Christian Fellowship [TACF]), the Toronto Blessing quickly spread throughout North America, England, and then scores of other countries revitalizing diverse sectors of the P/C movement. It has proven to be an important catalyst for the dissemination of third-wave thought, practice, and experiences beyond the AVC to classical Pentecostal as well as to mainstream Charismatics and especially to independent charismatic churches and parachurch organizations.

By the summer of 1994, the planes flying into Pearson International Air-port carried pilgrims from around the globe, especially from the U.K. to TAV. News of the revival quickly made headlines in England when an affluent An-glican church in London, Holy Trinity Brompton, experienced what the British press dubbed the "Toronto Blessing"(Roberts 1994; Hilborn 2001). The newly available Internet coupled with more established communications media soon brought thousands of P/C faithful, as well as the curious and the skeptical, to see for themselves what was happening at the nightly revival meetings at TAV. Just as Azusa Street in Los Angeles had been the catalyst to launch Pentecostalism in the early twentieth century, TAV became a major force in its revitalization as the millennium came to a close.

The main task I have set for myself in part I is to provide a sociopsycho-logical account of the Toronto Blessing in historical and social context. This narrative comes from the word processor of a "stranger"—one whom sociol-ogist Georg Simmel described as being both "inside" and "outside" of a social group. As I have noted elsewhere (Poloma 1982; 1989; 2000), I have experi-enced the wind, been refreshed by the rain, and observed the fire of the P/C movement for over two decades. Yet as a phenomenologically oriented social scientist, I have tried to "bracket" (as best one can) my personal faith experi-ences as I sought natural explanations for what often appeared "supranatural" and (at least in part) may be "supernatural."

This search for comparative frames to describe what I have seen and heard have taken me beyond sociology to psychology, anthropology, history, and even to what might be considered "parascience." Sociology and psychology (social psychology), however, provide the overarching theoretical framework that I use to comparatively explore the nature and effects of the Toronto Bless-ing. While such comparisons with earlier revivals and experiences in other religions and other cultures will necessarily be more descriptive than explanatory, they do serve to demonstrate commonalities that have led some medical scientists to question whether humans are "hard wired for God" (Benson 1996; Begley 2001).

Foundational to this analysis is the premise that good description must precede scientific explanation. Comparative illustrations are useful to enhance this description of the 1990s revival movement but are not intended to explain them away. The stance I take as a sociologist can best be described by Ann Taves's (1999) "mediating tradition." Much of the discussion about involuntary religious experiences, notes Taves, has revolved around discerning "true" from "false" religion or distinguishing between "natural" and "supernatural" experiences or both. The instruments of science can resolve neither of these issues, but social science can take a "mediating" position that regards such religious experiences as "natural" and "true."[2] The experiences discussed in the first part of this book are found in varying spiritual traditions.

Although psychologists of an earlier era may have labeled them as delusional, these spiritual traditions have been found to be commonly natural when unchallenged by Enlightenment beliefs. Religious experiences can be assumed to be true in the sense that social psychologists have long known subjective experiences can have objective social consequences. It is my intent to describe the 1990s revival (with a particular focus on the Toronto Blessing) and to suggest naturalistic explanations where warranted. It must be emphasized, however, that the use of this approach is in no way intended to explain away the revival with simplistic assumptions and explanations.

Through the use of narrative, I hope to remain close to the experiences I am describing.[3] As Taves notes in the conclusion of her insightful historical analysis of *Fits, Trances and Visions:*

> The closer we are to the experience in question the more we can see the way it is imbedded and connected to other things. The more we abstract or disconnect "experience" from the *narrating of experience* in order that it may participate in more abstract discourses, the more it is fragmented or, as (William) James says, "decomposed." (Taves 1999, 360)

To guard against fragmentation and decomposition, accounts of institutional effects of the revival found in part II use accounts collected during some eight years of participant observation. Interviews conducted with leaders of the movement, content analysis of testimonies, sermons and music, Internet list serves and websites, and some quantitative data from surveys provide the content for the historical narratives and overarching metanarrative presented here on the P/C revival.

Through the information collected using tools of the sociological trade, I will first describe the Toronto Blessing. Individual experiences of the Blessing are foundational for moving to the more elaborate narrative histories presented in part II that assess the revival's impact. This study is a longitudinal one that begins with my first visit to TAV in November 1994 and is ongoing even as I prepare this formal manuscript.[4] It builds on over twenty years of research, writing, and personal involvement in the P/C movement. My status as an involved participant observer has both assets and liabilities, but I trust the benefits will outweigh the costs.

The remainder of this introductory chapter will be used to place the Toronto Blessing within the context of the larger P/C movement by providing some general background and a synopsis of its distinctive mystical worldview. Accounts of mystical experiences provide the narrative data throughout this work to discuss the ongoing dance between religious experiences and the cultural, structural, and institutional contexts in which they are imbedded.

WHO ARE THE PENTECOSTAL/CHARISMATICS?

Within the past one hundred years, the P/C community has evolved from a small band of believers to a global movement with an estimated one-half billion adherents and still growing.[5] It represents an increasingly diverse subculture that includes (1) classical Pentecostals or the "first wave" whose sects and denominations originated mostly in the first quarter of the twentieth century; (2) neo-Pentecostals (Charismatics) or the "second wave" of the 1960s and 1970s that can be found in Catholic and Orthodox churches, in most streams of Protestantism as well as in newer independent or nondenominational churches and church networks; (3) "third wave" adherents who established new churches, independent ministries, and quasi-institutional networks that revivalized the P/C movement in the 1980s and 1990s; and (4) countless syncretistic groups (particularly in developing nations) that have adapted Spirit-filled Christianity with their indigenous cultures (Hollenweger 1997). In some respects the movement is evolving so rapidly that it is not entirely clear which distinctive hallmarks of early Pentecostalism still hold (Hunt, Hamilton, and Walter 1997). The position taken here is that what delineates the P/C movement is not a single leader, institution, or doctrine, but rather its worldview—a worldview that proves to be a good fit with both premodernism in developing countries and postmodernism in the Western world.[6]

At the center of this distinctive worldview expressed in diverse cultural contexts is a particular "core spirituality" (Land 1993; Albrecht 1999). Daniel Albrecht describes this diversity within unity as follows:

> In asserting an underlying spirituality, I understand that each "species" of Pentecostalism has a particular type of Pentecostal spirituality. However, I do believe that amidst the many Pentecostal spiritualities there is a *core* spirituality, as experience in and of the Spirit that unifies the vast variety. The core or underlying spirituality mixes with many theologies, traditions and cultures to produce a wide range of types of Pent/Char spirituality. (Albrecht 1999, 28–29)

The worldwide P/C movement can thus be regarded as "one single cohesive movement into which vast proliferations of all kinds of individuals and communities have been drawn in a whole range of different circumstances" (Barrett 1988). At the heart of this movement is a particular and peculiar worldview reflected in a common spirituality.

In combining the terms *Charismatic* and *Pentecostal,* however, it is important to note that there are distinctions sufficient enough to cause many (at least in the United States) to identify with either one group or the other but not with both. In North America the term "Pentecostal" usually refers to persons in denominations born out of or changed by the Azusa Street Revival during the first three decades of the twentieth century. They are adherents of the churches or denominations resulting from the so-called first wave. The term "Charismatic" on the other hand refers to those in mainline and independent churches who embraced a neo-Pentecostal worldview in the mid-twentieth century or later. Charismatics are those who identify with the "second wave" and possibly the "third wave" of the P/C movement. In the United States, some 23 percent of all evangelical Protestants, 9 percent of mainline Protestants, 13 percent of Roman Catholics, and 36 percent of Black Protestants claim to be "Spirit-filled," a more generic term designed to capture all three "waves" of the American movement. Americans who claim to be Spirit-filled tend to self-identify as "Pentecostal" (4.7 percent of the total respondents) or as "Charismatic" (6.6 percent of respondents), but much less frequently as both

"Charismatic and Pentecostal" (0.8 percent), reflecting differences that do exist in different streams of this growing movement (Green et al. 1997).[7]

Although identifying common characteristics of all the P/C constituents is probably impossible (especially when considering non-Western cultures where the P/C movement is experiencing its most rapid growth), scholars have sought classifying categories and created "ideal types" for heuristic purposes (Cox 1995; Hollenweger 1997; Anderson and Hollenweger 1999). The terms "Pentecostal" and "Charismatic," as we have shown with the preceding statistics, do appear to have different meanings for insiders, but those outside the movement are less likely to note the nuances. What can be said generally about the movement ever since its inception, as has been already noted, is that that it is more about a distinct "spirituality" rather than about "religion" (Larson, Swyers, and McCullough 1998; Hill et al. 2000; Slater, Hall, and Edwards 2001). It is more about a shared transcendent worldview than a particular denomination, set of doctrine, or defined ritual practices.

This worldview is a curious blend of premodern miracles, modern technology, and postmodern mysticism in which the natural merges with the supernatural. Signs and wonders analogous to those described in the premodern biblical accounts are expected as normal occurrences in the lives of believers. Rejecting a Cartesian dualism that separates body from spirit, supernatural phenomena are regarded to be a "natural" experience for the P/C Christians. Although its worldview is not readily adaptable to philosophical tenets of modernism, the P/C movement has pragmatically embraced features of modernism to further its goals (and to accommodate to the larger culture) throughout much of its more recent history (Lyon 2000; Wacker 2001).

At its core, however, the P/C worldview has always been somewhat ambivalent about modernism and aligns better with premodern (in its early history and in developing nations) or postmodern thought (in contemporary industrialized nations). As a form of mystical spirituality rather than a single strong religious organization, the P/C movement better resonates with the shift toward a postmodern paradigm, sharing the latter's ideological reactions against modernism and its epistemological assumptions.

Although concerned about the power of postmodern thought to relativize Christian "truth," some Pentecostal scholars have recognized the potential of postmodernity to free indigenous Pentecostal theology from its restrictive Fundamentalist trappings that have historically affected the P/C theology as both battled against modernity (Dempster 1999). Despite the debates about the acceptability of a postmodern paradigm among scholars, the P/C move ment with its emphasis on personal and often dramatic encounters with God, its use of narrative (rather than prepositional) logic, and its frequent denunciation of the "dead religion" that is said to quench the Spirit, all illustrate ways P/C followers join in a postmodern rejection of monolithic institutions and modernist thought.

P/C Christianity (unlike Christian Fundamentalism), however, is not primarily a reaction to modernism. It has proactively developed certain characteristics that taken together make its worldview somewhat distinct from other forms of Christianity, both of the liberal and conservative stripes. As already noted, the P/C worldview is experientially centered, with its followers in a dynamic and personal relationship with a deity who is both immanent and transcendent. "The Spirit-filled believer has a predisposition to see the transcendent God at work in, with, through, above, and beyond all events. Therefore, all space is sacred space and all time is sacred time" (Johns 1999, 75). God is seen as active in all events past, present, and future that work together in a kind of master plan. It is a worldview that tends to be "transrational," professing that knowledge is "not limited to the realms of reason and sensory experience."

Consistent with this transrational characteristic, P/C Christians also tend to be anticreedal, believing that "knowing" comes from a right relationship with God rather than through reason or even through the five senses. Theirs is a God who is in a personal relationship with each believer, a divinity who can and often does defy the laws of nature with the miraculous and unexplainable. Without doubt the Bible holds an important place in the P/C worldview, but for many it serves as a kind of catalyst and litmus test for personal and corporate experience rather than a manual of rigid doctrine and practices. (Revival leaders are sometimes heard to quip that "many Christians think the Trinity is made up of the Father, the Son, and the Bible," alluding to the replacement of the creative work of the Holy Spirit with a rigid reading of the text.)

The draw toward a Fundamentalist dogmatism has been and continues to be ever present, but the belief in and experience of a creative Spirit who is with the Word appears even stronger. During times of revival, renewal, and refreshing, the Spirit (through mystical experiences) and the Word (of the Bible) are dynamically involved in creative play. As Johns (1999, 79) notes about the P/C worldview: "In summary, a Pentecostal paradigm for knowledge and

truth springs from an experiential knowledge of God which alters the believer's approach to reading and interpreting reality." For the P/C adherents, as
for postmodernists (albeit from very different perspectives and assumptions),
reality is not what it appears to be. Miracles, mystery, and what some might
call magic are all part of what the P/C followers experience—especially those
who actively seek the wind, rain, and fire of revival.

PENTECOSTALS AND CHARISMATICS AS MAIN STREET MYSTICS

Mysticism is what Robert Ellwood terms "a modern intellectual development." According to Ellwood:

> The modern responsibility for one's interior self has led to rebirths of mysticism
> and paramystical processes, from psychotherapy to positive thinking. Because
> religious institutions have also been affected with the cool engineering model
> of organization, they too have often seemed unable to deliver an adequate self-
> validating subjectivity. But in the face of alienation people have never needed such
> subjectivity more and have on their own responsibility turned to techniques
> brought out of mystical traditions of the past that seem to offer connections with
> larger realities. As a result many modern people live double lives as technicians
> and as mystics or religionists of some kind. (Ellwood 1999, 70)

If indeed mysticism appears to be on the rise as Ellwood suggests, the P/C
movement has offered a way for millions of Christians to connect with a common mystical tradition within orthodox Christianity.

A common dictionary definition of a mystic is "a person who claims to attain,
or believes in the possibility of attaining, insight into mysteries of transcending
ordinary human knowledge, as by immediate intuition in a state of personal ecstasy" (*The Random House Dictionary of the English Language* [Second Edition]).
Such a commonly accepted definition allows for a variety of mystical experiences: experiences that range from simple intuition to visions and voices and
from a calm, passive "knowing" to ecstatic trances. Anthropologists and psychologists as well as philosophers and theologians have explored and expanded on
such common understandings to raise questions that have often polarized scholars. Is all mystical experience of the same essence? Has this essence been camou-
flaged by various interpretations dependent on the religious or the philosophical
framework of the mystic or both? Do some mystical experiences cut across such
cultural barriers? Or are there as many different types of mystical experience as

there are paradigmatic expressions of them? Are there even more "unique expressions" than there are general paradigms that have been used by some to frame discussions of mysticism? (Poloma 1995b; Ellwood 1999).

These unanswered questions point to a lack of a shared understanding about the nature of mysticism, differences that appear to be deeply rooted in assumptions and paradigms found in different academic disciplines. As Taves notes in her excellent work exploring "the interplay between experiencing religion and explaining experience":

> Various academic disciplines have developed distinctive discourses to designate the general sort of experience in question. Psychiatrists most commonly refer to dissociation (or more distantly hysteria); anthropologists to trance, spirit possession, and altered states of consciousness; and religionists to visions, inspiration, mysticism, and ecstasy. (Taves 1999, 7)

Conflicting assumptions about mysticism reflected in the discourse of diverse fields of study have tended to polarize scholars into accepting either a classical/essentialist or a constructionist/contextual view of mystical experience. The classical or essentialist approach assumes that behind the multiform descriptions and interpretations of mystical experiences there is a common core of experiences that is essentially unaffected by the individual mystic's particular historical situation, social status, cultural environment, and religious commitments. It maintains that "mystical experience is first of all a pure, indescribable experience to which an interpretation drawing from the experiencer's religious presuppositions is added" (Ellwood 1999, 21). At the other end of the pole are those who subscribe to a contextualist or constructionist approach, which emphasizes that the relationship between context and content, interpretation and experience, and religious doctrine and religious experience is reciprocal (Hollenback 1996). As such, there is no single core experience, but rather many mysticisms dependent on individual personal makeup and myriad social contexts. Increasingly, however, a more middle ground is being advocated that acknowledges both seeds of universality and content-specific factors in mystical experiences.

Mysticism remains a complex phenomenon that emanates from deliberations about the nature of its essence. Even with more scholars concurring about the need to consider mysticism within its respective context, the nature of these "contexts" include a natural context (rooted in nature, such as, beautiful sunsets, the miracle of birth, or the music of waves crashing against a beach), the use of pharmaceutical products (drug-induced mysticism), or widely varying religious traditions (represented in all the world religions). Clearly, mysticism has different faces expressed in divergent ideas, in special practices, and in its sociological narrative. For Ernst Troeltsch (1931), as for his sociological contemporaries Max Weber and Emile Durkheim, mysticism clearly has a sociological component. It is not simply an individual experience, but it is part of society—the third face of religious expression (with the other two being church and sect). According to Troeltsch (1931, 734), mysticism has two forms: a "narrow, technical, concentrated sense" that undercuts structure and forms new groups and a "wider form" that is diffuse and supports the prevailing religious structures.

The stance on mysticism taken in this discussion is consistent with Troeltsch's sociology of mysticism as well as Taves' (1999) "mediating position" discussed earlier. Mysticism is regarded here not only as a common and "natural" experience but also as one that differs in form, interpretation, and expression among different cultures, religious traditions, and over time. Although for heuristic purposes some similarities between experiences and testimonies of the Toronto Blessing will be compared with those of other mystical streams, the focus of this work will be a contextual one that describes not only the experience but also the social milieu in which it was elicited. It seeks to link the "mystical self" with its religious context and in turn with the revitalization of that context, namely, the P/C movement.

As can be gleaned from the preliminary description already provided of the P/C worldview, basic to this worldview is the belief that God is active in an ongoing way in the world. It is a worldview that moves beyond the commonly accepted *belief* that God can perform miracles to common *personal experiences* of a divinity that walks and talks on the planet earth. The seemingly paranormal experiences of glossolalia, healing, prophecy, and diverse "miracles" are "supernaturally natural" signs that God is always available, working collaboratively with humans. Such experiences have been an ongoing part of the P/C way of life even when the big waves of renewal have receded, but these mystical experiences seemed more commonplace and intense with the revival meetings of the 1990s.

The protracted meetings and scheduled conferences welcomed the strange bodily manifestations accompanied by accounts of the miraculous, but it was a closer relationship with God that served as the major focus for the revival testimonies. The vast majority (some 90 percent) of pilgrims to Toronto who responded to surveys in 1995 and again in 1997 reported that as a result of their pilgrimage to Toronto they experienced God in particularly intense ways, leaving them with a sense of being "more in love with Jesus than ever before" and "knowing the Father's love in a new way" (Poloma 1996, 1998a).[8] Perceived encounters with "ultimate divine reality"—the Father, Jesus, the Holy Spirit—is at the heart of the Toronto Blessing and its tributaries.

Descriptions of mystical experience can be quite diverse, reflecting the language and worldview of the mystic. P/C mysticism is framed by both the metaphor and myths of the Judeo-Christian tradition as well as elements from the larger non-P/C culture. When the Toronto Blessing is placed within the context of North American culture, for example, it reflects not only Christian tradition but also the worldview of the popular New Age subculture (although the language and metaphors used to describe the seemingly similar experiences may be quite different). Within such comparisons, however, there must always be sensitivity to differences in language and underlying mythology that reflect differences in the worldview.

Hollenback's (1996) comparative study of mysticism aligns well with Ellwood's call for sensitivity to mysticism's fundamental contextuality. His "broad comparative historical treatment of mysticism," however, goes beyond many more limited discussions that include only the mystics of the large historic religions (Christianity, Islam, Buddhism, and Hinduism). Hollenback extends his analysis to compare the mysticism of traditional religions with that of minority religions, an analysis from which he derives a list of universal traits for identifying mysticism in diverse contexts. The five distinctive contextual features of mystical experiences listed by Hollenback are readily apparent in common experiences reported by those involved with the Toronto Blessing. Each of them will be discussed briefly and coupled with a narrative selected from a book of articles edited by TACF pastor John Arnott (2001a) in which authors shared their Toronto experiences.[9]

1. Change in Mode of Awareness

After reviewing diverse accounts of mystical experiences, Hollenback (1996, 42) noted how the "mystic's mode of awareness underwent a dramatic change while he was in the midst of a waking state of consciousness." This state is "transsensory," one in which mystics seem to perceive the objects of their visions and locutions by means of some faculty other than the five senses. In short, this change of awareness can be described as a *radical, trans-sensory metamorphosis of the subject's mode of consciousness that takes place while he or she is awake.*

Scott McDermott, one of the contributors to John Arnott's (2001a) book on the Toronto Blessing reported the process through which he moved into this changed state as follows:

> When John (Arnott) came to me, nothing happened at first. He began to pray, "More, Lord. More of the Lord." Nothing happened, and I was actually quite okay with that. John then began to pray for the person standing next to me. That person fell over, but I just closed my eyes and said to the Lord, "I'm not going to look around; I'm just going to focus on You, Lord." Just then, John stepped back to pray for me. To my amazement I soon found myself on the floor! As I extended my hands heavenward, my arms began to tremble slightly. At first I wondered why my arms were trembling, but my attention was soon drawn to the fire dancing on my eyelids. Quickly my mind referenced the biblical passages on fire to better comprehend the significance of what I was experiencing. (McDermott 2000, 16)

McDermott was aware of Arnott's praying for him, his leaving to pray for others, and his periodic prayers for the entire room. During one such prayer Arnott asked for the "fire of the Spirit to come into the room," and McDermott reported hearing God say to him, "You be the oil and I'll be the fire."

> No sooner had I heard this than I began to feel gentle, pulsating waves of the Spirit move over my body. One gentle wave after another came, delicately and slowly flowing from the top of my head to my feet and then back again. From somewhere in the room, John lifted his voice and prayed again, "We welcome the wave of the Spirit here in this room. Let the waves of the Spirit just come. One wave after another." (McDermott 2000, 16)

What followed was a series of visions that seemed to come in the "waves" prayed for by Arnott.

2. Privileged Access to the "Ultimately Real"

Hollenback (1996, 47) observes that "mystical experiences give the subject both privileged access to and knowledge of what religious traditions regard as ultimately real." For McDermott this knowledge came through visions in which he was a runner in a race that took place in the Holy Land. McDermott (2000, 16–17) describes entering the visionary state as follows:

The next thing I knew I was standing in the brown and desolate Judean wilderness, not far from the city of Jericho In front of me stood a large and deep canyon that was part of the Wadi Qelt. As I looked across the wadi, my eyes began to focus on an area of contrasting green vegetation that flourished on the canyon wall. There in the middle of all the green, I saw a steady stream of water gushed out of the hillside into the canyon below. As I stood transfixed by this refreshing and compelling contrast, the Lord said to me, "I want you to be living water to the people I have given you to pastor. Be like fresh water to them."

The scene then changed and McDermott found himself running:

I found myself running on the road that leads from Jericho to Jerusalem. This road runs 18 miles along a winding a mountainous terrain, ascending nearly 3,300 feet as it makes its way from the Jordan Valley to the heights of Jerusalem. At times the roadway skirts the edge of the adjacent canyon, while at other times it slowly curls through the Judean hillside. Despite the hills and the difficulty of the road, the run was easy. Even when the hills seemed steep and difficult, it felt as if I were running downhill or as if the roadway itself were pushing me along.

I began to cry for the wonder of what I was experiencing. I asked the Lord, "Why is this so easy?" He replied, "Your heart is set on Jerusalem, and when your heart is set on Jerusalem the hills are light." (McDermott 2000, 16–17)

Hollenback describes this second context in terms of the mystic's *being given both privileged access to and knowledge of those things that his or her particular culture and religious tradition regards as ultimately real and having utmost importance for human salvation.* Like countless other accounts of encounters with Jesus reported by Toronto mystics, McDermott's reflects important Christian teachings. In this case it seemed to impress on the visionary that doing the work of God is effortless when one is called to the work and empowered by the Spirit.[10]

3. Knowledge Is Relevant to Subject's Religious Tradition

The content of McDermott's experienced vision and locutions fits well with its Christian context. It reflects the characteristic described by Hollenback as *a content that validates the mythology or metaphysic that the mystic takes for granted as being self-evidently true.* The place is the Holy Land, the focus is Jesus, and the event is a race. (The Apostle Paul [Acts 20:24] used the metaphor of a race to describe his own spiritual journey.) Surrendering burdens to God and allowing God to exchange the heaviness of life's demands for a "yoke that is easy and a burden that is light" is a basic spiritual principle. While experiencing this mental vision, McDermott was simultaneously demonstrating somatic reactions; he reports that "my arms and my legs were moving as if I were actually running." Although physical manifestations were a common occurrence at the Toronto revival, McDermott's were so intense that it brought observers, including Arnott:

> John walked over to me, bent down and said, "Scott, what is God doing?" I explained to him, "I'm running the road from Jericho to Jerusalem." Then I added, "I'm running uphill, but it feels like I am running downhill." John repeated my words to the others. With a quivering voice and tears gently streaming down my face, I told him that the Lord said the road was easy because my heart was set on Jerusalem. (McDermott 2000, 18)

McDermott (2000, 18–19) then went onto another scene in the vision in which he was being cheered on by spectators that opened the way for his going through the "finish line" and into an experience demonstrating yet another interrelated mystical characteristic discussed by Hollenback.

4. Mystical Experiences Are Laden with Affect

Mystical experiences are often laden with affect. Results from the surveys of Toronto Blessing participants revealed an array of emotional responses, especially feelings of peace, joy, and happiness, but also sadness and embarrassment (Poloma 1996; 1998b). Weeping and laughing are both common expressions of the emotional feelings occurring during the P/C revivals. McDermott's emotional response was one of weeping and tears that contrasted with the laughter he saw around him in his vision. He described his crossing the finish line as follows:

> As I approached, I could see the once walled and sealed city gate was now open. Stretched across the opening was a finish line. And there, on the other side, stood Jesus with his arms outstretched and beckoning, a smile of delight radiating from His face. I collapsed across the finish line into my Savior's loving arms. Jesus held me ever so tightly, laughing with delight while I wept in His arms. (McDermott 2000, 19)

Tears and sobbing continued throughout this part of the vision during which McDermott (2000, 19) reports "feelings of unworthiness filled my being" followed by more intense experiences of divine love. "With each word and each look, there was an impartation of irresistible and indescribable love. That love filled my entire being until it made even my unworthiness surrender to the bidding of his will."

5. Mystical Illumination

The fifth characteristic, one that Hollenback devotes considerable attention to, is that of mystical illumination, an *illumination that is both literal and metaphorical*. According to Hollenback:

> One of the most common phenomena associated with mystical states of con-
> sciousness is a preternatural illumination that can take several different forms.
> Sometimes it becomes manifest as a brilliant aura that seems to emanate from
> either the mystic or the particular beings that the mystic encounters in the spir-
> itual world. At other times it seems as though it is the whole environment that
> is suffused with radiance rather than individual beings within it. On other oc-
> casions, the preternatural illumination seems to be localized within a system of
> subtle physiology (for example, kundalini energy seems to be a peculiar liquid
> light that is located within the spinal canal). (Hollenback 1996, 56)

Although testimonies can be found given by Toronto mystics in which light plays a significant role, there does not appear to be the emphasis on a literal illumination suggested by Hollenback. Examples of metaphorical illumination, however, are widespread. As illustrated by the excerpts from McDermott's narrative—a narrative not unlike countless others presented verbally at revival services or printed in books and magazines—Toronto testimonies are rife with metaphor. Metaphors are commonly used to present linguistically what Hollenback (1996) describes as mysticism's *"amorphous quality in that there is no predetermined form."*[11]

One other characteristic of mysticism merits mention in reporting on the Toronto Blessing. A "deep sense of unity," often included in descriptive definitions of mysticism, is a factor to be added to Hollenback's list of content characteristics. Unity with God, self, and others, is a frequent theme in recent P/C revival testimonies and narratives. It finds expression at the individual level in a new sense of integration and wholeness, in a deeper unitive relationship with God, and in improved relationships with and greater compassion for others. At a corporate level there is an emphasis on minimizing the rifts and bridging over the differences that have developed in different sectors of the P/C movement. It could be said that the recent P/C revivals, for which

Toronto was a kind of epicenter, are primarily about a deeper unity with God that finds concrete expression in improving interpersonal relations and working toward the breaking down of walls that have fragmented the P/C movement. While the coming kingdom of God prophesied by the leaders appears to be slow in coming, for many followers the first payment of the promise of the coming kingdom can be found in changed personal lives and enhanced personal relations.

SUMMARY AND CONCLUSION

P/C mysticism exists within a religious social context rooted in Christianity. It fits well with the thirteenth-century theologian Thomas Aquinas's simple and classic definition of mysticism as "knowledge of God through experience." Anyone who experiences ultimate reality can be called a mystic, but not all mystics have experiences of the same form, intensity, frequency, or duration. Comparison of mystical experiences across traditions is complicated by the fact that mystics describe their experiences in language cloaked with metaphor and myths derived from the social context in which they were experienced. The phenomenon at the core of the experience is assumed by a growing number of scholars to be of a similar essence.[12]

P/C mystics believe they are refreshed with the Holy Spirit and this refreshment is personally empowering. Countless numbers who participated in the Toronto Blessing revivals and its tributaries assert that this time has been one of extraordinary personal refreshing and institutional revitalization. Intense experiences of God, including those that brought prophetic words, divine healing, and alleged visible signs of God's presence, fanned the cooling embers of revival experiences that birthed the P/C movement over one hundred years ago. These experiences have been empowering, providing some spiritual entrepreneurs with a sense of risk taking and abandonment to establish and promote new organizational structures that are revitalizing the P/C movement.

The revival that broke out early in 1994 at TACF (then known as the Toronto Airport Vineyard [TAV]) is but one strand of a reticulate and web-like social movement that has covered the entire globe within one hundred years of its founding. From its humble beginnings at the Azusa Street Revival in 1906, it now comprises the second largest communion of Christian believers in the world. At the heart of this movement are dramatic experiences of God underlying a common spirituality and worldview that might be described as a "shared mysticism." These perceived experiences not only have had an impact on individuals who have them but also have had a revitalizing effect on the larger P/C movement. While the latest wave of the 1990s appears to have reached its peak, it has left behind institutional consequences that will continue to have an impact on the movement.

Central to P/C renewal rituals both present and past is music. Although the contemporary sound of love ballads set to string and drum preceded by celebrative songs set to heavy metal sounds are somewhat different from the music of earlier P/C revivals, music continues to play an important role in contemporary revivals as it has throughout the history of the P/C movement. In the next chapter we will explore some commonalities between music and mysticism in relation to the P/C movement. In short, music serves as a facilitator of mystical experience as it offers experience-evoking sounds wed to accepted metaphors and myths. Music thus becomes a vehicle for transmitting what Walter Stace (1960) has termed *introvertive mysticism* while providing lyrics to describe what has been said to be indescribable.

NOTES

1. At the outbreak of the Toronto revival in 1994, the Association of Vineyard Churches consisted of a network of over four hundred U.S. congregations, with nearly fifty more churches in Canada and over one hundred others scattered throughout the globe. It was a significant force in what has been called the third wave of the P/C movement.

2. The reader interested in learning more details about my interactive stance in studying the Blessing may choose at this point to read the concluding chapter (10) on "Narrative and Reflexive Ethnography: A Concluding Account."

3. This position is in accord with Yamane's (2000) observation that social scientists cannot actually study "religious experiencing" but only religious experience in real time. Such studies necessarily include retrospective accounts presented through linguistic representations found in narrative.

4. My interest in the movement continues as I pursue research on Blood-N-Fire (ministry discussed in chapter 9) funded by the Institute for the research on Unlimited Love and participate in the Healing Rooms of Greater Cleveland (see chapter 8).

5. Throughout this discussion I will use the terms "Pentecostal" and "Pentecostal/Charismatic" (P/C) interchangeably. "Pentecostal" is sometimes used as a generic term to include both Pentecostals and Charismatics, although it is more commonly reserved for

adherents of traditional Pentecostalism. The term "Charismatic" is generally used for neo-Pentecostal groups that developed after 1950.

6. Karen Armstrong (2000) has described "the battle for God" as one in which *mythos*, a "mode of knowledge rooted in silence and intuitive insight which gives meaning to life but which cannot be explained in rational terms" (p. 376), is challenged by *logos* or "rational, logical, scientific discourse" (p. 376). The P/C movement's involvement in this "battle" is somewhat different from both Christian Fundamentalism and liberalism. Despite the difficulty of maintaining *mythos* and the P/C tendency to drift toward fundamentalism, the regular waves of revival that wash on P/C shores contribute to the dialectical dance between the intuitive and the rational.

7. The figures on persons involved in the P/C movement are not without ambiguity (see Grant Wacker's "Appendix: U.S. Pentecostals," 2001). Those classified as Pentecostal are usually done so on the basis of membership in a Pentecostal church. Charismatics are generally determined by reported self-identification with the P/C movement.

8. In 1995 a survey was prepared for distribution through *Spread the Fire,* the magazine published by the Toronto Airport Christian Fellowship, to be completed by those who had visited this renewal site. This same questionnaire was included in the "Catch the Fire" (October) and "Healing School" (November) conference programs. A total of 918 useable questionnaires were returned. Twenty-five percent of the respondents also included qualitative information that supplemented the questionnaire data. In 1997 a follow-up survey was conducted for the 1995 respondents who indicated a willingness to participate in this survey by providing a name and mailing address. Of the 690 questionnaires mailed to the original respondents, 364 (53 percent) were returned to the researcher. Findings from these two surveys are used to address issues raised throughout the book.

9. This account was written by Scott McDermott, senior pastor of Washington Crossing United Methodist Church in Pennsylvania. McDermott holds a doctorate in New Testament studies from Drew University and serves as an adjunct professor at Southern Methodist University.

10. Although McDermott does not use Scripture to support his vision, one passage that readily comes to mind is Jesus' (Matt. 11:28–30) call to the weary: "Come to me, all you who are weary and burdened, and I will give you rest. Take my yoke upon you and learn from me, for I am gentle and humble in heart, and you will find rest for your souls. For my yoke is easy and my burden is light." Narrators often do weave in Scripture passages, seemingly to link private revelations with biblical authority.

11. The mysticism described here best fits with what Walter Stace (1960) has defined as *extrovertive,* providing more elaborate details about and interpretations of the religious

experience. This type can be compared with *introvertive* mysticism, often described in terms of "pure consciousness," "nothingness," and "loss of self." In reviewing hundreds of testimonies from the TACF pilgrims, it would appear that introvertive and extrovertive forms of mysticism often occur in tandem. Visions and voices provide materials for interpretations, but the experiences themselves are often said to be "indescribable." In accord with Stace's unity thesis and the empirical research of Ralph Hood and his colleagues (2001), these testimonies suggest that a common phenomenology underlies the experiences at TACF and other reports of mystical experiences.

12. See Hood et al. (2001) for a comparison of mysticism in the United States and Iran that offers general support for Stace's "unitive" phenomenology of mysticism.

2

Faces of God in Revival: Music, Mysticism, and Metaphor

We find that the decision to listen to pure music involves a particular attitude on the part of the listener. He stops living in his acts of daily life, stops being directed toward their objects. His attention toward life has been diverted from its original realm; in Bergson's terminology, his tension of consciousness is changed. He lives now on another plane of consciousness.

—*Alfred Schutz*

Music is said to take humans into a "rarified sphere, beyond concepts, representations, and objectivity" (Stambaugh 1989, 167). Whether enjoyed alone or in community, music's peculiar sociality is not dependent on conceptual thought or rational logic. As noted in the excerpt taken from the works of phenomenologist Alfred Schutz (1964), music has the potential to lift the hearer (and the performer) to "another plane of consciousness." In his discussion of "Making Music Together," Schutz observes how "performer and listener are 'tuned-in' to one another, are living together through the same flux, are growing older together while the musical process lasts" (Skarda 1989, 87). Music thus often generates a shared experience of what Schutz calls "inner time" that binds people together.

What has been said about music and particularly about the "mutually tuning-in relationship" could also be said about mysticism in general and Pentecostal/Charismatic (P/C) revivals in particular. Mutually tuning in is a form of social interaction that is precommunicative and nonconceptual. It can neither be grasped by, nor does it directly enter into, the process of communication. As Skarda (1989, 81) notes, "It forms the substratum of human interactions, so to speak, and the possibility for the emergence of language as the paramount vehicle of communication."

Although Schutz used music to illustrate the "tuning-in" relationship, the revival services at the Toronto Airport Christian Fellowship (TACF) often appear to be conducted on a similar "substratum of human interaction" that is not readily accessible to existing data-gathering instruments. Two important components of TACF-like renewal services during which music plays a significant role are (1) so-called worship, the initial hour or so of music and song, and (2) receiving prayer from a prayer team, a time during which individuals wait in personal prayer before being prayed with following the formal service. During worship and postservice prayer, congregants are most likely to connect with what Schutz has termed "inner time" made possible through "mutually tuning in"—times during which music facilitates a personal altered state of consciousness that brings many into a heightened sense of mystical unity with God and with other worshipers.

Comparing mystical experience to musical experience is more than an analogy. James Spickard (1991; 1993) contends that the Schutz's discussion of music provides an important basis for a sociology of religious experience, especially experiences during religious rituals. Musical experience and religious experience are both "patterns of inner time; like all patterns of inner time, they can be shared" (Spickard 1993, 199). It is the extended time of music (which P/C Christians refer to as "worship") that is catalytic for a sense of close communion with the divine. Sociologist Don Miller (1997, 87) has described this link between P/C music and mystical experiences based on his field research in so-called third-wave congregations in Southern California where "worship may be viewed as a form of sacred lovemaking, transcending the routinized rituals that so often structure the human divine communication." As will be demonstrated in the chapters that follow, accounts of the experiences shared by pilgrims to Toronto provide countless examples of this inner time that demonstrates both corporate and personal dimensions.[1]

This chapter seeks to build on observations about the interplay of music and P/C mystical experiences. It explores the role music plays in contemporary revival rituals, its relationship to the mysticism enjoyed during the gatherings, and the metaphors used to describe the face of God found in revival lyrics. Music is not only a vital component of the P/C ritual and its accompanying experiences, but it also serves as a bridge to the more cognitive expressions of metaphor and myth.

MUSIC IN PENTECOSTAL/CHARISMATIC CONTEXT

Music has been central to the P/C movement ever since its inception early in the twentieth century. Religious historian Edith Blumhofer (1993) discusses the important link between the joyful spirit of early Pentecostals, its lively and diverse music, and the attraction of new converts in early Pentecostalism in a manner that also reflects the affect, functions, and diversity of contemporary revival music:

> The conviction that "Jesus had come" in a vital way into their circumstances seemed to imbue participants with limitless joy and reckless courage. Joy typically found expression in enthusiastic, fast-paced "infectious" singing. . . . Parham's [one of the founding fathers of Pentecostalism] associate Howard Goss appreciated the role of music in attracting converts: "Without it," he claimed, "the Pentecostal Movement could never have made the quick inroads into the hearts that it did." Pentecostals sang holiness songs, gospel music, and Charles Wesley's majestic descriptions of Christian experience. Some of the earliest Pentecostal creativity took musical form. David Wesley Myland and Aimee Semple McPherson were among the more prominent of many who claimed to have been divinely "given" songs in tongues and interpretation that achieved a degree of popularity. Within a decade, Pentecostals also began writing popular gospel songs that captured and popularized their fervent hopes. (p. 92)

The musical style of early Pentecostalism reflected the time and social origins of its followers, eventually becoming an anachronism for many of its descendents and newer converts. It did, however, demonstrate the importance of using music that was culturally relevant in its rituals, a lesson that has not been lost on present-day revivalists. While the second and third waves of the P/C movement produced music that was unfamiliar to many descendents of the early Pentecostalism who had isolated themselves from much of the larger culture, many in traditional Pentecostal denominations have slowly adopted first the choruses of the second wave and now the newer musical forms of the third wave.

Like the founders of Pentecostalism, contemporary music leaders of the third wave recognized that "tradition" (even Pentecostal tradition) has limited appeal. Miller (1997, 17) astutely notes how "tradition is more often a negative than a positive word" in P/C circles. He further comments that while a few boomers may like Bach and Mozart, "most groups grew up on bands and singers, not orchestras and choirs, and it is not surprising that they seek out churches with contemporary music." A new form of contemporary worship music grew out of the Association of Vineyard Churches (AVC), parent to TACF revival, that has become a hallmark of the revival of the 1990s.[2]

Vineyard music varies in style, reflecting a range of contemporary music, including differences found in geographic locale and according to age cohorts. Some mellower forms employ acoustic guitars, while much of it is soft rock or jazz oriented that utilizes electric guitars and drums. Youth bands are more likely to emulate heavy metal with more of a rock edge to the music, while adult bands may be more seventies-like or adapt the sounds of New Age music. The music of TACF (formerly the Toronto Airport Vineyard [TAV]) reflects these stylistic differences, with its artists mixing and matching forms that reflect regional adaptations that can be found throughout Canada, England, Australia, and the United States. A description found on the TACF website (www.tacf.org) of a recent TACF recording, "Catch the Fire 7—Dancing with the Father," speaks specifically of the relationship between music, the mystical worship experience, and the common articulation of such experiences:

> The production carries the intimacy and passion of the worship experience at TACF. . . . Toronto's hallmark is the drawing together of powerful worship songs from around the world and adding songs written here to help facilitate the listener's receiving a unique encounter with God. "Catch the Fire 7" is an album that is a demonstration of God's love and power and a catalyst in your worship experience.

Ritual and Music in Social Context

A premise on which TACF operates and reflected in its worship is that the so-called Toronto Blessing comes through the power of the Holy Spirit. Revival rituals (music, testimonies, preaching, etc.) are seen as conduits through which the power flows, being thus a means rather than an end. Although relying almost exclusively on contemporary religious music, it is noteworthy that successful revival meetings have not rested on a particular music leader, band, preacher, ministry team, or even particular physical place. Especially during the early months of the revival at TACF, the church was forced to use musical groups from other local churches to meet its needs (including some that sounded like high school bands) without dampening the revival spirit. Over the years, however, there has been an increased professionalism with nightly services led by resident music ministers Jeremy Sinnott (the original leader) or Rob Critchley (who joined Sinnott on the TACF staff in 1996). Other internationally known worship leaders and bands often accompany the TACF staff musicians during regularly scheduled conferences. Reliance on unproven groups of uneven quality from local churches to meet the needs of nightly renewal services has long become a thing of the past.

A ritual form, variations of which are used worldwide, provides a stage for the nightly visitation of the Spirit at TACF and other revival tributaries. Miller describes well the model for Vineyard worship that is foundational for most revival services that have spun off from the Toronto church:

> Regardless of the Vineyard one enters, the pattern of worship is similar. The service opens with a brief prayer, inviting the people to enter into the presence of God. Then for the next thirty to forty minutes, a worship team comprised of several vocalists and a small band of musicians leads the people in singing worship songs. The lyrics are simple and are projected onto a screen or wall where all can see them. There are no hymnals or prayer books to occupy one's hands. Posture is a matter of personal preference and changes as individuals respond to their spiritual yearnings. Looking around the audience, one may see some people standing with arms raised, and others sitting. On some faces, tears trickle down cheeks; others possess a radiant smile. This period of worship is a time of both great interiority and divine connection. (Miller 1997, 91)

Often lasting an hour or more at the beginning of a gathering, music plays a vital role in the revival ritual. Contemporary music (with the expected degree of amplification and beat) sets the mood for "making a joyful noise unto the Lord," giving permission to worshipers to dance, sway, and play before a divine Father who loves his children. Engaging the whole person, including emotions and the physical body, revitalized P/C worship requires more than a cognitive assent. It is during the worship time that many appear to enter into the "collective effervescence" that Emile Durkheim recognized to be the heart of ritual. Praise and worship of God is believed to be the medium through which the presence of God is made manifest, as reflected in the oft-cited scripture verse, "God inhabits the praises of His people."

Since the earliest days and months of the renewal, Jeremy Sinnott, the senior music pastor for TACF, has taught classes for pastors, music leaders, and others on how to conduct TACF-style worship. Sinnott's definition of worship guides his actions: "Worship is a personal and intimate meeting with God in which we praise, magnify and glorify Him for His Person and His actions. It is the act of freely giving love to God. We meet God and He meets us" (Sinnott 1995). He emphasizes that worship is "only for God's glory," and all must be evaluated in light of that purpose.

Although Sinnott insists that he does not want anyone "to pick up a formula," an acknowledged normative pattern has developed to ensure the smooth flow of worship. For example, the opening music tends to consist of songs that are electrically charged, proclaiming in loud and exuberant song what God is doing or about to do. Then begins the process of "bringing it down," moving toward quiet worship songs that allow the worshiper to enter into a time of contemplative intimacy with God. Sinnott notes it would be "rude" to end worship and move into the announcements on this note. (A select piece of music may last ten minutes or more before moving onto the next selection, allowing affect to build, especially during the more contemplative pieces.) The music tempo is then brought up a bit to allow the move to the next phases, typically announcements, testimonies, and preaching before the altar call and prayer with team members at which time the music typically resumes (Sinnott 1995).

The music team is also charged with providing music during the elongated time of prayer time with teams praying for individuals following the altar call. The music chosen for the time of prayer ministry is "quiet intimate love songs to Jesus." The intent is to keep the music "relatively quiet to allow those who want to worship to do so." As more and more people came to revival meetings seeking nightly prayer at TACF, a greater emphasis was found on instructing people to remain in a worshiping mode as they awaited someone to come and pray with them. Pilgrims were reminded that many people, without seeking the assistance of prayer ministry teams, were ministered to during this time directly by the Holy Spirit. Once prayed with, pilgrims were encouraged to remain in a receptive mode "soaking in" the blessings being poured out upon them. A live worship band generally played for an hour or so and then was replaced with CD music.

A common distinction is made in renewal circles between *a musician* and *a worshiper*. Ideally, the music leader should be both, but there is an expressed preference for someone who knows how to worship and to lead others into a sense of God's presence over a skilled concert musician who may be tone deaf to divine leadings. A recent revival song titled "The Heart of Worship" (with subtitle "When the Music Fades") captures the sentiment of many worship leaders and followers of the revival about music and revival:

When the music fades
All is stripped away
And I simply come
Longing just to bring something of worth
That will bless your heart
I'm coming back to the heart of worship
And it's all about you, Jesus. (Redman and Smith 1999)

Music, while a facilitator for worship, is not identical to worship. Believers are frequently reminded that true worship is not found in any ritual component but only in a personal relationship with the divine. Having said this, the fact remains that music unquestionably plays an important role in revival services in facilitating a kind of communal mysticism or (to use a Durkheimian concept) a sense of "collective effervescence."

Music and Altered States of Consciousness

Music appears to be related to the altered states of consciousness (ASC) experienced by many who attend the P/C renewal services. Revival experiences have been noted to commonly include one or more of the following: an alteration in thinking or in perception of time, a loss of control, a change in emotional expression, dissociation between mind and body, perceptual changes, feelings of profound insight, a sense of the ineffable, feelings of rejuvenation, and hypersuggestibility (Helland 1996). During such times the temporal dimension seems to fade and the spiritual dimension is enhanced. Often this altered state of consciousness is accompanied by physical manifestations (the subject of the following chapter), including falling to the ground, loud belly laughter, intense weeping, and even animal sounds. The most common manifestation is falling to the ground (commonly referred to at TACF as "carpet time") while being prayed for by a prayer team and laying prone (sometimes for an hour or more) while "waves of the Spirit" wash over the person.[3] Throughout this prayer time, worship music, usually played live for the first hour or so followed by CD recordings, can be heard in the background. It is during this time, as will be illustrated throughout the next two chapters, that many of those who received prayer report having encountered the divine in extraordinary ways.

Music is an important triggering device for the ASC commonly experienced in revival rituals. Worshipers and leaders of worship are likely to recognize when the musical section of the service reflects a special "anointing" or when a particular piece of music carries such an "anointing" in bringing about an altered state of consciousness. With the service and surroundings being very simple (no fancy churches, icons, stained glass, candles, or incense), music assumes an even more important role than it does in liturgical churches where religious triggers are more diffuse. As Miller (1997, 81) notes: "In the very emptiness of these worship places, music becomes central as a triggering device. Music connects to very deep strata in human consciousness; the interaction between performer and listener is nonrational and 'right brain' rather than rational, objectively verifiable, and 'left brain.'"

Although the social context and its triggering devices can be described, care must be taken not to impute unwarranted causation to these observations.[4] Social context, including traditions, expectations, even the "right music," does not automatically ensure the success of a revival. Like musical experiences, mystical experience cannot be reduced to the context in which it occurs— some aspects of both mysticism and music remain free of the conditioning power of tradition. Having cautioned about the inherent causal limitations of this discussion of music and revival, I feel it is important to add a word about the significance of looking at music within its social context. It remains the task of social science to explore social relationships that provide a better understanding of the seeming miraculous, and music appears to provide an important key for understanding the shift from ordinary consciousness to ASC.

TOWARD A BIOPSYCHOLOGICAL UNDERSTANDING OF MUSIC

In seeking to account for the potential effects of music on religious experience, psychologist David Wulff (1991, 76–82) has brought together four complementary explanations. These include auditory driving, subauditory components, a Pavlovian model, and the role of endorphins. Again, it is important to sound a cautionary note at the onset of this discussion. Researchers do not claim that music alone will produce religious feelings, induce ASC, or launch revivals. Music of some form seems to be a necessary correlate of P/C revivals but is not sufficient to explain the ebb and flow of charisma. Wulff (p. 78) astutely observes that most people "strongly doubt that any one factor such as auditory driving will be shown to be of sole, or even predominant importance in possession states; rather such states are likely to be caused by a number of interrelated factors, from psychological to cultural, which vary greatly from one setting to another." To this list of potential causes, I would like to add another one suggested by J. Bowker in 1973 and reiterated more recently by Ralph Hood (1995, 3): "[I]t is still not unreasonable to suggest that part of our sense of God comes from God."

The four explanations identified by Wulff are overlapping and interconnected. Quite probably they play significant but partial roles in fueling revival fires. *Auditory driving* refers to "the loud and rhythmic music and especially the beat of the drums that so often accompanies these ecstatic practices [which] may directly affect neural functioning" (Wulff 1991, 76). Popular revival music, especially the selections used to open or close the worship time that sing about revival, fits this general description of shamanistic sounding music that has moved humans for centuries. The more meditative music that is played during much of the service and during the final extended time of prayer seeks to bring the worshipers into the divine presence. This time of worship is much less likely to make use of loud rhythmic forms, sounding more like soothing New Age music than rhythm, rock, or rap.

It may be that auditory driving is a prelude to still other auditory or subauditory mechanisms. *Subauditory components*, notes Wulff, have a commonality with thunder. "With sufficient distance, thunder may be inaudible to the ear yet deliver powerful infrasonic waves that trigger the brains reticular activating system without providing sensory clues to their origin (Wulff 1991, 77–78). Ritual music throughout the ages, ranging from the majestic pipe organ to the modern rock bands." has been able to recreate sensations "of the intrinsically mysterious, which humans resolve by attributing the origin of these feelings to the supernatural." My observations over the years suggest that most adults are more likely to be moved to an altered state through more meditative music than through the beat of heavy metal.[5] Having noted a tendency, I must add that I have seen numerous cases of ASC without the aid of music—before any music is played at the start of a session and after it has become silent. In the height of the renewal, expressions of ASC could be witnessed without any musical accompaniment in airplanes en route to Toronto, in hotel lobbies, in restaurants frequented by pilgrims, and even in parking lots.

The *Pavlovian model* takes a somewhat different tack by examining the overall effects of religious rites on their participants. Wulff (1991, 78) claims, "We may safely predict that the vigorous and prolonged movement patterns that commonly occur in ecstatic rituals, in combination with the excitement or stress that frequently accompanies them, will increase heart and breathing rates, modify blood chemistry, and sometimes disturb the sense of balance and equilibrium." This proposed explanation might have particular relevance for the common experience of falling down and doing carpet time when being prayed for by a prayer team.

Those seeking prayer sometimes stand for long periods of time with eyes closed and hands open while worship music plays in the background before being approached by a team of pray-ers. Having been both prayed for and been involved in praying with others on countless occasions at TACF, again I must caution about too simplistic a use of the Pavlovian model. I have had similar responses to my prayer offered for others (not previously involved in the renewal) in the classroom when teaching at a Christian college, in offices, in restaurants, and in private homes (to name a few places) where no music was being played.

Finally, the *role of endorphins* seems to play a role in the altered states of mind that occur for many during revival meetings. Music is known to affect endorphins, the pain-relieving and euphoria-inducing properties, found in the brain. As Wulff (1991, 81) notes:

> A number of researchers now speculate that endorphins play a major role in trance states and other phenomena associated with ritual. Prolonged physical exertion, as in ritual dance; loud, rhythmic music or other acoustic stimulation; fear-inducing procedures such as handling snakes or fire, whipping or piercing of flesh, or preaching of eternal damnation—such practices as these, especially if joined with extended fasting, thirsting, sleep deprivation or stimulus reduction, or hyperventilation, are thought likely to facilitate the production of endorphins and thereby the achievement of euphoric altered states of consciousness.

Of the practices mentioned by Wulff as related to the release of endorphins, music serves as the primary stimulant in revival rituals.[6]

Building on the explanations just discussed, more recent research in musicology recognizes not only that music is a universal phenomenon but also that it may predate humans and is found among animal species. Particularly through work done in biomusicology where the neurosciences and behavioral biology, as noted by the editors of *The Origins of Music* (Wallin, Merker, and Brown 2000, ix), "have made significant strides in areas relevant to the foundations of musicology. Thus, there is now hope in gaining an understanding of the processes of musical cognition as well as biological factors that, together with cultural determinants, shaped mankind's musical behavior and the rich global repertoire of musical structures it has produced." Those searching for the origins of music, for the most part, have abandoned earlier suggestions that humans simply mimic animal musical sounds, but rather they emphasize a complex interrelationship between biological and cultural factors that have developed over time. Freeman (2000, 422), for example, presents a neurological argument to suggest the neurobiological role of music in social bonding. He asserts that "music and dance originated through biological evolution of brain chemistry, which interacted with the cultural evolution of behavior." Geissmann (2000, 118), in a related article, traces the evolution of music through song and the human voice. He closes his discussion with the following observations:

The most widely distributed (albeit not universal) function, and probably the most likely function of early hominid music, is to display and possibly reinforce the unity of a social group toward other groups. In humans, this function is still evident today whenever groups of people, be they united by political, religious, age, or other factors, define themselves by their music. National hymns, military music, battle songs of fans and cheerleaders encouraging their favorite sports teams, or the strict musical preferences of youth gangs may serve as examples of this phenomenon, whose origin may go back to the very beginning of human evolution." (Geissmann 2000, 119)

The field of evolutionary musicology may hold important insights for understanding the role of music in cultural development, including the role music plays in the culture that develops around the P/C renewals and revivals.[7]

MUSIC AND EMOTIONAL AROUSAL

It has been theorized that music, with its roots deep in a physiology shared with other animals, predates human language. Whether this theory of origins survives further scientific scrutiny, it has alerted scholars to the relationship between physiology, neurology, emotional arousal, and musical sound. Music not only can be a catalyst for the body to sway, hands to clap, and feet to tap, but music can and does affect human emotions. This relationship between music, the subsequent release of chemical substances in the brain, and emotional arousal is relevant for describing changes in the mystical self, including somatic responses (see chapter 3) and emotional, mental, and physical healing (see chapter 4).

Scholarly recognition of the relationship between types of music and emotional responses goes back to the ancient Greeks who developed a typology for categorizing music. Building on this typology, contemporary scholars can now relate these changes in the emotional state to chemical changes in the brain (Freeman 2000). According to the ancient Greeks, Phrygian music, using the sound of trumpets to incite action in battle, is accompanied by feelings of fear and rage. Such music is now recognized as a catalyst for the release of norepinephrine in the brain. Lydian music is "solemn, slow, plaintive, and religious, with a reliance on flutes instead of trumpets" and is reportedly correlated with a contemplative and relaxed mood that releases serotonin in the brain. Ionian music is "convivial, joyful, and, according to Plato, effeminate, relying on drums to induce dancing." Ionian music appears to bring about the pleasurable states now associated with the release of dopamine and endorphins (Freeman 2000, 417–18).

Most contemporary revival music tends to be either Ionian and celebrative or Lydian and contemplative, with both being used extensively during a single service. Ionian music is played largely as a prelude to a time of Lydian, more contemplative music. Ionian music is also played as an interlude after the announcements and testimonies have been given and before the sermon (while ushers pass the collection baskets). Lydian music is more likely to be played during the time of prayer with prayer teams that follow the altar call and can be considered a kind of postlude to the formal part of the two-hour or more service. It is likely that the music played during the revival rituals can cause a neurological response that may be related to emotional, mental, and physiological changes in worshipers. This is particularly significant for the discussion of healing found in chapter 4.

In sum, revival music can be analyzed in terms of Schutz's (1964) inner time being captured by the sound of instruments. Instrumental expression, however, is but one component of music, and the lyrics that accompany the melody also warrant some attention. It is through language set to music that revival experiences find another, but intimately related, mode of expression. Music and religious experiences may well be involved in a dialectical dance, with music both facilitating revival experiences and also capturing in memory that which has already occurred. The medium used to relate the experienced inner time of music and mysticism to the chronological time of culture and its social context is metaphor.

REVIVAL METAPHORS SET TO MUSIC

There is a critical distinction between *reality* (what is really out there, whatever that may be), *experience* (how that reality presents itself to personal consciousness), and *expressions* (how individual experience is framed and articulated) (Bruner 1986). The tools of social science can do little to determine the reality of religious experiences during revivals. The best researchers can do is to describe the religious experiences people claim to be having during religious revivals through full participant observation or by asking others about the experiences or both. Although such soft methodology may leave some scholars uneasy, it reflects the "unscientific" way in which humans live and interpret their everyday lives. As Edward Bruner (1986, 7) notes, "Some experiences are inchoate, in that we simply do not understand what we are experiencing, either because the experiences are not storyable, or because we lack the performance and narrative resources, or because the vocabulary is lacking." (This difficulty was noted a number of times in secular publications where reporters themselves enjoyed some of the emotional and even physical manifestations reported by pilgrims to TACF, but then were at a loss to frame them within their master secular paradigms.) A common popular device for sharing lived religious experiences through the ages has been through the use of metaphor.

Metaphors are ordinarily selected to fit a preexisting and culturally shared model, serving an important role in complex reasoning about familiar but abstract domains. Quinn (1991) has succinctly described the relationship between the abstract domain, its cultural context, and the metaphors used in discourse:

> Particular metaphors are selected by speakers, and are favored by these speakers, just because they provide satisfying mappings onto already existing cultural understandings—that is, because elements and relations between the elements in the source domain make a good match with elements and relations among them in the cultural model. Selection of a particular metaphor for use in ordinary speech seems to depend upon its aptness for the conceptual task at hand. (p. 65)

Not surprisingly, the metaphors selected by P/C Christians to talk about their experience are usually biblical concepts or narrative. Common metaphors used when referring to the renewal/revival are based on the basic earth elements that are also used repeatedly in the scriptures and in accounts of earlier revivals: rivers, rain, wind, and fire. Popular renewal songs include titles such as "Light the Fire Again," "Let It Burn," "Fire, There's a Fire," "Revival Fire," "The River Is Here," "Let the Winds Blow," "Sweet Wind," "Let the River Flow," "Your Love Flows Like a River," "Let Your Love Rain Down," "Let It Rain," and "Rain Down on Us." Appropriate lyrics are set often to Ionian-like music that celebrates the revival and are used primarily at the beginning and end of the elongated time of singing that opens the service. Some are set to Lydian-like music of more quiet, contemplative supplication that are said to move the worshiper into (to use another metaphor) the "throne room of God." It is in this sacred space that the Bridegroom (Jesus) woos his bride (revival pilgrims) in a divine romance.

The references to rain, rivers, wind, and fire are often mixed, even at times within one song or disk recording. The renewal is seen as "Times of Refreshing" (the title of another popular song by Bob Baker [1994]) that comes from a gentle wind or rain. But this "time of refreshing" is also one of refinement and purification. "Light the Fire Again," (Brian Doerkson 1994), a piece frequently sung during the earliest years of renewal (on the same compact disc as "Times of Refreshing"), cries out to God for a refinement by fire:

> You know my heart, my deeds
> I'm calling out
> Light the fire again
> I need your discipline
> I'm calling out
> Light the Fire again.

Perhaps the best illustration of the use of all three popular metaphors of wind, fire, and water within a song can be found in "Sweet Wind," another song written in 1994 by popular worship leader and CD artist David Ruis:

> There's a wind a-blowin'
> All across the land
> A fragrant breeze of Heaven

Blowin' once again
Don't know where it comes from
Don't know where it goes
But let it blow over me
Oh, sweet wind
Come and blow over me.

There's a rain a pourin'
Showers from above
Mercy drops are comin'
Mercy drops of love
Turn your face to heaven
Let the water pour
Well let it pour over me
Oh, sweet rain
Come pour over me.

There's a fire a burnin'
Falling from the sky
Awesome tongues of fire
Consuming you and I
Can you feel it burnin'
Burn the sacrifice
Well let it burn over me
Oh sweet fire
Come burn over me. (Ruis 1994)

The seemingly disparate metaphors of water, wind, and fire each reveals an important face of the revival. "The river is here," proclaims a particularly popular early renewal song by Andy Park (1995)—it "flows" and brings "refreshing"; it "sets feet a-dancing," "fills hearts with cheer"; and "mouths with laughter." Water imagery reflects the refreshment and joy that comes from experiences of the divine, referred to as "mercy drops of love" in the lyrics of "Sweet Wind" cited in the preceding. Wind, as implied in the title of this selection from Ruis's (1994) recording *Winds of Worship 3,* suggests that the presence of God is a "gentle breeze from heaven" that goes where it will. The imagery of water and wind is supplemented with fire that burns away the old to make way for the new (as found in the David Ruis lyrics cited in the preceding). The imagery of fire at times is linked with powerful winds as "revival fire" sweeps over the earth. Sometimes the focus is on individual spirituality, as found in the lyrics to "Light the Fire Again": "Don't let my love grow cold. I'm calling out—light the fire again" (Doerksen 1994).

Water, wind, and fire can be seen on one level as metaphors about faces of the revival, but when they are used in Lydian music, they tend to be about the felt presence of God. Prayers of longing and waiting for more of God's holy presence characterize much of the more contemplative music used in revival services, spawning another complex set of metaphors about the bride and bridegroom.

The Song of Songs (Song of Solomon) is a book of the Old Testament that only infrequently finds its way into a typical Sunday sermon. God is not mentioned by name in its chapters, and on the surface it seems to be simply a love story, presumably about King Solomon. Christian mystics, including Bernard of Clairvaux, John of the Cross, and Madame Guyon, have recognized its metaphoric qualities and applied the love story to the soul and the divine. Those involved in the latest revival have used it, as well as other metaphoric images of the church as the bride and Jesus as the bridegroom, as a trope for the P/C movement. Based on the Book of Revelation, Jesus is coming back for a bride that is spotless, thus the call for fire to purify hearts. Three of TACF pastor Jeremy Sinnott's new CDs from TACF are titled *Intimate Bride, Passionate Bride*, and *Warrior Bride*, complementing single selections about the bride that have been popular both as celebrative songs and especially as songs for contemplative worship.

Romantic lyrics set to Lydian music make up much of the heart of worship time. David Ruis's popular CD *True Love* (1992) includes songs professing "I Want to Know What Love Is," "Jesus, I Need to Know 'True Love,'" and "'His Love' is higher than the highest of mountains." Later popular recordings by other artists continue this love theme: "No One Like You" (*Light the Fire Again*, 1994); "Arms of Love" (*Do It Again Lord*, 1995); "My Jesus I Love Thee" (*Winds of Worship 4*, 1995); "You Are the Love of My Life" (*What a God!*, 1997); "Only One Love" (*Shake Off the Dust*, 1999) and "I Could Sing of Your Love Forever" (*Festival Generation*, 1999).

These love songs are sometimes addressed to Jesus and at other times to God the Father. Identifying the face of God addressed in the lyrics is seemingly less important than experiencing the love of God. The metaphor of the "Father's heart" remains an important one, as illustrated by the series of 37 CDs released as the *Father's Heart Series*. (It is also worthy of mention that at the time of this writing, the series 1–16 has been discontinued. Songs are quickly adopted and quickly discarded, but the message and metaphors appear to remain the same.)

Although this overview of renewal music fails to capture all the varied themes that can be found, it does provide examples of common metaphors that have been set to music. Providing illustrations of the CD titles and lyrics gives the reader some idea of how metaphors are used within this wave of the P/C movement to capture the longing for and experience of intimacy with the divine.

Mixing Metaphors: A Caveat

A caveat needs to be added to this cursory analysis of renewal CD titles, song titles, and lyrics about the nature of religious metaphors. The rationalistic reader who abhors the use of mixed metaphors may find them disjointed and confusing and fail to see how they operate to bring together individual mystical experiences with images shared by the collectivity. Rather than regarding each metaphor as representative of a single phenomenon, seemingly disparate and fragmented, it may be more productive to note the power of mixed metaphors to integrate and unify.

James Fernandez (1986) contends that "religious culture cannot be expressed satisfactorily in any one metaphor" (p. 172)—that religious movements always mix metaphors. He then uses the metaphor of music to describe the common practice, particularly in religious revivals.

> To take up the musical metaphor again, the shift from domain to domain is like the shift from instrument to instrument in orchestral performance, each in their domain following the basic melody—the overall order of things in that culture— but each adding the different properties, the complementary qualities of their domain of expression. No instrument and no domain can "make music" alone, but performing together they create a vital—or revitalized—cosmological harmony out of iteration, replication, and wide classification. (p. 178)

Paradoxically, the mixing of metaphors brings about a sense of wholeness. There is a play of tropes, a dynamic interaction among tropes that gives people the impression of coherence. The love of the bride and bridegroom is one trope found in the illustrations used here; another image that is used in dance with the biblical romance is the coming of God's kingdom. The "harvest" is ripe ("souls" ready to give their hearts to Jesus), but the Evil One works against this expansion of Christianity. Jesus, however, has won the battle against Evil and is a Warrior Bridegroom; his followers are not only the "Passionate Bride" and "Intimate Bride" but also a "Warrior Bride" (titles of Jeremy Sinnott's CD trilogy mentioned earlier). This same unitive process can be seen in the lyrics addressed to the Father and Jesus as well as the Spirit without a sense of division or fragmentation in the triune Godhead.

The one God is a passionate lover, a father, a sweet wind, a bridegroom, a warrior—to name a few of the images woven together to express Christian myth. Unity, one of the traits of mysticism, is a theme that sometimes subtly and sometimes more directly permeates the renewal/revival movement. There is a sense in which "dividing walls" between and among people are "falling," in which personal fragmentation is "being healed" and in which love is being poured out on the larger world. Unity within the triune Godhead, unity between God and humans, unity among disparate groups of people are all frequent themes that can be found in revival music. Mixed metaphors are important building blocks of myth that facilitate, in Fernandez's phrase (1986), "a returning to the whole."

MUSIC, METAPHOR, AND MYTH

Myths are figures of speech that according to the late scholar of world myths Joseph Campbell (1987) perform several functions, including that of rendering a cosmology. Myths offer accounts to help humans "make sense" of the universe. Armchair scientists of the past who studied myths often perpetuated the opinion that myths were essentially fairy tales. This understanding of myths can be traced back to the early Christian church and its attempt to distinguish its "true myth" from the "false myths." The practice of dichotomizing myths into one of two categories according to its alleged truth or falsity was expanded during the Enlightenment to include the myths of Western religion as well as those of the ancient world.

The anthropologist Bronislaw Malinowski was one of the first to challenge this line of thinking by studying the context in which myths were used in various tribal societies. He discovered that within the living context of ritual myths were highly significant forms of expression that functioned to confirm traditions, to interpret crucial events, to give reassurance to both individuals and groups in times of great stress, and to provide a horizon of meaning within which a group's patterns of social action made sense (Sadler 1970, 18). The social importance of myths has often been obscured by Western society's failure to see myths as a means of communication through much of the history of humankind. The dominance of rationalistic language and objective facts over myths and storytelling has left modern men and women speaking from their ("left") brain rather than as whole persons.

Just as social science cannot distinguish "true" religion from the "false," it lacks both the mandate and the ability to distinguish "true" myth from "false" ones. As first noted by Malinowski and accepted by most cultural anthropologists, myths play an important role in all societies. The difficulty, according to many social commentators, is that (to adapt an old Durkheimian phrase) "the old myths are dying or already dead and the new ones are yet to be born." Put another way, for most modern urbanites myth (including Christian myth) has lost the ability to "make sense" of the universe or to perform its "cosmological function." The problem of finding plausible replacements is reflected in the title of psychoanalyst Rollo May's (1991) thought-provoking book, *The Cry for Myth*. Western society suffers from ways to communicate about "the quintessence of human experience, the meaning and significance of life." According to May (1991, 20):

> Myths are our self-interpretation of our inner selves in relation to the outside world. They are narrations by which our society is unified. Myths are essential to the process of keeping our souls alive and bringing us new meaning in a difficult and often meaningless world. Such aspects of eternity as beauty, love, great ideas, appear suddenly or gradually in the language of myth.

There is a widespread assumption, as already noted, that the old myths—including those of the Bible—have lost their power to captivate the modern rationalistic mind. Rollo May and Joseph Campbell (among others) contend that the old myths have failed and new ones must rise up to meet the human need for meaning and purpose in life. While this may be the case for secular society—in a sense the old myths have failed and the new ones are yet to be born—many mystics involved in the P/C movement are successfully breathing new life into old myths. Contemporary style music, in tandem with traditional biblical metaphors, tends to work together to evoke positive experiences that reinforce seemingly outdated myths.

The narratives in the chapters that follow continue to tell the story reflected in music and metaphor of the role mystical experience plays in the ongoing revitalization of the P/C movement. The seemingly individual mystical experiences found in contemporary revivals share a collective consciousness. They reflect what the late anthropologist Victor Turner (1986a) referred to as *lumen*, or a threshold—a "no-man's-land betwixt and between the structural past and the structural future." Metaphor and myth set to music is but one medium for carrying the revivalists to Turner's threshold. Revival preaching/teaching can be another. It was neither the music nor the preaching, however, that brought the religious seekers, the curious, and the news media to Toronto in the mid-1990s, but rather the somatic responses to the perceived presence of God that swept nightly over the congregation. It is through the lenses of Victor Turner's theory that sought to reconcile "culturology" and neurology that the controversial manifestations and their relation to the mystical self will be presented in the following chapter.

NOTES

1. In his insightful analysis of three different P/C ritual forms, Daniel Albrecht (1999, 143) provides another illustration of a vehicle for sharing "inner time," namely, the religious icon. He suggests that similar processes may be occurring in the veneration of icons and listening to music when he refers to P/C music as an "auditory icon." Albrecht notes that music "embraces the Pentecostal worshipers in an analogous fashion to the manner in which icons visually surround the Eastern Orthodox faithful in their sanctuaries."

2. Kevin Springer, a key figure in the AVC, provides an interesting and relevant statement to this effect in Miller's (1997, 83) study of the emerging denomination: "You don't understand the Vineyard if you don't understand the worship music. That is probably the greatest contributor to the growth and advancement of the Vineyard movement. More than healing, more than books, more than tapes, it's Vineyard music. That's my experience based on what people tell me. John Wimber, if he's really technically trained at anything, it's as a musician. He's the one who developed and set the tone to the music that's gone all over the world and touched Christians from all kinds of traditions."

3. This practice and its accompanying experience have been given varying labels during the course of different P/C revival waves, including "falling under the power" (traditional Pentecostal), being "slain in the spirit" (Latter Rain movement), and "resting in the spirit" (Charismatic movement). "Carpet time" seemed apropos for the playfulness of the early stage of TACF revival (where people were encouraged to remain on the floor and "soak" once they fell). In time the more generic "soaking" replaced the earlier term and included the practice of assuming a prone position voluntarily or involuntarily, alone or in a worship setting, with or without a prayer team to minister, and to expect similar experiences of the divine.

In a recent *Spread the Fire* article, Arnott (2003b, 5-6) deals with the question, "What is soaking?" He describes it succinctly as follows:

> During previous revivals people referred to it as "waiting on the Lord" or "tarrying" as they lingered expecting God's revival blessings. Although "soaking" includes waiting on the Lord, in this present move of the Spirit it means much more than that. To "soak" in God's presence is to rest in His love rather than to "strive" in prayer. As the person receiving a touch from God begins to connect with the reality of the Holy Spirit's presence, he often responds by falling or simply lying on the floor. As he rests expectantly in God's presence, often the Holy Spirit hovers over the person to reveal more of God's love and to renew and repair areas of a person's life. As the believer soaks in God's presence, the Lord takes control and begins to draw his attention to God's word either in the scriptures or through internal audible impressions or pictures he sees in his mind's eye.

4. If the social context alone were responsible for revival events, there would not be the ebb and flow that can be readily found in the revivals and their tributaries since the outbreak of the Toronto Blessing in 1994. Some pilgrims "took the Blessing" back to their home churches and experienced Toronto-like meetings for weeks, months, or even years. For whatever reason, most churches were not able to keep the revival going at their local churches indefinitely. While the revival movement seems to have lost much of its earlier momentum by the birth of the new millennium, there are congregations who only recently "got into the river" (a popular revival metaphor), years after the "fire of revival" (another popular metaphor) had been reduced to dying embers in other congregations.

5. The youth conferences I have attended can have a very different sound and pattern of worship. Moving to an altered state for the young who tend to engage in energetic and ecstatic dance seems to usually be accompanied by loud rhythmic sounds.

6. With the exception of music, most of the practices included in the cited quotation are rarely found (if at all) in P/C revival services. Two of the list are worthy of a passing note. Fasting enjoyed a period of widespread popularity, especially forty-day fasts where only liquids were taken, but they did not enter the picture until two years after the revival began. In fact it was often noted that the revival at TACF was unexpected—it came without the serious extended periods of fasting and prayer that preceded many early revivals. Moreover, as we will see in the overview of lyrics to revival music that follows, the preaching of hellfire and brimstone found in earlier American revivals does not characterize the Toronto stream of the P/C movement.

7. Attempts to utilize its theories to explain revivals to date, however, have fallen short. For example, Sargant's often-cited claim to document striking similarities between brainwashing "techniques and those used to arouse the fervor of dancers in preliterate tribes and parishioners

of evangelistic churches in congregations from the seventeenth century to the present" would be misleading if applied to the revival at TACF. Although emotions are aroused, it is not achieved by fear of devils, severe physical exercise, or sensory overload, as claimed by Sargant (1957) and recently quoted by Freeman (2000, 118).

The Spirit at Play: The Body and the Mystical Self

The mighty winds of Hurricane Opal that swept through Toronto last week (were) mere tropical gusts compared with the power of God thousands believe struck them senseless at a conference at the controversial Airport Vineyard church. At least with Opal, they could stay on their feet. Not so with many of the 5,300 souls meeting at the Regal Constellation Hotel. The ballroom carpets were littered with fallen bodies, bodies of seemingly straightlaced men and women who felt themselves moved by the phenomenon they say is the Holy Spirit. So moved, they howled with joy or the release of some buried pain. They collapsed, some rigid as corpses, some convulsed in hysterical laughter. From room to room come barnyard cries, calls heard only in the wild, grunts so deep women recalled the sounds of childbirth, while some men and women adopted the very position of childbirth. Men did chicken walks. Women jabbed their fingers as if afflicted with nervous disorders. And around these scenes of bedlam were loving arms to catch the falling, smiling faces, whispered prayers of encouragement, instructions to release, to let go.

—*Leslie Scrivener,* The Toronto Star *(October 8, 1995)*

The Toronto Airport Christian Fellowship (TACF) (formerly the Toronto Airport Vineyard [TAV]) drew the worldwide attention of both believers and nonbelievers with the unusual physical manifestations that were seemingly ubiquitous during the early years of the revival. Knowledge about the more peculiar manifestations (e.g., wild shaking, laughter, rolling) in revival history was limited largely to historians of Protestant revivals. The more common expressions (e.g., glossolalia, being "slain in the spirit," prophecy), however, were familiar to many within the various Pentecostal/Charismatic (P/C) traditions. Whether discussing the common or the peculiar manifestations, the duration, intensity, and diversity of the various somatic responses seen and experienced at TACF were unexpected. Even those in the Association of Vineyard Churches (AVC), where a wide range of manifestations had occurred since John Wimber founded the denomination in the 1970s, were caught off guard by the revival at TACF.[1] There were many who were drawn to TACF yet who questioned, "Why can't we have revival without those manifestations?" (Fish 1996, 36). Any number of answers—some theological, some biblical, and some allegorical—were provided in an attempt to explain the somewhat embarrassing and intensely controversial religious expressions.

The story of the revival and its attendant strange manifestations at TACF begins with its pastor, John Arnott, his wife, Carol, and their quest for more of the power of the Holy Spirit. In 1987, while Arnott was pastor of a Vineyard church in Stratford, Ontario, the Arnotts reportedly "felt called" to plant a church in Toronto. Together with Jeremy and Connie Sinnott, the Arnotts began a home group in Toronto. By 1990 the congregation grew to the point where the church was able to rent a space at a warehouse/office complex near the Toronto airport. After commuting between their two churches for four years, in 1991 the Arnotts left the Stratford congregation to an associate and gave their full attention to the Toronto church. The focus of the new church was on counseling their new parishioners, inner healing, and deliverance, the outcome of which the Arnotts were reportedly less than satisfied. As Arnott (1998, 4) describes it, "Somehow battling the darkness had become our focus rather than dispelling it with light. Inadvertently, the devil had become too big, and God, too small."

Like many of the pilgrims who would eventually flock to TACF, John and Carol Arnott reportedly were "dry spiritually" from the intensive demands and limited success of pastoral responsibilities. They saw other ministers who they believed were powerfully anointed for ministry, and they prayed earnestly that they might be similarly empowered. Responding to what they believed was the voice of God, they began to spend their mornings in prayer and to interact with others who were "powerfully anointed." Their quest took them to a revival in Argentina in November 1993 where they attended meetings with some of the Argentine evangelists. It was here that Claudio Freidzon, an Assemblies of God evangelist and a leader of the Argentine revival, singled out John from the

crowd asking him, "Do you want the anointing?" As he gave his affirmative response, John reported something "clicking in my heart and receiving the
anointing and power by faith." It took two months for this power to be experienced in a dramatic way at John and Carol's new church in Toronto—an experience that launched the so-called Toronto Blessing (Arnott 1995).

Meanwhile, a Vineyard pastor from St. Louis, Missouri, Randy Clark, experienced a special anointing of his own through a series of meetings held by the
former South African evangelist, Rodney Howard-Browne who came to the
United States in 1987 as a "missionary to America." Howard-Browne, who is
commonly referred to "God's bartender" because of the frequent demonstra-
tions of seemingly intoxicating experiences at his gatherings, had been conducting revival meetings in which uncontrolled laughter frequently swept
through the congregation.[2] His revival meetings soon became known as the
"Laughing Revival," an appellation it later shared with the revival at TACF.[3]
Clark reluctantly went to a Howard-Browne meeting in August 1993 and was
surprised when he succumbed to "holy laughter." Later that same year Clark
attended a Howard-Browne meeting in Lakeland, Florida, where he experienced what he believed to be a fresh and powerful anointing from the Holy
Spirit through the evangelist's prayer.

After hearing about Clark's experience and the transformation of his ministry at the annual meeting of the AVC in November 1993, Arnott invited
Clark to preach four meetings at TAV. Clark arrived on January 20, 1994, and
the unexpected happened to the approximately 120 persons gathered there. As
Arnott (1998, 5) reports: "It hadn't occurred to us that God would throw a
massive party where people would laugh, roll, cry and become so empowered
that emotional hurts from childhood would just lift off. Some people were so
overcome physically by God's power that they had to be carried out." Unknown to them, the seeming pandemonium experienced on January 20 would
recur nightly (long after Clark's delayed departure three weeks later) during
the months and years that followed. Hundreds of thousands of visitors from
around the world would be touched by the revival, with untold numbers carrying its spirit back to their local churches.

One of the early visitors to the renewal at TACF in February 1994 was Guy
Chevreau, a Baptist minister who had studied revivals while pursuing his Th.D.
at Wycliffe College, Toronto School of Theology. Chevreau (1994) quickly
linked what he observed with Jonathan Edwards and the manifestations that

occurred during the First Great Awakening. He became the in-house theologian who could respond to queries about the controversial physical manifestations through his preaching and teaching classes at TACF and through itinerating around the globe. While the manifestations remained controversial and divisive for many outside the P/C movement as well as some within, Chevreau was able to provide some legitimacy for those who came, experienced, and believed they had been touched by God.[4]

FITS, TRANCES, AND VISIONS

Some readers may find the controversy that soon surrounded the manifestations to be a modern replay of the controversy surrounding "enthusiasm" reported at earlier trans-Atlantic revivals. Descriptions of "enthusiastic" behavior by observers of eighteenth-century revivals in the United States and in England sounded, as Chevreau (1994) astutely noted, much like what was now occurring at the Toronto renewal. (There are also noteworthy differences; it would be difficult to imagine a laid-back Vineyard minister preaching in the style and rhetoric of Jonathan Edwards as he gave his famous sermon "Sinners in the Hands of an Angry God.") Although the cast of characters differed from the 1800s, the arguments have a certain similarity.

There are those who would have sided with Jonathan Edwards' moderate position on the manifestations, some with John Wesley's more radical acceptance, and still others with opponent Charles Chauncy's condemnation. What Ann Taves noted about the divide between natural and supernatural explanations of the historical explanations of "enthusiasm" also would apply to the debate about the Toronto manifestations played out in conservative Christian publications and on the Internet. "True" religion had "true" revivals with manifestations that were from God; "false" religion had counterfeit revivals, with manifestations coming from human abnormalities or from the devil.[5]

A similar scenario that sought to distinguish "true" from "false" revivals was played out during the early years of Pentecostalism. The Chauncy-like position was taken by the holiness and reformed churches from which many early Pentecostals were forced to leave once they experienced glossolalia, or "speaking in tongues." Perhaps more directly relevant to P/C revivals, however, is the split over revival manifestations that occurred between the two most significant players in the outbreak of Pentecostalism early in the twentieth century. Charles Parham is often credited with conceptualizing the doctrine of tongues as the "physical evidence" of Spirit baptism while William Seymour is credited with the Azusa Street Revival that launched Pentecostalism into global orbit. As Taves (1999, 328) notes: "If Charles Parham, preoccupied with counterfeits, was (loosely speaking) the Jonathan Edwards of Pentecostalism, then William J. Seymour was Pentecostalism's John Wesley." While Edwards and Parham both accepted limited somatic expressions as authentic work of the Spirit, Wesley and then Seymour were far more willing to let the weeds grow along with the wheat than to quench what they believed to be the activity of the Holy Spirit. John Arnott, pastor of TACF and leader of its revival stream, can be said to demonstrate a Wesley–Seymour stance on revival manifestations.

The managing of the manifestations at Toronto, however, was more a matter of common sense than a fine-tuned theology or a systematic study of revival history. Most leaders of TACF-style revivals, although unschooled in the nuances that could be found among revivalist leaders of old, fell into the Wesley–Seymour camp. Rather than spending time and effort in sorting through "real" and "counterfeit" manifestations, those in the TACF stream of the renewal preferred testimonial narratives to elaborate theological defenses. The physical manifestations were judged by their fruits, with testimonials to demonstrate their probable authenticity. Many P/C believers soon accepted the manifestations as signs that the Spirit of God was moving in powerful ways, while simultaneously acknowledging that not all that occurred was genuinely of the Spirit. Any rules that were established were done so in the interest of safety rather than theology.

Similarly, revival practices and reflections on them, while commonly checked against biblical stories, were more likely to be considered and discussed in narrative context than under the microscope of systematic theology. Nightly, in the church auditorium and often in parking lots, restaurants, and hotel lobbies, people could be seen laughing and rolling, falling and jerking, and shaking and grunting, as onlookers stood around praying, "Give them more, Lord—more, Lord—more, Lord." In this playful atmosphere, it is not surprising that one of the meanings given to the outbreak of these phenomena in its earliest days is that "God is playing with his kids." A cursory look around at the hundreds of bodies on the floor at any given time, however, would quickly reveal that not all were frolicking in delight. While one person would be lying on the floor consumed with playful laughter, the person next to her could be heaving sighs from deep, uncontrolled weeping or shaking violently as if experiencing lethal shocks, thus providing the visuals to support the mixed metaphors found in revival language. God, the Father who loved to play with his children, was also a God of power and might.

It was the violent shaking, witnessed during many testimonials and often continuing after the pilgrim had fallen to the ground, that gave rise to discussion of God's power being reflected in some of the manifestations. Arnott offered the following hypothesis on the violent shaking that could often be seen at TACF:

> People often shake when the power of God hits them. Why are we so surprised that physical bodies react to God's power? It is a wonder to me that we do not explode and fly apart. God's power is real power—the *dunamis* of heaven. (Arnott 1995, 153)

One of the most dramatic examples I personally witnessed of what some ministers called "getting blasted" occurred on January 21, 1996, and was reported by Roger Helland, a Canadian Vineyard pastor in his book on the revival. Helland had observed and experienced many of the revival phenomena some years before visiting TACF. Shortly after the onset of the Toronto Blessing in March 1994, he had his first experience of being "drunk in the Spirit" after a couple in his church prayed for him—an experience he described as follows:

> As they prayed I could feel the presence of the Holy Spirit. I had felt his presence many times before and I had been "slain in the Spirit" before. I stiffened my knees, but I couldn't resist. I fell on my side on the floor. After about ten minutes I decided to get up. One problem: I couldn't. I could only lift my head. I started to laugh, and I also felt tremendous waves of love. A couple of men helped me up and put my arms around their necks as they supported me. I could not speak clearly. My speech was slurred, my eyelids were heavy, and I could not stand or sit without falling over. . . . I felt a tremendous freedom and joy and a spiritual euphoria which I can't describe. My mind was clear and my spirit was alive. I was then inspired to begin writing this book. (Helland 1996, 15)

It was about the book and his experiences of revival that Helland and I conversed for several hours during the afternoon before he experienced what some would call the "baptism of fire" at TACF's evening revival service. The worship time of the evening service had ended, announcements and testimonials were given, and the main speaker was about to begin his sermon. Helland described what happened next as follows:

Then suddenly, like a bolt of lightning, I was struck down by God's Spirit, and I was lying on my back across several chairs in the second row. I began to shake violently and uncontrollably. I ended up on the floor as my body twitched, heaved, and shook like bacon in a frying pan. . . . Waves of the Holy Spirit's power were causing my whole body to go into the most wild contortions and reactions imaginable. I felt a surge of holy energy and revelation gush from my inner being. People who were near me fell back or began to shake as the Spirit's power spilled over into them too. I felt as if I were the Incredible Hulk bursting with God's power, or Popeye after eating his can of spinach, ready to go and fight Brutus! This lasted for three and a half hours non-stop. (Helland 1996, 15–16)

Helland, recognizing that many might be asking the point of such an experience, offers the following response: "But God took my life and reordered it. The fruit of that experience was that I felt humbled and literally shaken to the core of my being. I experienced the fear of God. I was full of prophetic revelation that blessed people. I wanted to give away to others whatever God was doing in me. I laughed, I cried, I worshipped" (Helland 1996, 16–17).

Whether expressed as play or work (power), those who gave testimonials about the manifestations interpreted them as experiencing the Divine Presence. A common, related rationale for the seemingly bizarre manifestations reasoned that God was using the signs and wonders to wake up a disillusioned and complacent church (Fish 1996). It is difficult to ignore groups of people laughing uncontrollably like hyenas, standing in a corner roaring like a pack of lions, running seemingly without purpose like Forrest Gump through the church auditorium, or lying on the floor shaking as if a piece of bacon over a fire as reported by Helland.[6] The widespread eruption of the strange manifestations and the testimonials accompanying them were edifying to some and scandalous to others. For those who believed, a community of revivalists assured the believer that the manifestations were indeed from God and that more of God's power and presence was soon to come.

Still another interrelated explanation contended that the manifestations are much like a flashing sign saying, "Spirit at work. . . . Spirit at work. . . . Spirit at work." Whether a sign of God's power or his playfulness, the manifestations primarily are regarded as *signs* or even *sacraments*. Although spokespersons for the Toronto Blessing, coming as they do from nonliturgical traditions, would be hesitant to use the term *sacrament* for these phenomena, their attributions fit well the accepted definition for the term as a "visible sign of inward grace." Whether they were the *signs* of semiotics or the *sacraments* of ecclesiastical theology, the physical manifestations cannot be separated from the mystical experiences that occurred and still occur through the Toronto Blessing.

Although the TACF leaders were frequently criticized for encouraging the manifestations and for permitting or even encouraging them to be modeled during testimonials, the official position was that the revival was not about manifestations. The verbal emphasis has remained more or less focused on a simple theme—one of God's mercy and love. As people began to testify what was happening within them as they engaged in seemingly bizarre behavior, the motto originally selected for TACF before the revival began was highlighted: *That we may walk in God's love and give it away.* TACF believes it has been blessed by the renewal and remains committed to "giving it away" as a prime ministry.

MANIFESTATIONS AND THE SURVEYS

I saw a picture of Jesus weeping and weeping. It hit me that I was blaming God for all the bad stuff in my life. I then began to weep, as I never purposively desired to blame God. I loved God with all my heart. I repented and asked for His forgiveness.

Almost immediately my body started rocking and shaking. I felt like something was coming from my belly. I grabbed a pillow as I felt like something was now coming out of my mouth. Then this strange language ("tongues" as I understand it) came forth with uncontrollable sobbing. I cried and talked in this strange language. I laughed and laughed. I couldn't understand how I could be sobbing and then laughing. This went on for one and a half hours. I could think in English, but I couldn't speak in English. I opened my eyes, thinking it would go away, but it didn't. I took a drink. It was still there. I was getting very exhausted, but I could tell it was toning down—and I felt more peaceful than I had ever felt in all my life. The first words in English finally came out: "Thank you, Lord. I love you, Lord. There really is a Spirit of God. HE is alive!" I was ecstatic!

But you know, the most wonderful thing is that for the first time in my Christian walk, I feel victorious and not defeated. I am joy-filled, no longer negative. I have a desire to share the love of God with everyone and anyone. That was two years ago. And it has never died. I am alive in Christ! (Written testimony submitted by Case #264 with the structured survey.)

In 1995 a survey was completed by nearly one thousand Toronto pilgrims, with a follow-up survey conducted in 1997. Although not a random sample of the hundreds of thousands of visitors who have come to TACF over the years, it does provide some insightful data on the pilgrims and their reports of the physical manifestations.[7]

Particularly worthy of note is that 95 percent of the respondents described themselves as "charismatic or Pentecostal Christians," with 87 percent reporting that they had spoken in tongues, and 70 percent had experienced resting or "being slain" in the Spirit ("carpet time") before their first visit to TACF. The majority was personally familiar with the more common manifestations, and many had firsthand experience of some of the more controversial ones. Over one-third reported they had experienced deep weeping (46 percent), holy laughter (38 percent), and dancing in the spirit (34 percent). Fewer reported firsthand experience with the more or less common and more controversial manifestations, including being "drunk in the spirit" (24 percent), intense shaking (22 percent), uncontrolled jerking (11 percent), rolling on the floor (7 percent), or roaring like a lion (4 percent).[8]

While interesting, such statistics provide only a skeletal portrait of the revival experience. They demonstrate that most visitors were familiar with at least some of the manifestations and that these experiences do wax and wane. By themselves, however, statistical data are unable to reflect the complexity of the revival phenomena. Within the woman's report used to open this section, for example, we find a rich description that includes visions, emotional responses, physical manifestations, and a change in emotional well-being. Among the several manifestations reported was her first experience of glossolalia, or "tongues," often regarded by classic Pentecostals to be the "initial physical evidence" of Spirit baptism but treated less doctrinally by those in the so-called third wave of the P/C movement. Of particular significance for those seeking the "fruits" of the somatic manifestations, we see in this testimony that violent shaking, glossolalia, holy laughter, and weeping preceded being filled with a peace and joy that has never left her. She attributed the action to God who remains present and active in her life at the time of the follow-up survey two years later.

Although the statistics from the surveys do provide important background information (see Poloma 1996, 1998a, 1999 for additional data), they also tend to deflect from the narrative qualities of revivals. The dramaturgical theory of the late anthropologist Victor Turner provides a heuristic paradigm to frame revival experiences that maintains the dynamic qualities of revival. Turner, in seeking to integrate neurology and "culturology" within his social scientific model of ritual, provides a framework for describing the manifestations and assessing their relationship to healing and wholeness, a topic introduced in this chapter and developed further in chapter 4.

VICTOR TURNER ON BRAIN, BODY, AND RITUAL

Victor Turner saw the world, and particularly ritual performance, as an unfolding drama. In contrast to many theorists of his day, Turner refused to limit his conceptualization of society to an abstract static system, preferring to frame it as an interrelated and dynamic process. Society, according to Turner (1969, vii) "is a process in which any living, relatively well-bonded human group alternates between the fixed and—to borrow a term from our Japanese friends—'floating world.' Human beings have had to create spheres of action that take them out of the normative, routinized, structured worlds." In Turner's language, these floating worlds are "antistructural" and "liminal."

For Turner, "liminality" is a qualitative dimension of the ritual process that often appears in efficacious ritual, operating "betwixt and between" or "on the edge of" the normal limits of society. Liminal conditions create an antistructure that makes space for something else to occur. Much like the earlier American revivals, the P/C rituals, and especially its revival rituals, have sought to create the space to approach the "lumen."[9]

I would venture to say that Turner would have been fascinated with TACF revival with its blend of structure and antistructured ritual. The primal ritual behavior seen in the manifestations usually (but not always) occurred to the tune of amplified contemporary Christian rock music worked together to produce an antistructured ritual that was fluid and molten. It is within Turner's paradigm, beginning with some of his observations on ritual and then focusing on one of his last essays titled "Body, Brain, and Culture" that we will now turn to discuss the role that manifestations play in revitalizing the mystical self.

Liminality and the Spirit at Play

Yet, there are still times when the direct ministry of the Lord needs to blot out or at least soft-pedal all the hymn singing, preaching and passing of collection plates [in the respondent's formal Anglican liturgy]. We all have a built-in hunger to be dealt with One on one. . . . At Toronto the timetable was still there.

Many of the timetable events—workshop, meal, talk, ministry—were filled with grace. Some were not. It really didn't matter! For again and again, God dropped me out of the singing and listening or ministry by gently but firmly dropping me to the floor and keeping me pinned down there for extended periods. So I am a faulty and inaccurate witness to all that may have happened on the platform or in the hall during the conference. From my place down on the carpet, God directly (a) taught me, (b) healed me, and (c) empowered me by withdrawing me from the heady new routines of TACF. (Narrative supplement to survey case #745.)

The ritual at TACF, as reflected in the preceding quotation provided as a survey supplement by an Anglican priest, seems to illustrate well Turner's understanding of liminality as "betwixt and between" the structure of much contemporary religious ritual and the antistructure of revival. There is a sense within the congregation that God is at work—or perhaps better expressed, God is at play. (Both the concepts of "work" and "play," as we have already seen, appear in TACF's discussion of the manifestations.)

The reported experience of God's love, often accompanied by strange physical manifestations, transcended whatever was actually going on during the ritual, binding the participants into "communitas" that extended beyond the church walls to restaurants and hotel lobbies where it was not unusual to see people "drunk in the Spirit." Who was preaching, what was being said, the kind of music ministry, and the decor of the auditorium did not seem to matter. What did matter (to the respondents, and the critical point for a better understanding of the process taking place) was the *meaning* pilgrims were ascribing to their unusual experiences. For them God was visiting TACF in an unusual way and was changing their lives through the power of the Holy Spirit. As a sociological starting point, however, the ritual framework within which these experiences originate (although they may be actually experienced after leaving TACF) is of particular relevance.

Testimonies were regularly given at renewal services (often while the interviewee was performing spiritual gymnastics before an amused audience) that highlight how lives had been changed through the Toronto Blessing. While the interviewee might be laughing, jerking, or exhibiting some other unusual somatic sign, the focus of the questioning was on what has come to be called the "fruits of the renewal." The narratives included countless stories of personal spiritual refreshment; inspirational reports of increased holiness, wholeness,

and healing; and tearful accounts of repentance, forgiveness, and restored relationships. These narrations based on personal experiences and interpretations are the primary material from which other secondary accounts develop.

I have elected to provide ethnomethodological accounts for two of the more
controversial manifestations, namely, prophetic mime (roaring, crowing/cluck-
ing, and barking) and spirit drunkenness. Some physical manifestations, although unfamiliar to those outside the P/C movement, are well-known
experiences for those who claim to be Spirit baptized. The most common is
tongues, or glossolalia, an experience regarded by many as a litmus test for being Spirit filled. Falling under the power of the Spirit (being slain in the spirit,
resting in the spirit, or doing carpet time) has also been experienced by many
veteran P/C believers over the decades, as have jerking and shaking by many
older Pentecostals. These relatively familiar manifestations stand in stark contrast to prophetic mime and drunkenness, with the latter providing new charismatic script for the reality construction process, just as the older manifestations
provided a reality construction challenge for Pentecostals of generations past.

Prophetic Mime: Those Animal Sounds

As already noted, many of the physical manifestations experienced during
the Toronto Blessing were not new to revival history. Most had been experienced in early American revivals, including the Azusa Street Revival that
birthed Pentecostalism and, more recently, at the AVC in both North America
and in England beginning in the early 1980s (White 1988). Although continually being modified, the basic construction of social reality around glossolalia, being slain in the spirit, and, to some extent, jerking and shaking,
occurred much earlier in P/C history. It was the challenge of providing meaning for the animal sounds (which were relatively infrequent at TACF revival
meetings) that proved to be the straw that broke the proverbial camel's back
and led to the split between the Toronto church and the Vineyard.

Arnott (1995) reported his first encounter with roaring, a phenomenon that
broke out at TACF about five months after the manifestations first began. Arnott
was out of town and had called to see how things were going at his church, when
someone told him that a man "roared like a lion last night." He immediately
asked a series of questions like, "Did he hurt anyone?" "Was it demonic?" "Did he
attack anybody?" "Did you stop it?" The person on the other end of the phone
responded negatively to each query, concluding with the assessment, "We felt it
was from the Lord." Arnott recounted the rest of the story as follows:

When I arrived back in Toronto later that week, the man who had roared was still at our meetings. I interviewed him in front of the church. He was Gideon Chiu, a prominent Cantonese Chinese leader from Vancouver, Canada, a pastor's pastor, very honored and well-respected. He shared what he was feeling and how he had come to Toronto desperately hungry for more of God. Suddenly this meek and mild pastor started roaring again, right in front of everyone. He moved back and forth across the front of our church, roaring and lunging like an angry lion, crying, "Let My people go! Let My people go!"

When he was called to the microphone, he testified that the Chinese people had been deceived by the dragon for hundreds of years, but now the Lion of the tribe of Judah was coming to set His people free. Our church immediately exploded into volumes of praise as they bore witness to what the Spirit of God was saying. (Arnott 1995, 168–69)

Pastor Chiu's account provided the necessary material to help to create order out of what initially appeared to be a disorderly experience. Through the use of personal narratives, other seemingly bizarre behavior was explained and accepted in regular revival ritual.

Crowing rooster and clucking hen sounds soon followed the roaring lions in renewal services. On one occasion I was present at a TACF service when a man who was clucking like a chicken came up to the microphone, struggling to share what he believed God was saying to him. He would try to speak but a clucking noise would interrupt. He stammered and clucked (much like someone with a serious speech impediment), and then he would begin again to try to speak. The prophetic message that finally emerged in this struggle was a simple one: "God is saying that I am going along the ground scratching like a chicken for whatever little I can find while He has set a banquet table. He is telling me to feast at the banquet table." The image of the banquet table (here referring to the revival) is a biblical metaphor, one that proved to be an acceptable interpretation for this visible sign for the gathering. The Spirit-led prophetic mime was seen as a sensual wrapping to present a very simple message in a most memorable manner.

What can be seen from such accounts is how the interpretation of the animal sounds began by soliciting the meaning ascribed to the action by the actor and then evaluating it in light of the reported accounts. If the outcome was judged good, the story was accepted not so much for the animal sounds as for message being imparted. As Arnott (1995, 40) has noted, "these sounds are most often made in the context of prophecy, vision, and revelation." The sounds and gestures are regarded as being a means through which God is speaking to people, not unlike the way a donkey was reportedly used to speak to Balaam in the biblical account (see Num. 22:21–39). Put another way, the animal sounds can be regarded as visible signs of a fresh work of the Holy Spirit, much like glossolalia became the preeminent sign for the earlier P/C movement.

Spirit Drunkenness: Being Inebriated with the Divine

Widespread divine inebriation in the early 1990s began with the ministry of God's bartender, Howard-Browne, and soon became linked with the Toronto Blessing and the revival at TACF. In his discussion of the revival manifestations in history, Chevreau (1994, 13), reported an account of his wife's experience of Spirit drunkenness:

> She was down on the floor, repeatedly, hysterical with laughter. At one point, John Arnott, the senior pastor prayed that she would stay in this state for forty-eight hours. She was that, and more—unable to walk a straight line, certainly unfit to drive, or to host the guests that came for dinner the next evening.

The guests arrived to be greeted by a hostess acting very strangely and decidedly unprepared to serve them. When Chevreau came home to find the table was not set and no dinner was in preparation, he excused himself and went out to buy fish and chips. When he returned, the table was still not set, and leaving the fish and chips on the table, Guy went to gather some eating utensils. As he began setting the table, his wife methodically began portioning out the fries on the table and tossing the fish from the container to their guests— all the while thinking this was incredibly funny!

Janis Chevreau described her own state and feelings about this extended period of Spirit drunkenness when she later appeared on a television talk show ("Toronto Airport Vineyard and Revival," *Donahue Show*) on September 19, 1995. She and her husband had been copastoring a Baptist church just outside of Toronto when they had heard about what was happening at the then TAV. Both were having a very difficult time with the work they were doing when they decided to pay a visit to the renewal:

> Janis Chevreau: We went about a week into it. I was too desperate to be skeptical. We were having a hard time in the church we were working at, and we just decided to go because I had been away the weekend prior with two friends who had been taken by this the week it had begun. And they laughed the whole week-

end, and I thought, "Well," I said, "God, I really need You, but I don't think I want that." But we went the first day, and when it came time for prayer, someone prayed for us and I just—my knees got all wobbly and wiggly, and I just kind of fell over, and next thing I know, I woke up and was just in a fog. And I thought, "Well, I don't know what this is but that's okay." And I went home and we got invited back a day later, we went up to pray again. And they invited pastors and wives who kind of burned out, and that was us, so we jumped up. And they prayed for us, and the men came forward, and there was [sic] about 50 men, male pastors, and about two of us women, and he didn't get over to me and I was on the floor, and that began the laughter for about four hours.

Phil Donahue: You laughed for four hours?

Janis Chevreau: Four hours. . . . There was an intense—I would describe it as joyfulness. I will just briefly tell you I'm a very uptight person. I'm not someone who has a lot of fun as a rule. I'm very serious about life; I saw the heavy side of it. . . . And to see me there [in that state of Spirit drunkenness] was absolutely a miracle in itself. But, yeah, it's just such an intimate time of having fun. . . . But there was some embarrassment. I was always trying to cover my face and crawl under chairs. . . . You're conscious of what's going on, but everything is funny. It just doesn't matter. So I was trying—I was embarrassed a bit, because I thought, "What am I doing? Am I that much in need? Do I need people's opinions of me, or what is it?" So I'd go home each time, wondering what this was about, but there was also—I would go home and literally that first night, there was a joy that came over me. Our circumstances hadn't changed—and there were some hard circumstances we were in—I had a lot of pain, but it lifted right off. And I walked around for months with it lifted.

In his book *The Father's Blessing,* Arnott (1995) told of how people of another congregation were being affected somewhat similarly by Spirit drunkenness. A pastor from Quebec shared how children and adults were experiencing outward manifestations of being drunk while being changed inwardly:

"Every time they go down, it's like they had another glass of booze, but it isn't that at all. It's the Lord's Spirit. If it was just limited to that, I guess that would not necessarily be special in and of itself, but it goes much, much further. While people are under the Spirit they are delivered of all sorts of problems. They go into the heavenlies. They come back, and they are no longer the same. They are transformed" (Arnott 1995, 146).[10]

As with the examples of prophetic mime, there is no single explanation given by those who experience Spirit drunkenness. Some, like Janis Chevreau, are filled with joy; others offer prophetic words; others find it a time of worship and praise; and still others experience forgiveness and different types of healing (discussed in the following two chapters). As rational beings in a culture still heavily influenced by Enlightenment thought, humans are quick to move beyond simple experiential narratives in an attempt to uncover more systematic explanations. Initial social scientific attempts to find patterns, however, have not been successful. Psychiatrist John White began his investigation with the assumption that he would uncover some patterns when he studied the manifestations exhibited in John Wimber's gatherings in the mid-1980s and reports: "But the more I have interviewed affected people and pondered their stories, the more mysterious the matter has become. To force my observations into a coherent theory is at present impossible. I suspect that even rigorous research would not clarify the matter" (White 1988, 104).

VICTOR TURNER AND REVIVAL RITUAL

The quotations used throughout this chapter suggest that Turner's succinct description ritual as being "antistructural, creative, often carnivalesque and playful" (Schechner 1986, 7) fits well in the Toronto-style worship. It provides an opportunity for liminality—Turner's "betwixt and between" threshold that reflects celebrated feelings of "spontaneous communitas." The *lumen*, or threshold, according to Turner (1986a, 41–42) "is a no-man's-land, betwixt and between the structural past and the structural future as anticipated by the society's normative control of biological development." Turner (1986a, 41–42) goes on to describe the liminal phase

> as being dominantly in the subjunctive mood of culture, the mood of maybe, might be, as if, hypothesis, fantasy, conjecture, desire—depending on which of the trinity of cognition, affect, and conation is situationally dominant. Ordinary life is in the indicative mood, where we expect the invariant operations of cause and effect, of rationality and common sense. Liminality can perhaps be described as fructile chaos, a storehouse of possibilities, not a random assemblage but a striving after new forms and structures, a gestation process, a fetation of modes appropriate to postliminal existence.

What has often drawn the pilgrims is a curiosity about the open display of emotion and seemingly bizarre physical manifestations—a ritual context that allows for catharsis quite atypical of modern society. The focus of testimonies given during the ritual itself like those that accompanied the survey responses, however, is much less likely to be on the physical manifestations than on the changes brought about in self-identity. Of the 1995 survey respondents, 70 percent agreed with the statement that "family and friends have commented on the changes that have been observed in me [as a result of the renewal]" (Poloma 1996). In the words of one respondent whose testimony has been repeated time and again by visitors to the revival:

> Personally I am ecstatic at the love, mercy and favor God has been poured out on me by His grace! I've come from a place of somewhat forsaking life, not being suicidal but one where death seemed appealing. I was losing all hope for change and transformation; I was tired and all of the fight was wrung out of me. Being clueless as to why, I was losing the fight and giving up ground. But God in His kindness and mercy began to visit me with His presence and began to help me, opening my eyes and delivering me from the assault of the enemy and the deception in my heart. (Case #832)

THE TRIUNE BRAIN AND RENEWAL MANIFESTATIONS

There is always a danger of biological reductionism in isolating religious experiences from the social contexts in which they occur. While neurology and psychology provide important pieces of the puzzle for understanding religious experience, fascination with the working of the brain can lead to a distorted description. Without either invoking the explanation of the Holy Spirit or discounting the possibility of divine activity (both clearly outside the scope of both natural and social sciences), Turner's (1993) exploratory essay on "Body, Brain, and Culture" (written shortly before his death in 1983) can be used to demonstrate the importance of adding the cultural factor to the somatic and cerebral factors when studying mysticism.[11]

Turner's (1993) use of cerebral neurology and anthropology to fashion a new synthesis on the process of religious ritual predates the new study of neurotheology that seeks to link the brain and spirituality. Recognizing the two schools of seemingly opposing thought on ritual—one insisting that ritual is culturally transmitted and the other that it is genetically programmed—Turner attempts to integrate cultural factors with those of biology. He (p. 83) describes this approach as "a kind of *dual control* leading to . . . a series of symbiotic coaptations between what might be called culturetypes and genotypes."

At the center of his discussion is Paul MacLean's theory of a triune brain. As Turner (1993) notes:

> According to his model, MacLean sees us as possessing three brains in one, rather than conceiving of the brain as a unity. Each has a different phylogenetic history, each has its own distinctive organization and make-up, although they are interlinked by millions of interconnections, and each has its own special intelligence, its own sense of time and space, and its own motor functions. MacLean postulates that the brain evolved in three stages, producing parts of the brain which are still actively with us though modified and intercommunicating. (p. 83)

Turner's discussion of the triune brain—described as the *instinctual brain,* the *emotional brain,* and the *cognitive brain,* with its right and left sectors—warrants closer examination as applied to the manifestations.

Instinctual or Reptilian Brain

The physical manifestations discussed in this chapter would appear to be a result of the activity of what Turner refers to as the instinctual or reptilian brain. Among other things the instinctual brain (1) contains nuclei that control processes vital to the sustenance of life (i.e., the cardiovascular and respiratory systems; (2) is concerned with the control of movement; (3) is responsible for the storage and control of what is called "instinctive behavior"; and (4) is responsible for alertness and the maintenance of consciousness (Turner 1993, 83). The illustration and discussion of the bodily movements experienced by participants in the renewal appear to be closely related to the functions of the instinctual brain. Although some of the thrashing, rolling, falling down, deep laughing, and so forth, that has come to characterize this renewal can become learned behavior, reports suggest that at least some of the initial activity may be involuntary. As demonstrated through the quotations from Toronto pilgrims found in this chapter, the manifestations at times are somewhat voluntary but at other times worshipers find themselves unable to get up off the floor, to curb laughter and tears, or to control violent shaking and jerking.

Involvement of the body in religious ritual can be found throughout human history and among countless cultures.[12] As already discussed, somatic manifestations had been part of earlier American religious revivals (see White 1988; Riss 1997; Taves 1999) where sinners fell to the ground and saints shouted in the felt presence of God. Strange bodily manifestations are also found in shamanist activity (Kakar 1982; Pierce, Nichols, and Dubrin 1983), some psychoanalytic accounts (Scheff 1979; Pierce, Nichols, and Dubrin 1983; Orcutt and Prell 1994), as well as reported by practitioners of kundalini yoga (St. Romain 1994). It might be argued that these seemingly diverse contexts tap into a single primal vestige of the human brain.[13] Although the causal mechanisms remain obscured, it appears that MacLean's reptilian or instinctual brain is responsible for triggering the physical or bodily manifestations observed in psychoanalysis as well as diverse religious rituals.

Emotional or the "Old" Mammalian Brain

The genetic roots of human emotions are seated in the "second brain" of MacLean's model—the "old" mammalian or emotional brain. In the emotional brain are found "the most important components of which are the limbic system, including the hypothalamus (which contains centers controlling homeostatic mechanisms associated with heat, thirst, satiety, sex, pain and pleasure, and emotions of rage and fear), and the pituitary gland (which controls and integrates the activities of all the endocrine glands in the body)" (Turner 1993, 84). While the older reptilian brain has been defined as a "stream of movement," the newer mammalian level has been called the "stream of feeling." As can be gleaned from the narratives found in this chapter, the manifestations had both a somatic and an emotional component.[14]

Although the renewal at TACF has often been referred to as a "laughing revival," there has always been much more than laughing going on. In an attempt to tap the varied emotions that lay beneath the effervescent renewal services, survey respondents were asked to select the physical manifestation experienced at TACF that left the most lasting impact. Resting in the spirit and somatic shaking, jerking, jumping, and so forth, tied for first place, each with 22 percent of the respondents selecting them for first place. The ranking of some other manifestations was as follows: deep weeping (16 percent), speaking in tongues (16 percent), holy laughter (9 percent), being drunk in the Spirit (6 percent), and roaring like a lion (3 percent).

After the respondent selected the single manifestation that left the most impact on their lives, they were provided with a battery of thirty emotional responses and asked to indicate which of them were experienced during the manifestation. There is some evidence that some physical manifestations are correlated with positive affect while others are related to negative emotional responses. As might be expected, laughing was positively correlated to feeling happiness, joy, and peace and was negatively related to feeling fearful, guilty, or sad. Similar correlations with positive affect were found for those who selected being drunk in the Spirit as the most memorable manifestation. Those who chose holy laughter and Spirit drunkenness as the predominant manifestation found the experience to be totally refreshing, as reflected in an increase in scores for positive affect and a decrease in scores for negative affect.

Respondents who reported on weeping and birthing, however, demonstrated statistically significant feelings of negative affect, such as pain and sadness. Their scores on items of positive affect (feelings of happiness, joy, and peace) were negatively correlated to these manifestations. The 16 percent of the survey sample who chose weeping as the most memorable manifestation not surprisingly were statistically more likely to report feelings of sadness, grief, depression, and shame. Similarly, the 6 percent who chose birthing as the most memorable experience reported more negative emotional responses than those who chose laughter or Spirit drunkenness.[15] (See Poloma 1998a for further information.)

What is important to note here is that emotional responses to the varied manifestations did differ in expected ways. Furthermore, the manifestations and their accompanying emotional responses do seem to affect the brain and may be important factors in holistic healing models. This topic will be explored further in the discussion of holistic healing that follows in chapter 4.

The Cognitive or Neomammalian Brain

The cognitive or neomammalian brain "achieves its culmination in the complex of mental functions of the human brain" (Turner 1993, 85). It is responsible for cognition and sophisticated perceptual processes as opposed to instinctive or affective behavior. As we have seen, respondents can and do reflect on their experiences and seek meaning and interpretations for them framed by their P/C worldview.

The cognitive brain is further "split" into two hemispheres. Turner uses the succinct distinction provided by Barbara Lex's overview of the literature to describe the functioning of the respective spheres:

In most human beings, the left cerebral hemispheric functions in the production of speech, as well as in linear, analytic thought, and also assesses the duration of temporal units, processing information sequentially. In contrast, the specializations of the right hemisphere comprise spatial and tonal perception, recognition of patterns—including those constituting emotion and other states in the internal milieu—and holistic, synthetic thought, but its linguistic capacity is believed absent. Specific acts involved complementary shifts between the functions of the two hemispheres. (Turner 1993, 87)

Religious myth is embedded in ritual and can be discussed in terms of the two hemispheres, where the left-hemispheric level works to describe the "ecstatic state and sense of union," which the right-hemispheric level recognizes is literally beyond verbal expression (Turner 1993, 91). Religious myth and structured ritual are more akin to the "serious work of the brain" performed by the left hemisphere than the "play" that characterizes the right hemisphere. (Much of what appears in this book might be described as left-hemispheric narrative attempting to convey playful experiences found in the Toronto Blessing that cannot be adequately expressed in verbal language.)

"Play," as described by Turner, is "a kind of dialectical dancing partner of ritual." Antistructured play has had a prominent place in the TACF ritual, as may be gleaned through the left-brain accounts of the religious experiences described by respondents throughout this analysis. These playful experiences, however, seem to cry for interpretation. (I have described at length elsewhere [Poloma, 1996] how intellectual "order" is made out of the playful "disorder" caused by some of the manifestations.) The following narrative serves as one account of an attempt to "make sense" of the manifestations as experienced by a middle-aged British male respondent:

> From roughly that time onward (a particularly intense experience at a renewal service which included a range of manifestations), I began noticing the manifestation of "bowing forward" continued even outside the service. I had viewed it with curiosity in others, but had never experienced it in twenty-three years of Spirit-filled life. I manifested this again most of the day, and to a lesser degree in my own church after we flew home. I do not yet understand exactly the significance of this manifestation, but I find it subtly unexpected, and nearly without out a sense of my own muscles making the muscular contraction. All bowing has been in slow motion by my sense, meaning that it is not "jerking" or sudden extreme motion, but a quiet, slow bow, much like the British might do if they were to bow to the king or Queen. The bowing does not necessarily seem to coincide with specific words, spoken or words sung, but I have noticed that the name of Jesus and the words "wonderful" and "glory" seem to cause me to manifest more than not. (Case #741)

Manifestations and music (as discussed in the previous chapter) appear to have a similar function in renewal ritual practices, namely, divine worship. Both involve participating in an alternate reality, an antistructured flow, and a minimizing of the social self in interacting with the deity. While cognitive expressions reflect diverse perceptions and accounts of these experiences, there is a seeming commonality beyond the words that involves a sense of Other, or Non-self, that participants believe is the Divine Presence.

SUMMARY AND CONCLUSION

Turner's use of "lumen" and "liminality" to describe the "floating world" of human reality can be regarded as another way of approaching the phenomenon underlying Schutz's phenomenological study of music discussed in the previous chapter. There is a liminal, antistructural quality to the "inner time" to which musicians and lovers of music "tune in." In many revivals, including the recent one at TACF and its tributaries, physical manifestations and music often work together in an antistructure in which unusual physical responses as well as attendant mystical experiences occur.[16] The physical manifestations triggered in the reptilian brain are accompanied by emotional responses of the limbic system and expressed through the efforts of the cognitive brain.

The physical manifestations experienced during religious rituals do more than provide mechanisms for somatic expression and emotional catharsis. They appear to cloak the road to transcendence from one reality to another. As with Turner, we have no intent of "reducing ritual to cerebral neurology" or of saying that "ritual is nothing but the structure and functioning of the brain writ large." There appears to be more happening than some form of cerebral gymnastics. Turner attempted to account for this "more" by discussing a Jungian-inspired *collective overbrain*. For Turner (1993, 104) this collective overbrain was said to be a "global population of brains . . . whose members are incessantly communicating with one another through every physical and mental instrumentality." The overbrain is reflected for Turner in both ritual and community.

Turner's attempt to integrate neurology and culturology is probably not subject to empirical verification. As Schechner (1993, 18) notes, it is a model that seeks "a synthesis not mainly between two scientific viewpoints but between science and faith," a model that moves outside the narrow confines of the scientific paradigm. What the model does permit us to do, however, is to

take a nonreductionistic stance in describing revival ritual practices. It is
through the antistructured worship ritual with its song, dance, and physical
manifestations that Turner's *communitas* may be experienced.
The next chapter will provide a link between personal revival experiences and
the social life of *communitas*. The P/C experiences known as "inner healing,"
"healing of memories," or sometimes "emotional healing," in which fragmented
selves are made whole and broken relationships are mended can be regarded as
building blocks for *communitas*. The mending of psychic and interpsychic brokenness, as we shall see, also appears to play a role in physical healing, reports of
which have been on the rise as the revival continues to run its course.

NOTES

1. Although John Wimber did not found the Vineyard, it is his leadership that brought the
emerging denomination into the P/C spotlight. Wimber's church was initially affiliated with
Chuck Smith's Calvary Chapel, changing affiliations after some disagreement with Smith over
the display of the gifts of the Spirit in church services. In 1982 Wimber moved his congregation
to a small network of congregations called The Vineyards formed in 1974 and then overseen by
Ken Gulliksen.

2. Rodney Howard-Browne was largely unknown until he led revival meetings at the
Carpenter's Home Church in Lakeland, Florida, in 1993. (Carpenter Home Church, an
Assemblies of God congregation, had been a flagship for the Charismatic movement in the
1970s.) During the meetings Howard-Browne reportedly "would just point at people, and they
would fall to the ground writhing in uncontrollable laughter" (Bruce 1999, 75).

3. Play and laughter are phenomena that have a decidedly limited role in liturgical Christian
services and seemingly fare little better in nonliturgical evangelical services. The seeming
frivolity of the Toronto Blessing came under frequent attack in some Christian circles, most
notably from Hank Hanegraaff ("Mr. Bible Answer Man") whose radio program had a large
conservative Christian following. For an interesting and relevant account of C. S. Lewis's
approach to laughter and play in Christianity, see Terry Lindvall's (1996) *Surprised by
Laughter.*

4. The management of the physical manifestations was the primary reason given for the forced
separation of TAV from the AVC. In December of 1995, John Wimber ousted the Toronto church
for a failure to adhere to "Vineyard values." Although Wimber visited TAV only once during the
nearly two years of revival before "releasing" it from the AVC (and his visit was as speaker who
reportedly remained somewhat aloof from the revival itself), tension had been mounting as the
spotlight continued to shine on TAV. Wimber, who himself was recovering from a stroke and was

watching his son dying of cancer, seemed to have little energy for or interest in mediation and due process. In a seemingly arbitrary move (and after writing an endorsement for the book—which he later told me in a personal interview that he had not read), Wimber used Arnott's (1995) discussion of the animal sounds as one of the primary examples of a conflict of values between TAV and AVC.

5. Taves (1999, 45) described the controversy over manifestations during the Awakening—a description that also fits well the controversy surrounding the Toronto Blessing:

> A comparative method undergirded the search for naturalistic explanations and formed the bedrock of the attack on false religion. When the bodily exercises of the transatlantic awakening were compared with the bodily exercises of such evidently false manifestations of religion as the Montanists, the French Prophets, or the Quakers, this undermined the credibility of the revival phenomena. Comparison of Protestant bodily exercises to the "fits" of the mentally ill had much the same effect. Christian thinkers in this period tended to assume that authentic supernatural revelation was (by doctrinal definition) "unique" and thus incomparable, while false revelation was in some sense all "the same" and, thus, comparable. Comparable phenomena, it was assumed, shared a common naturalistic explanation, whether or not science was yet able to provide it. If some found animal spirits uncompelling as an explanation of such phenomena, that did not make the "fits" of Methodists, French Prophets, and the insane any less compelling. (Taves 1999, 45)

6. I found myself at the center of a dramatic example of physical manifestations when John Arnott asked me to share some of the survey findings on TACF revival with some four thousand people who had gathered for a revival conference in 1998. Although manifestations were still commonplace at that time, they were no longer as dramatic as they once had been. As I took the microphone and began reporting and interpreting some common statistics, I noticed a man who began running around the perimeter of the auditorium, up the stairs, down the stairs, and through the middle aisle. This Forrest Gump-like character seemed to have no agenda, save to run! As he passed by rows of people, some began to laugh uncontrollably, others shouted, while still others fell under the power of the Spirit. Arnott encouraged me to continue with my presentation despite the pandemonium that had developed. I did so for about ten minutes before returning the microphone to Arnott who then preached. The intense manifestations continued unabated throughout the entire service.

7. For some preliminaries about the surveys, see endnote 8 in chapter 1. The respondents were from twenty different countries, with the majority coming from the United States (54 percent), Canada (26 percent) and England (11 percent). Visitors represented over forty denominations and sects, with more than one in four (28 percent) coming from nondenominational/independent churches. The demographic profile of the respondents is skewed toward being married (71 percent), female

(58 percent), middle-aged (average age, forty-five years), and completing a minimum of sixteen years of formal schooling. The demographic profile reflects a respondent who tends to be well educated and mature, the majority of whom were either pastors (18 percent) or involved in church leadership. (See Poloma 1998a for further details.)

8. The overall incidence of somatic manifestations before coming to the TACF by respondents ranged from none (only 7 percent) to more than ten (3 percent), with a mean average of four and a median of three different manifestations reported. As already noted, the vast majority of respondents had at least limited experience with the charismatic manifestations that marked the Toronto Blessing before, during, and after their pilgrimage. There is some indication from the follow-up questionnaire completed two years after the initial survey that the intensity and range of manifestations began to decrease by 1997, a decrease that is apparent to visitors of renewal gatherings and churches throughout North America. From 1995, the date of the original survey, to 1997, the date of the follow-up survey, there was a decided drop in the range of physical manifestations to an average of 2.5 (down from 4), with a median of 1 (down from 3).

9. Taves's (1999, 107) description of the Methodist camp meeting of the nineteenth century as "the final step in a process of creating a public time and place where . . . 'the very presence of the Deity' was manifested in and through the bodily exercises and extravagant emotions of the faithful" is descriptive of contemporary revivals as well as historic ones.

10. At the "Catch the Fire" conference held in Dallas in August 1995, I had an opportunity to observe as a participant another firsthand account of intense Spirit drunkenness. The young woman who had picked me up at the airport came over to greet me in the hotel ballroom during the time of prayer immediately following the formal service. As she hugged me long and hard, she suddenly crashed to the floor—her keys going one direction and her camera in another. I gathered her belongings and sat on the floor next to her for nearly an hour, watching as she jerked, shook, writhed, and intermittently seemed to be pulling in a rope with hand motions made in the air. In her case there was no laughing; her face often looked pained, but the pain would dissolve into a look of peace. Pained pulling on the rope—then peace—more pulling— and then a peaceful respite.

An unexpected time of expressive worship broke out in the middle of the prayer time as I sat in vigil on the floor. As the crowd began to get more animated in the hotel ballroom, dancing in wild celebration around the room in worship, I became more concerned about my new friend's (and my) precarious position on the floor. I motioned to a man and asked him to help me get the young woman on her feet. As we stood her up, she began to laugh uncontrollably. I knew she was drunk in the Spirit. Although aware of her state, she seemed to be enjoying it too much to do any-thing about it. Seeing her in this drunken stupor, she did not seem to be capable of safely driving a car. I decided to have her brought up to my hotel room for the night. It took three of us to get her into a wheelchair we borrowed to get her out of the auditorium and up to my room where she immediately fell asleep.

The next morning I asked this now very together and composed young woman what she had experienced. She responded, "There was a lot of junk inside me that I didn't even know was there. Jesus was pulling out hatred, anger, bitterness, and resentment from the depths of my stomach. It just kept coming and coming! Jesus was pulling on what seemed to be yards and yards of ribbon in which these negative feelings were attached. I did not know I had those ugly feelings within me." I then asked why she thought God allowed her to get so drunk in the Spirit. She replied, "It was probably an anesthetic. It was the only way I could stand it as God removed all that stuff from within me."

11. Neurotheology, the study of the neurobiology of religion and spirituality, has only recently developed as a field of study (Begley 2001). Works like James Austin's (1998) *Zen and the Brain: An Understanding of Meditation and Consciousness* and Andrew Newberg, Eugene d'Aquili, and Vince Rause's (2001) *Why God Won't Go Away: Brain Science and the Biology of Belief* provide empirical evidence of a cranial "spirituality circuit." While such work has sought to integrate neurology with biology, describing what happens when people encounter a reality different from, or higher than, the reality of everyday experience, it still is unable to tell us exactly why these experiences occur.

12. For a comparison between animistic and Pentecostal beliefs see J. C. Ma (2002), similarities that are said to explain the success of the Pentecostal mission among animists. Both share a similar vision of the spiritual world and the role of spirits in human problems and their resolution.

13. For a detailed presentation of a neurobiological analysis of shamanism, see Winkelman's (2000) *Shamanism: The Neural Ecology of Consciousness and Healing*. Winkelman asserts that "shamanism is not just an ancient practice nor is it limited to simpler societies." Although shamanism was supposed to disappear with the development of modern rationality, it is on the increase with neoshamanistic practices. Winkelman's word provides a detailed description of the brain systems, their functions, and their relationship to intuitive powers.

14. Within the past two decades, sociologists, particularly social interactionists, have come to recognize the importance of taking emotions into account when studying human behavior. Criticisms of an overcognitized conception of human behavior in sociology fell on fertile symbolic interactionist ground, even yielding a subspeciality known as the sociology of emotions. While tending to stress the social component of emotions over the biological (cf. Reynolds 1990; Denzin 1984), sociologists of emotion finally have begun to build on early symbolic interactionist theory. This increased interest in human emotions on the part of social scientists complements the model Turner provides by downplaying the biological while placing

emphasis on the social factors of learning and expressing emotions (cf. Reynolds 1990; Denzin 1992; Johnson 1992). Turner's model seeks a synthesis between body and emotions as well as between genetic and social factors in emotional expression.

15. Birthing is a manifestation where women and sometimes men lie on the floor crunching and groaning as if in labor. It seems to have a prophetic dimension that was not usually reported with any regularity for other somatic activities. When I questioned these individuals, they often reported feeling burdened by some world problem for which they travailed in prayer. The emotions reported reflected the travail and sorrow of giving natural birth. These respondents were more likely to report emotions of fear, grief, embarrassment, and confusion than the larger sample.

16. Sociologist Peter Berger (1970, 58) similarly suggests a connection between surrendering play and encountering "signals of transcendence" with the following observation: "In playing one steps out of one time into another."

4

Divine Healing: Healing of Memories, Relationships, and Physical Ailments

---

The anti-supernatural bias of western culture extends as far as North America, Europe, to many of those nations that were part of the British Empire and sadly to many cultures we have touched. The relative lack of healing in these affected nations also reinforces cultural doubts about healing. The Church, living in those nations, has consistently demonstrated that it struggles with healing much more than the Church living in Asian, African, or even South American cultures. The extent of the effect of culture upon us personally is difficult to discern until revelation begins to penetrate our hearts and minds. It is as though we are too close to the trees to see the forest.

—*Roger Sapp*

Despite the Western "anti-supernatural bias" described in the preceding by Roger Sapp (2002, 26), divine healing has always had an important place in the Pentecostal/Charismatic (P/C) movement in America.[1] With each new revival wave has come a renewed and revitalized mandate to pray for the sick. The revival of the 1990s is no exception. As the effects of the Toronto Blessing and other streams of the recent revival continue their ripple effects, healing ministries, particularly those that focus on the democratization of healing practices, have been spreading across America. Although most would acknowledge the efficacy of ministries of healing evangelists like Benny Hinn and Oral Roberts, there is an increased interest in the approach of the late John Wimber in "equipping of all believers" to exercise divine powers.[2]

Although P/C practices include praying for physical healing, healing is treated holistically and in a broader context. The Cartesian split between mind and body that has permeated modern medicine and filtered into modern religion does not mirror the belief and practices of P/C Christians. Reflecting recent research that relates spirituality to health, models of P/C healing present a holistic view of the person as an integrated composite of soul, spirit, mind, and body.

COMPONENTS OF DIVINE HEALING

Spiritual Healing: Healing Personal Relationships with the Divine

Consistent with most other contemporary spiritual healing practices, healing for P/C Christians is more than the curing of physical ailments. Recognizing the intricate interweaving of soul, mind, body, and spirit, this perspective places a personal relationship with God at the center of its model. Healing, as understood by those involved in the P/C movement, is somewhat different from a common use of the term where it is often equated with "curing" medical maladies. As Meredith McGuire (1988, 43) observed during her study of charismatic Christians in suburban New Jersey, a medically diagnosable condition is not necessary for the experience of healing. Healing is primarily a spiritual experience with "the key criterion of healing" involving "a process of becoming closer to the Lord" (see also Csordas 1988). Establishing a vertical relationship with God is the base for healing of self as well as of horizontal relationships with family, friends, and coworkers. When relations are in good order, personal healing of a person's spirit, mind, and body is expected to follow. Important to the thesis that P/C spirituality is a form of mysticism is that, as McGuire (1988, 43) has noted, "healing 'works' first and foremost as a spiritual experience; physical and social-emotional changes are hoped-for, but secondary, aspects."

The focus of the Toronto Blessing and its many tributaries, as we have discussed in earlier chapters, has been on mystical experience of the divine. The initial experience of salvation (i.e., coming to "know Jesus" in a personal way) is recognized as being only the beginning of an exciting spiritual journey. The renewal brought some who were "unsaved" into this basic experience, but a vast majority who came to Toronto and to other revival sites were already P/C Christians who had experiences of salvation, Spirit baptism, and a range of the gifts of the Spirit.[3] Many pilgrims to renewal sites reported, however, that they had become spiritually "dry" and were in need of a fresh touch of the Holy Spirit (Poloma 1998a). This longing for more of the divine presence can be seen from an addendum to a questionnaire supplied by a fifty-year-old airline pilot— a testimony that reflects what others repeatedly heard during the revival:

We came into the first service late. The atmosphere was charged with excitement and expectation. The Lord's presence was awesome! I don't remember who the speaker was, but the Lord began speaking to me soon after we entered the service. We had missed worship, and through the speaker I heard the Lord say to me that I didn't realize it, but I was pitiful, poor, blind and naked. It was as if at this point I knew why I was there.

My relationship with the Lord had grown routine, and (honestly) somewhat boring. Of course, the problem was my heart, which was so weighted down with the cares of the world. In that instant I knew that all I wanted—the only thing that was real in my life—was my relationship with the Lord. As I purposed to lay down everything in my life that separated me from him, I began to cry out to Him to forgive me, to change me, to deliver me. I wanted to be consumed by Him! (Case #586)

Spiritual healing for P/C believers is the most significant form of healing and the base on which other forms of healing rest.

Although the vast majority of those who came to the renewal/revival services were born-again Christians, repentance is a theme that frequently ran through the testimonies. As men and women believed they encountered the presence of God, like the ancient prophet Isaiah, they were left undone. Clifford, a policeman from England, shared his feelings of unworthiness as he experienced the Toronto Blessing:[4]

I woke three mornings crying and groaning from my belly at my sinfulness in the presence of a glorious holy God. I didn't before, but I know now a measure of what Isaiah was conveying when he felt "undone" in the presence of God. It was the most distressing but holy time I have experienced in thirty-three years as a believer. It broke my heart in the times of worship with love for Jesus and the sense of His presence. (Case #203)

John, another middle-aged male respondent, similarly described how his experience of the holy opened his eyes to the sin that still could be found in his life after repeatedly experiencing God's presence at TACF:

Certain besetting sins of lust of the eyes and imagination and fits of anger were being dredged up like garbage and being disposed of. Then I understood—just by passively receiving—that God has a relentless, unending love for me personally and for every other person in the universe. When I "came to" (after resting in the Spirit for some time) following one of these sessions on the floor, I said to Jim: "The reason Israel knew the face of God would kill them wasn't his righteous holiness and justice; it is because His total unfiltered love would burn you to a cinder!" (Case #745)

Spiritual healing involves a greater intimacy with God, reflected in a deeper sense of God's presence and love that is often accompanied by an awareness of personal sinfulness and a fresh sense of divine forgiveness.[5] Experiencing the presence of God has always been the focal point of the revival meetings, although increasingly there is a greater articulated emphasis on a need for personal holiness and spiritual healing to create a hospitable environment for the divine presence. The data suggest that the awareness of the need for spiritual healing was present at TACF revival even before it became the topic of conferences and meetings. "The closer I come to God, the more I am aware of my sinful condition" was a common theme reflected in the testimonies that supplemented the structured questionnaires.

Malcolm, a forty-eight-year-old Anglican and teacher from England, is one of many respondents who reported experiencing a dramatic re-conversion while participating in the renewal services. Malcolm had an initial conversion experience some thirty years earlier and had gone on to develop a successful Christian ministry. "Over the years," he reported. "I ruined everything I did. It's difficult to compress the daily anguish and much more over more than 20 years into a few lines, but believe me, I could go no lower." Malcolm sent in the following narrative as an addendum to the TACF survey to describe his experience:

Well, no sooner had the man [who came up to pray with him after the service] started speaking than the Spirit of the Lord came on me; I was filled with the most incredible sensation—and was sent crumbling to the ground. Although he was a total stranger, the Spirit enabled him to pray such specific prayers for me, my past relationship with God, forgiveness, healing, guilt, self-loathing, condemnation, and even for my family far away—though there was no way he could have known that I was from another country.

I cannot describe the wonder. . . . The party started and gets better daily. Instant delivery from drugs, depression, and sexual sin; a transformation so radical that friends, colleagues and scores of my high-school students started making enquires about what happened to so change me. Healing of sleeplessness (which had led me to an addiction for illegally-obtained sleeping tablets);

even a change to my life-style, driving attitudes, work, language (gutter, marine-type tongue); deliverance from high anxiety and stress for which I was well known. I experienced a profound sense of total forgiveness, cleansing, and reconciliation with God. And now, a love for the Lord so deep that sometimes it literally aches; a passion for the souls of my school students and others who don't know Christ; a sense of praise and worship that has me singing songs of adoration as I wake up in the morning. (Case #574)

Although Malcolm's account may be more dramatically Pauline than most, similar conversion narratives are common in renewal circles, with some being shared during revival services, others being written up in renewal periodicals, and still others being transmitted in cyberspace to the thousands who were on various renewal list serves and in chat rooms. The TACF survey figures also attest to the commonality of conversion experiences despite the fact that, unlike the stereotypical profile of historic revivals, the topic of sin was rarely a theme of the preaching. TACF, especially during the earliest years of the revival, was a place where party and playfulness set the emotional tone (see Poloma 1997 for further discussion). Despite the seeming levity of the services, the 1995 TACF survey reports 68 percent of the respondents acknowledging that they had experienced a new sense of their sinful condition as a result of their involvement in Toronto revival services. An even greater percent of respondents (81 percent) reported experiencing a "fresh and deep sense of God's forgiveness" at the TACF revival site. The vast majority (92 percent) could report two years after the initial 1995 survey that their visit to TACF resulted in a "positive change in their relationship to God."[6] Throughout the years of renewal, spiritual healing has been a core revival experience.

Repentance from sin, forgiveness and reconciliation with God is but one of two prongs of the phenomenon known as spiritual healing, with the other being forgiveness of others.[7] Healing testimonies and teachings commonly include a model of and instruction about the importance of forgiveness for healing and wholeness.

Spiritual Healing and Forgiveness

One of the important links between spiritual healing and other healing forms (inner or emotional, mental and physical) is forgiveness. After years of misunderstanding and neglect by the secular mental health community, forgiveness is now widely acknowledged as an agent of "transformation" and an "act of re-creation" by psychologists. Pargament offers the following psychological description of forgiveness and its relationship to religious coping that fits well with experiences of the TACF worshipers:

> Forgiveness is designed to produce a radical change from a life centered around pain and injustice. It is a method of coping that involves a shift of both destinations and pathways. Implicit in the act of forgiving is the effort to transform significance. . . . In forgiveness, the individual pursues the possibility of peace of mind, that is, the hope that painful memories can be healed, that the individual will no longer be held emotionally hostage to acts of the past. Forgiveness also offers the possibility of peace with others. Coming to terms with the hurt and injury inflicted by another person opens the door to a future of more fulfilling relationships. (Pargament 1997, 262)

The love of God experienced by devotees at TACF often went hand in hand with being able to "let go" of past hurts and to forgive those who wronged them. As with the topic of sin, it was not so much a matter of preaching being centered on the issue of forgiveness but rather its being modeled and experienced. Reports of experiencing divine forgiveness were often linked with finding less need to judge others. In the words of one TACF survey respondent:

> One of the most outstanding experiences for me has been *finally* receiving His forgiveness—realizing that God is *merciful*, full of mercy, even for me. Understanding that means to live in God's grace and translating that understanding to mean others live in God's grace also. There is no longer a need to fear condemnation or to condemn others. I am rejoicing that His wisdom is greater than all! (Case #009)

Forgiveness cannot be self-induced or manufactured, but P/C Christians do believe it can be willfully elected and then received as a gift of God. Testimonies abound to illustrate the diverse ways in which forgiveness had been experienced and received at TACF. At times it is directed toward God or toward oneself, but more often forgiveness is directed toward others who have wounded the person. TACF pastor John Arnott (1997, 5) summarizes the relation of forgiveness to the Toronto Blessing in a chapter titled "Mercy Triumphs over Justice." In it Arnott links the mystical experiences of the Toronto Blessing with inner healing and outreach to others:

Forgiveness is a key to blessing. Forgiveness and repentance open up our hearts and allow the river of God to flow freely in us. We need to give the Holy Spirit permission to bring to our minds those things that need to be resolved in our hearts.

Three things are vital to seeing a powerful release of the Spirit of God in our own lives and in the world around us. First, we need a revelation of how big God is. We must know that absolutely nothing is impossible for Him (Luke 1:37). Second, we need a revelation of how loving He is, how much He cares for us and how He is absolutely committed to loving us to life (Jer. 31.3). I delight to tell people that God loves them just the way they are, yet loves them too much to leave them the way they are.

Finally, we need a revelation of how we can walk in that love and give it away. A heart that is free has time and resources for others. (Arnott 1997, 5)

Inner (Emotional) Healing and the Human Spirit

Inner or emotional healing is closely linked with spiritual healing, particularly the ability to forgive. Although the hurts inflicted by others may be long past and may have even been forgiven, P/C Christians claim that a residue may remain in the memory that can serve as a catalyst for other problems.

"Inner healing," also commonly known as "healing of memories" or "emotional healing," traces its recent origins to the writings of an Episcopal laywoman, Agnes Sanford (1950, 1958), in the early 1950s. Unlike many Christian counseling techniques that focus on the cognitive (especially an application of the Bible to particular problems), inner healing has been more holistic with its focus on emotions as well as cognition. Garzon and Burkett have defined the healing of memories as follows:

[Healing of memories is] a form of prayer designed to facilitate the client's ability to process affectively painful memories through vividly recalling these memories and asking for the presence of Christ (or God) to minister in the midst of this pain. While the processing of these memories and the ministry given often take on the form of visual imagery, at times other elements of the client's sense experience predominate. (Garzon and Burkett 2002, 43)

Numerous models of healing of memory prayer have developed over the years, many if not most within the larger P/C community. They all stress an emphasis on a holistic restoration of the person with an expectation that Jesus Christ will function as healer and deliverer. Although they share an emphasis on the Holy Spirit's "gifting and power" (i.e., leaving room for the healing to occur through the gifts of the Holy Spirit) and a biblical worldview, inner healing models freely incorporate principles and techniques of select secular counseling approaches.[8] To some extent, all healing of memory practices resemble psychotherapy in its remembering past life events, evaluating and fully acknowledging them and the role they may be playing in a current problem. They move beyond the cognitive in their use of imagery and emotions to affect the healing process.

The experience of inner healing in revival services, however, differs somewhat from the inner healing (counseling) prayer that became popular in P/C circles during the last quarter of the twentieth century (sometimes critiqued within the movement as having become "more counseling than prayer"). Those trained as "pray-ers" at revival sites were encouraged to refrain from asking questions and providing counsel during the time of prayer following the formal service. It was expected that the Spirit of God would do the healing work without the pray-er being aware of a person's needs. The prayer time following the formal service was to provide an opportunity for an encounter between the divine and the one being prayed for, with the pray-er being a conduit of God's power rather than a counselor.

Unlike many prayer counselors who use inner healing techniques, the pray-er at TACF revival was generally limited to the role of offering short prayers intended to simply bless what God was already doing in the person. "More, Lord" or "Go deeper, Lord," were the kind of ejaculatory prayers that could be heard around the room as pray-ers prayed for those seeking the blessing. Given the number of people seeking prayer and the relatively small number of prayer teams at each service, prayer with a prayer team member was of much shorter duration than most inner healing counseling prayer. The religious experience usually continued long after the pray-er(s) had gone on to pray with another seeker, with fruits similar to the experiences reported in earlier, more structured attempts to use inner healing to bring inner healing to a person's life.[9]

The following testimony given at a local Episcopal church illustrates what the anthropologist Thomas Csordas (1994, 75) has termed "therapeutic imagery"—an experience "typically evoked during moments in a healing session devoted to prayer." Visions (and manifestations with their prophetic mime quality) appeared to facilitate emotional healing by, to use Csordas's (1994,

75) description, constituting "the experiential resolution of the problem."
Elizabeth (not her real name) opened her testimony as follows:[10]

> I am 36-years old—and I have not really lived. I have existed and survived.
> When I was 12 years old, I gave up all hope of being emotionally accepted and
> belonging, and I went inside the walls of a castle and disappeared. The pain of
> rejection was too great, so little Elizabeth went inside and big Elizabeth was cre-
> ated on the outside to cope with what was going on in the inside.

Elizabeth then shared with the congregation a series of visions she had while at
the TACF conference, all of them related to the emotional healing that took
place as "little Elizabeth" was freed from this captivity created by a fear of rejection and as "big Elizabeth" correspondingly became less angry and more receptive. One scene involved the Heavenly Father carrying her out of the castle in
which she had been imprisoned into his castle. As the Father carried her in, she
heard cries of "Alleluia" both in her vision as well as from a person somewhere
inside the church auditorium. She continued her testimony as follows:

> Now this is the strangest thing—suddenly this man started barking. At the ex-
> act time he began to bark, I saw a picture and heard a dog barking in my vision.
> I had a dog when I was in the 5th grade, and my parents had him destroyed
> while I wasn't around. I never got to say good-bye, and I didn't know how bad
> that hurt me. In this picture a dog runs in and starts jumping and barking.
> (That man will never know why he was barking!—laugh.) God was returning
> my dog to me, and the child in the picture really perked up. She was able to
> walk. It was so healing. And in my picture, I looked around, and suddenly all the
> signs and smells came to life.

In a series of five specific therapeutic visions that came without human assistance and lasted more than two hours, Elizabeth reported that she experienced inner healing that allowed her to "really live for the first time."

Of the respondents to the 1995 survey, 78 percent reported having experienced "an inner or emotional healing" as a result of prayer at TACF, and the
vast majority were able to report two years later that the "healing" had staying
power. In the 1997 follow-up questionnaire, 94 percent of the respondents
who had claimed to receive an inner or emotional healing experience said that
they remained "healed" of the emotional trauma(s) that had afflicted them.

Those who indicated that they had experienced inner healing were more likely to report that they had an intense experience of spiritual healing (i.e., a fresh sense of God's love, their own sinfulness, and God's forgiveness) while at TACF than those who reported lower levels of spiritual healing or none at all.[11]

Accounts of emotional healing include narratives about a successful experiential resolution of inordinate fears and anxieties, sexual abuse, and depression. Diane, a forty-one-year-old widow, provides another example of emotional healing that illustrates the role physical manifestations and emotional response may play in such healing:

> Before my first visit to the Airport church, my life was in the state of despair. The preceding year my husband of 21 years shot himself in the head. Although he had many problems, including alcoholism, I had been trusting in God to intervene and to restore. . . . My faith was shattered, and I had grown extremely depressed. I considered taking my own life, but didn't want to hurt my family any more than they had already been hurt. I came seeking to Toronto, but found myself brought to the end of my rope that first night. I wept for hours and hours.
>
> I told God that if I got prayed for one more time and all I would do was cry, I would never ask for prayer again! The following night God started flooding me with his joy, and I haven't been the same since. His joy is so overwhelming in my life that I have been labeled the "church drunk." I am so in love with Jesus! I want to share this love with the world and see them set free. God is a wonderful merciful God! (Case #609)

While only a few of the qualitative accounts attached to the quantitative surveys were as instantaneous as Diane's, the reported results are similar. It is as if healing begins slowly and goes on to deeper and deeper levels. Many believed the process was begun before their visit to Toronto (often with the assistance of prayer counselors or professional therapists), but that the pace picked up dramatically due to prayer at TACF. A forty-year-old woman (Toni) told how she had been going to a Christian counseling center before coming to Toronto for the purpose of "dealing with severe trauma I suffered as a child." Her counselor's reaction to the change she observed in Toni was a theme that can be found in other reports: "One of the counselors working with me said she's never seen as much healing take place in a week as she saw with me. She said she's worked with several clients this year who have visited the Airport church, and time spent there seems to make the healing process go faster and at deeper levels" (Case #588).

Experiences of inner healing such as those described here share commonalities with other forms of "religious imagination," including shamanistic vision, hallucination, dreams, active imagination, hypnosis, possession, and other altered states of consciousness. It would be a mistake, however, to reduce all religious imagination to a single form that ignores the autonomous quality of imagination as expressed in revival testimonies. Imagination can remain a nebulous phenomenon or it can be (according to Michelle Stephens) "autonomous." Csordas's summary of Stephen's distinctive traits found in "autonomous imagination" (as compared with ordinary imagination) is worth repeating here:

> *Autonomous* imagination stands in contrast to the *ordinary* imagination in that its products are "vividly externalized," compelling," and "have their own momentum." In addition, it exhibits "a much greater freedom and richness of imaginative inventiveness and displays a different access to memory. Another important feature is its special responsiveness to external, cultural influence and direction. Furthermore, it exerts a special influence over mental and somatic processes. (Csordas 1994, 83)

The imagination found at TACF revival was not the guided imagery sometimes used by counselors to deal with emotional issues. For the most part it seems to originate from the psyche of the person being prayed with (rather than elicited by the pray-er). Not only did it engage the mind, but in many cases (as can be illustrated by testimonies found throughout these early chapters) it also often involved somatic response.[12]

The inner healing process is intimately interwoven with what Csordas (1994, 3) calls the "sacred self"—the dwelling place or "locus of efficiency" for the "experiential specificity of effect in religious healing." Within the sacred self can be found imagination, perceptions, and emotions woven together into a web that is not easily untangled without distorting the narrative of the healing process. Just as "self" develops within a social and cultural context, healing of memories involves not only the individual self but also relationships. *Inner healing* is thus but one facet of the larger genre of *healing of emotions*, with the other being *healing of relationships*.

Healing of Interpersonal Relationships

A widely distributed video by Christian film producer Warren Marcus, *Go Inside the Toronto Blessing* presents a visual account of the healing process described in this chapter. Marcus explains how his interest in the Toronto revival was peaked by the heterogeneity of the pilgrims he observed during his first visit:[13]

> What first hit me when I went to Toronto—there were people from all over the world there and not just nationalities and races but denominations as well—Catholics, Protestants, Pentecostals, Baptists, even Jewish people—they were all there together in one place loving one another. In my 18 years of religious broadcasting, I had never seen such a thing! (Marcus 1997)

Throughout the video, pilgrims are interviewed who have experienced inner healing and relational healing together with others who claimed to be healed of physical illness and clinically diagnosed mental illness. One segment was devoted to "restored marriages," providing testimonials to support the 1995 TACF survey data in which 88 percent of married survey respondents reported a noticeable improvement in their marital relationships as a result of prayer received while visiting TACF.

In a particularly striking scene, Marcus is seen interviewing a white couple from South Africa about the effects of the renewal when "the power of God fell." During the interview, which took place in the back of the church auditorium between renewal services, the couple began to shake and fall to the floor. First, the wife began to laugh uncontrollably as she reached out for her husband. When asked "What are you feeling—what's going on here," the wife (still laughing and "ooohing" in between words) replied: "It's like laughter, happiness, love." Then the couple fell to the floor, still laughing and locked in each other's embrace. Marcus made the following comment in his introduction to presenting the videotape of the scene:

> Then something happened that in all my years of a filmmaker had never occurred before. We were interviewing a couple from South Africa when all of a sudden the power of God fell. . . . I was stunned. No one was praying for these people. . . . There was no enthusiastic praise and worship. Basically nothing was happening so no one could accuse them of being caught up in an emotional frenzy. (Marcus, 1997)

When the wife sat up on the floor beside her still prone husband, she gave a testimony about what had transpired during their visit to TACF:

> We had a bad marriage. We were living together, but from day one it was like a hurricane. It was so bad! I wanted to destroy all his things. [When] I found something of his, I would burn it or break it. I'd chase him around with knives. . . . Marriage counselors all told us there was no way: "There is something inside you that nobody can get out." This [time at TACF] has changed my life. It has changed me so much that I want to burst open. I want to love everyone. I do love everybody—even all the people in South Africa. I want to love everybody. I want to love with a passion. [Then gesturing to her husband who still lay prone with eyes closed and a smile on his face, she exclaimed] Him—this is my big love!" (Marcus, 1997)

The clip of the South African couple in *Go Inside the Toronto Blessing* was framed by an interview with a Canadian mental health practitioner, Grant Mullen, M.D. Viewers are prepared for the scene by Mullen's "expert testimony" about how the somatic manifestations are interrelated to the inner healing process—"the physical changes that is seen to come over people when they are prayed for are actually the physical responses of the body to the presence of God." After the clip, Mullen offered testimony about how he first came to TACF. His patients were going to TACF for prayer and reporting back to him about the healings that were taking place there. "What convinced me I had to look into this," states Mullen, "is that people were coming free, suddenly or very rapidly—in a speed I had never before seen in my life." These clients had "tremendous emotional bondage" with "mood swings problems." Mullen adds: "In the last three years I have seen more emotional healing and transformations of people's spiritual life and emotional life than I have ever seen before."

As the video unfolded, there were more reports of "healed marriages" and restored relationships as well as cures of mental and physical maladies. The testimonies presented in the video not only reflected the experience of improved marital relations reported in the surveys (where 88 percent of married respondents affirmed a closer relationship with their spouses) but also tried to capture the diversity of the pilgrims (nationalities, denominations, age, and race) to visually support the "breaking of dividing walls" being brought about through the revival.[14]

Healing of Mental Illness

The category of "mental illness" undoubtedly overlaps territory with the healing of memories or inner healing. A separate question, however, was asked in the survey about whether a healing was received for "clinically diagnosed mental health problems." Six percent of the sample acknowledged having received such a healing. Reflecting the centrality of spiritual healing in P/C teachings on healing, those who had been healed from a clinically diagnosed condition were more likely to report having been spiritually healed than those who did not.

Although additional questions were not asked about the nature of the clinical diagnosis, testimonies suggest that many were from "mood disorders," especially from depression. Those who claimed a clinically diagnosed mental healing were more likely to have reported being "spiritually dry" when they first came to the revival, suggesting (as can be seen in the following testimony) that an angst about God may be at the base of some mental turbulence. Those who claimed to have received a healing from a clinically diagnosed condition were also somewhat more likely to report having received a physical healing. Although it is beyond the scope of this sociopsychological study to determine whether clinical conditions were in fact healed as claimed through revival prayer, evidence supports the fact that large numbers of people *believe* they have been healed of a variety of maladies as a result of prayer at TACF. It is important to note that this finding is not an isolated anomaly; it fits in well with the growing number of studies demonstrating a relationship between measures of faith and health, including mental health and familial relations (see for example Koenig, 1998a, 1998b; Kingsley 1996; Larson, Swyers, and McCullough 1998).

Melinda Fish, Christian author, editor of TACF's magazine *Spread the Fire*, and a popular renewal speaker, provides but one example of what is being discussed in this section. She has written the following description of her mental/emotional condition before visiting TACF:

> In the spring of 1994, I had major surgery and began to immediately suffer hormone shock. For the first time in my life, I began to experience panic attacks. I would wake up suddenly in the middle of the night with my heart pounding and a sense of impending doom smothering me. Bill would hold me until I stopped shaking. I was beginning to know the face of mental torment and wondered if I would have to check into a hospital for treatment. (Fish 2000, 111–12)

About the same time, the Fishes began to hear about the Toronto Blessing—and from their perspective, "It wasn't good. People were laughing and making animal noises in the meetings of some church up there near the airport." After being encouraged by good friends to check out TACF revival for themselves, they visited the church in October 1994. Melinda Fish describes her life-changing experience as follows:

> At the end of the service, we stood waiting for prayer. A ministry team member approached us, smiling, "May I pray for you?" he asked. "Certainly," we replied, trying not to appear too needy. Though I put on my best pastor's-wife smile, inside I was thinking, *Well, take your best shot, because I never go down.* Ron Dick simply reached out two fingers and lifted up the prayer that brought heaven down after 18 years of waiting. He said, "Come, Holy Spirit!"
>
> I felt a gentle pressure on my chest. Before this moment I had never fallen in response to prayer. I placed little value on the experience, having seen very little fruit from it. Now it was as though a gentle wind was pressing me backward. The man wasn't pushing us or intimidating us in any way. I now had a choice. I could either respond to God's presence and the way He wanted to touch me, or I could stiffen myself, resist and risk quenching the first powerful intrusion of God into my life in years. I fell backward onto the floor, completely surrounded by a sense of the love of God.
>
> In my mind's eye, I could see the shadow of Jesus bending over me. He was laughing! In my head I could hear him speaking, "Well now, you'll never be able to brag about not having been down under the power again, will you?" For over half an hour I felt too weak to get up. I didn't want to. The love of God was filling me for the first time in years. (Fish 2000, 115–16)

Not only did Fish report experiencing healing as a result of her perceived divine encounter, but she and her pastor husband Bill reported healings began to occur in their church after they returned from TACF—healings that were "confirmed by doctors and radiologists" (Fish 2000, 117). In a special issue of *Spread the Fire* on "Healing and the New Wine," editor Melinda Fish (1999, 2) wrote about a "discouragement in the area of healing" before the renewal and about some of the miracles she has seen since, concluding: "Everything that Jesus did when He walked on earth is happening again in this move of the Holy Spirit."

Testimonies such as Melinda Fish's are heard wherever people have claimed the experience of the Toronto Blessing. These accounts fit with the literature on religion and health, supporting findings reporting that "actively committed religious persons have better overall psychological development," that "religion is positively associated with a sense of well-being, healthier self-esteem, and better personal adjustment," and that "religiosity has the potential for the prevention of problems associated with mental illness and disorders" (Chamberlain and Hall 2000, 96). The Toronto Blessing provided an unusual milieu for both collective and personal religious experiences (it does not resemble the average Methodist or Lutheran service in the United States or a United Church service in Canada—or even a routinized P/C service)! TACF's laid-back style allows for cathartic practices that would most likely be very controversial in nonrenewal churches, where emotional release (and forms of healing) can occur with an expected frequency and intensity. The spiritual and psychological experiences at TACF not only appear to affect the spirit, emotions, and mind, but also were reported to have effects on the physical health of some pilgrims.

Healing of Physical Maladies

Reports of physical healing at TACF were off to a halting and somewhat questionable start during the earliest months of the renewal. Until its ouster in December 1995, TACF was a part of John Wimber's Association of Vineyard Churches (AVC) where physical healing was expected as part of the "normal Christian life" (Wimber and Springer 1987). Wimber provided a voice for others in the larger P/C movement who sought to downplay the role of healing evangelists and healing crusades that were characteristic of the 1950s healing movement, emphasizing instead that the power to heal was available to all Christians. There was an attempt to democratize healing, taking it out of the hands of a few and putting it in the hands of the masses. It was in this context that the "Toronto Blessing" was frequently said to be a "nameless and faceless movement"—a revival in which God could and did use anyone he chose to use.

Without a healing evangelist, TACF was dependent on personal testimonies rather than a charismatic individual or dramatic ritual to prime the healing pump. Some critics charged the leadership with being too eager in their earliest reporting of physical healings, repeating testimonies without verifying their accuracy.[15] Despite such controversy outside the movement, those leading the revival continued to press on with their prayer for healing, often with noticeable results.[16] More than one in five (22 percent) of the respondents to the 1995 TACF survey claimed healing of a physical health problem as a result of their attendance and prayer at the revival. Although this question was context and time specific, it falls within the 10 percent to 32 percent figures reported in other more general studies (Chamberlain and Hall 2000; Poloma and Hoelter 1998).

A testimony from Joe Durante, a former carpenter who fell off a two-and-a-half story building over fifteen years earlier, demonstrates the way one healing took place at TACF. Durante, who had been classified as permanently disabled, went to a healing conference at TACF in November 1998 "just to grow closer to God and have more of Him in my life." A fellow pilgrim from England planted a seed within him causing Joe, who was suffering from a herniated disk, arthritis in both knees, carpal tunnel syndrome, and bursitis in his shoulder, to make a silent personal prayer for healing. According to the testimony in *Spread the Fire* (1999, 24):

> During Marc Dupont's sermon, God spoke to Joe that he was going to heal him. As an act of faith, Joe asked the women standing next to him to pray for his knees.
>
> Suddenly as the women began praying, the Lord touched him. "My back went on fire." This was the third time that week that he had felt fire in his back during ministry times. "I politely thanked the women for praying for me and went back to my hotel room and lay down on the bed."
>
> "When I did, all at once the Holy Spirit fell on me and I began to shake slightly. My back went on fire again and for a while, I soaked in the presence of God. When I stood up I realized my back had been healed. I literally jumped for joy on my bed! Then I jumped on my roommate's bed and up and down the hallway in the hotel."

Durante reported that he was still free of back pain ten months later when interviewed for the special issue of *Spread the Fire* on healing.[17] Impromptu healing testimonies given in church tend to be for chronic medical problems, many of which modern medicine has few cures. Reports of cured migraines, arthritic conditions, back injuries, problems with joints, and respiratory ailments are common. Many testimonies suggest the pilgrim had suffered for many years and was cured as a result of prayer during revival gatherings. It is beyond the scope of sociological surveys to determine whether a medical cure was in fact received, but research has consistently demonstrated that a significant minority of Americans do believe they have received healing as a result of prayer. Some scholars, however, tend to be more skeptical.

Chamberlain and Hall (2000, 66–67) cite the following conclusion of Pattison, Lapins, and Doerr (1973, 297) as one that is "typical of the scientific perspective on faith healing":

> The primary function of faith healing is not to reduce symptomatology, but to reinforce a magical belief system that is consonant with the subculture of these subjects. Faith healing in contemporary America is part of a continuum of magical belief systems ranging from witchcraft to Christian Science. The psychodynamics are similar in all such systems; the variation is in the abstractness of the magical belief system. Within the framework of the assumptive world view in which faith healing subjects live, their personality structure and magical belief systems are not abnormal, but are part of a coping system that provides ego integration for the individual and social integration for the subculture.

Despite a language of discourse used to frame the preceding statement that may sound disparaging (depending on the ear of the hearer), it does provide a springboard for proposing a social scientific model for faith healing. Whether the underlying process is assumed to be *magic* (as in the preceding quotation), dissociation (Glik 1990a), relaxation response (Benson 1984), hypnosis (McClenon 1994), or neuroecology (Winkelman 2000) many who have observed healing in research fields from suburban North America to rural African villages recognize that "something" is happening. For Glik (1990b) this "something" was often a redefinition of the problems and a reconstruction of clinical realities by patients—or according to McGuire (1988) of creating "order out of disorder." As Chamberlain and Hall (2000, 71) have observed, this "process of redefining one's health problems may not be significantly different from how psychotherapy works well."

Although prayer for healing is not likely to replace medicine as a panacea for health problems, researchers have studied the relationship between faith and healing and recognize they are struggling with a "twisted knot" (Idler 1995). Rather than attempting to unravel the twisted knot, it has been suggested that the knot be viewed from different vantage points.

Anthropologist Victor Turner's application of Paul MacLean's theory of the triune brain to ritual performance (already discussed in chapter 3) offers a framework for viewing the twisted knot of P/C healing from varying vantage points. By weaving together somatic, emotional, cognitive, and cultural components into a single model, the danger of reducing healing to only one strand of the knot is lessened. The use of Victor Turner's insights moves the analysis away from a mechanistic one that focuses on curing to a dynamic holistic analysis that recognizes the complexity of the human healing process.

As a participant observer of the P/C movement for over two decades and of the stream known as the Toronto Blessing for eight years, I am convinced that some who seek curing are cured of medically diagnosed conditions, but many are not.[18] Believers are aware of this, but continue frequenting healing services and conferences. Two common misconceptions about alternative healing methods noted by McGuire in her study of ritual healing in suburban America cast an important light on the topic. Those who seek out alternative healing groups usually do not come with a prior medical condition for which they seek healing. As McGuire (1988, 5) notes: "Most adherents were generally attracted by the larger system of beliefs, of which health-illness related beliefs and practices are only one part." Second, McGuire observes that from a sociological stance, not only is religious reality "socially structured" but also medical reality is socially constructed and thus represents "relative" rather than "absolute truth": "This relativistic stance toward the 'truth' of biomedicine means that it cannot be used to explain nonmedical healing. One paradigmatic system cannot really explain another, although comparison may be useful as a legitimating device." Use of Turner's model permits a comparison between what may be gleaned from the scientific paradigm as it relates to healing and curing in a paradigm where the narrative of biomedicine is subservient to the dominant narrative of spiritual transcendence.

THE TRIUNE BRAIN AND PENTECOSTAL/CHARISMATIC HEALING

In their analysis of the data on healing from the 1995 and 1997 TACF surveys, Margaret Poloma and Lynette Hoelter (1998) used a multivariate statistical approach to generate a holistic model of healing that complements Turner's theory. The model includes spiritual, emotional, mental, and social well-being, as well physical healing. "At the center of the model," note the authors "is a relationship—namely a relationship with the divine—that must be in 'right order' before other forms of healing ordinarily takes place. Becoming aware of one's sinful condition, deliverance from demonic strongholds, and receiving a fresh sense of forgiveness for the P/C Christian are means of deepening the relationship with God" (p. 269).

It is important to emphasize that it was the measures of spiritual healing (rather than ritual participation, somatic manifestations, or emotional responses) that were most likely to be directly related to other healing measures. Those who reported a "healing" in their relationship to God were most likely to report they had experienced an inner and emotional healing, a healing from clinically diagnosed mental disorders, or a physical healing.[19] Although ritual participation, physical manifestations, and emotional responses did not directly affect physical or mental healing, they do appear to have an indirect relationship to healing of memories, mental problems, and physical ailments.

Participation in the prayer ministry at TACF (the measure used for the ritual dimension) was linked directly to the experience of somatic manifestations, with the intensity of the manifestations being accompanied by positive emotional responses. It appears that ritual participation facilitated somatic responses (physical manifestations) that tended to be accompanied with positive (rather than negative) emotional responses. The ritual prayer together with the accompanying manifestations and positive emotional affect all appear to be indicators of spiritual healing or an improved relationship with God. *In sum, it is spiritual healing that proves to be the significant factor in inner (emotional), mental, and physical healings.* The more intense the spiritual healing, the more likely the subject is to report having experienced healing of memories as well as healing from mental and physical problems.

The self-transformation from brokenness to wholeness described repeatedly by renewal/revival pilgrims can be said to be a path of liberation or a path of freedom. It involves what Csikszentmihalyi (1990, 20) has referred to in *Flow* as a "simple truth"—"that the control of consciousness determines the quality of life."[20] Without invoking the explanation of the Holy Spirit (an explanation proffered by P/C adherents but one that is outside the scope of social science), Turner's thesis allows us to stretch beyond the modernist paradigm with its presuppositions about physical reality and the nature of energy to suggest a process that P/C healing may share with other complementary healing models. It all begins in the reptilian brain.

Instinctual or Reptilian Brain

P/C ritual, as we have already demonstrated in chapters 2 and 3, is much more than a cognitively produced drama. We have discussed the role that music plays in transforming individual consciousness as well as the impact it is said to have on the limbic system. Shamans of all varieties have long known the effects of rhythm (especially drumming) in the healing process, and increasingly modern medicine is acknowledging the potential of music to facilitate healing. It appears that music not only is a cultural universal, but it may be universal in its curative powers (Campbell 1991; Crowe 1991; Lane 1994). Research on the role of music in the healing process is still in its relative infancy, but the preliminary positive findings it has on the brain and healing cannot be overlooked.

Andy Park (n.d.), one of the leading composers for the AVC Music Group, opens a short Internet article on the relationship between music and healing with a quote from Heinrich Heine: "Music is a strange thing. I would almost say it is a miracle. For it stands halfway between thought and phenomenon, between spirit and matter." Park notes that one of "God's purposes" of music is as "an agency of healing." The role worship leaders play is "the role of the ancient bard—singing songs that contain the breath of God." Park then moves away from metaphor to mix psychological and theological tenets to discuss the interworking of music and healing:

> From as early as the time of King David, we see music employed as a healing balm for the human soul. As David played his harp, evil spirits were driven away from Saul. This wasn't music alone—it was the anointing of the Holy Spirit.
>
> Music has the effect of bypassing our human defense mechanisms. Our hardened hearts soften up as we let melodies and harmonies wash over us. Music disarms us and taps into the sensitivities of our soul. Under the influence of songs of praise, our anxiety lifts, our mood changes, and we get in touch with our inner person and feelings. As we yield to the Lord and behold his beauty, we invite the Great Physician to come to us. . . . .
>
> As we worship the Lord, the healing power of God's kingdom comes upon us. God-inspired art, impacts the emotions and feeds the spirit. And I've seen God heal physical ailments in the midst of worship. Through our simple songs, God works wonders far beyond anything we could imagine.

Another element of P/C ritual mentioned earlier and used to measure ritual participation is prayer for the pilgrim by members of prayer teams. As noted earlier, the prayer was more intuitive (mystical) than cognitive. Words mattered little. There seemed to be a vital energy present that was channeled through the pray-ers to the one being prayed for with simple prayers like, "Come, Holy Spirit" or "Give her more, Holy Spirit." Pilgrims who may have been standing quietly lost in their own personal prayer often suddenly developed the somatic manifestations of quaking or shaking, sending out primal screams, or falling motionless to the floor when prayed with.[21]

It is impossible at this point to explain how music and prayer practices common to revival rituals affect somatic manifestations. The ritual or renewal/ revivals, however, clearly create the space for somatic responses that may have therapeutic value.[22] One of the most interesting theses about how somatic manifestations can directly or indirectly affect healing can be found in Levine's (1997) *Waking the Tiger*. In his thought-provoking discussion of trauma and healing, Levine challenges scholars to give "the body its due" in the resolution of trauma as he explores what he calls "somatic experiencing" as a natural healing process.[23] It is possible that the manifestations experienced at TACF and other revival sites reflect the "natural" response to overcoming the trauma of life events.

Emotional or "Old" Mammalian Brain

The genetic roots of human emotions, as discussed briefly in chapter 3, are seated in the "second brain" of Turner's model—the "old mammalian" or emotional brain. In the emotional brain are found "the most important components of which are the limbic system, including the hypothalamus (which contains centers controlling homeostatic mechanisms associated with heat, thirst, satiety, sex, pain, pleasure, and emotions of rage and fear), and the pituitary gland (which controls and integrates the activities of all the endocrine glands in the body)" (Turner 1993, 84). While the older reptilian brain has been defined as a "stream of movement," the newer mammalian level has been called the "stream of feeling."

We have already noted the role that emotions play in the Poloma–Hoelter analysis of the survey data on the TACF healing. Somatic manifestations and their attendant emotions may be important instruments in the healing process, supporting similar observations made on the healing effects of psychoanalysis and shamanism. Poloma and Hoelter (1998) found the manifestations to be positively related to reports of positive emotional responses (feelings of love, joy, gratitude, peace, being cleansed, self-forgiveness, strength, and compassion) while unrelated to negative affect (anxiety, frustration, depression, anger, shame and guilt). Positive affect (but not negative affect) in turn contributed to explaining inner healing.[24] What the ritual service appeared to do was operate along the same lines as effective psychotherapy in providing a place for catharsis to occur (Scheff 1979).

According to Nichols and Zax (1977, 8), catharsis has two dimensions related by separate components:

One is relatively intellectual—the recall of forgotten material; the second is physical—the discharge of emotion in tears, laughter, or angry telling. The cognitive-emotional aspect consists of the motoric discharge of emotion in expressive sounds and actions such as tears and sobbing of grief, or the trembling and sweating of fear.

It would appear that both of these dimensions of catharsis are often present in response to revival ritual.[25]

The Cognitive or Neomammalian Brain

It is not as if humans have three separate brains—or even one brain with separate compartments. There is exchange among the heuristically devised components that is apparent as the discussion of the "triune brain" continues. Interplay has already been observed between somatic manifestations and emotional responses. The same holds true for the "left" and "right" hemispheres of the cognitive brain (introduced in the last chapter). Turner (1993, 87) describes the activity within the cognitive brain as "complementary shifts between the functions of the two hemispheres." The playfulness of TACF revival is reflected in the somatic manifestations, including laughter and "drunkenness" and the accompanying positive cathartic responses. It could be said that those involved in the renewal somehow recognized that the experience of the divine is beyond verbal expression. Pilgrims were thus given space to dance out their experience (right hemisphere) over the rational dictate to develop doctrine (left hemisphere). Imagery and visions that permeate narrative testimonies also reflect activities of the right hemisphere.

Activity of the right hemisphere seems to be behind what Turner has called the "liminal phase." Turner (1986b, 41–42) notes how the liminal phase of ritual is "dominantly in the subjunctive mode of culture"—"the mood of maybe, might be, as if, hypothesis, fantasy, conjecture, desire." Ordinary life is in the indicative mood, "where we expect the invariant operations of cause and effect, of rationality and common sense." In this sense, revival happenings have more similarity with the subjunctive than the ordinary mode of culture. The creation of testimonies, attempts to develop systematic teachings and conferences around revival experiences, move toward the ordinary indicative mood and are reflective of a cognitive process found in the brain's left hemisphere.

Attempts (including this chapter) that seek to make social scientific sense of the renewal and its attendant experiences are the epitome of left hemispheric activity! In the process of bringing the liminal phase into ordinary life (whether it be by leaders of the movement or scholars who study it), most probably the experience itself becomes somewhat distorted. What Turner has noted about anthropology's being "deeply rooted in the subjective experience of the inquirer" can be applied to all the social sciences:

> Everything is brought to the test of self, everything observed is learned ultimately "on his [or her] pulses." Obviously, there is much that can be counted, measured, and submitted to statistical analysis. But all human act is impregnated with meaning, and meaning is hard to measure, though it can often be grasped, even if only fleetingly and ambiguously. (Turner 1986b)

If it does nothing else, hopefully filtering the qualitative and quantitative data on revival healing through Turner's model makes the reader more aware of the problems in translating one mode of discourse on healing into another. This is a lesson to be remembered and applied as we move onto the next chapter on prophecy and the revival.

NOTES

1. Roger Sapp, a former chaplain with the U.S. army, theology professor, and pastor, now is a full-time traveling minister. According to Arnott, Sapp's teachings come closest to what TACF is currently teaching about divine healing.

2. One mechanism that has developed out of the renewal to promote this ministry of "all believers" is the rise of healing rooms across the nation. Inspired by the ministry of the late John G. Lake who established healing rooms in Spokane, Washington, during the 1920s, healing rooms are being established in strip malls as well as churches for people who seek prayer for healing. The Healing Rooms of Greater Cleveland is described briefly in chapter 8.

3. According to the 1995 survey, only 1 percent of the respondents to the TACF survey made a first-time commitment to Jesus as Savior and Lord during their visit to TACF. This figure reflects my observations of responses to altar calls for salvation during the many services attended during the height of the revival. Twenty-nine percent reported recommitting their lives to the Lord during their pilgrimage.

4. Case illustrations (with pseudonyms) presented in this chapter are taken primarily from the supplemental qualitative responses provided by nearly a quarter of the 1995 survey respondents.

5. In his study of Catholic charismatic healing processes, Thomas Csordas (1988) identified four specific types of healing: (1) spiritual healing (forgiveness from sin and forgiveness of others); (2) physical healing; (3) inner healing that is psychologically oriented; and (4) deliverance from demonic oppression. Although most if not all renewal leaders are aware of, and may on occasion practice, deliverance, it has had much less visibility in the renewal of the 1990s than it did in the Charismatic movement of the 1970s. It was assumed that the strong presence of God forced the demons to flee and that (ordinarily) it is best not to focus on the demonic. The focus, believers were instructed, was to be on Jesus.

6. Poloma and Hoelter's (1998) test of a "holistic model of healing" on TACF survey reports found that those who had the most intense experiences of spiritual healing were more likely to "experience positive emotions, more bodily manifestations and [to be] prayed with often." Prayer by a prayer team, somatic manifestations, and positive emotional responses (happiness, satisfaction, joy, love, gratitude, peace, forgiveness toward self, compassion) all contributed to explaining variance in spiritual healing scores.

7. The limited research that exists on the relationship between intense religious experience (including conversion) and mental health reflects some ambiguity. Despite the fact that some scholars have assumed that intense religious experiences are pathological, no research evidence exists to support that unmitigated assumption. To the contrary, some studies suggest there may be positive psychological benefits to the conversion experience. See Chamberlain and Hall (2000) for a summary of recent research on conversion experiences (pp. 144–46) and the related topic of "grace and guilt" (pp. 153–54).

8. Beginning in the late 1970s through the turn of the century, other ministers, most notably, Francis MacNutt (1977) and John and Paula Sandford (1977, 1982, 1985) developed their own systems of inner healing from the principles found in Agnes Sanford's (1950, 1958) writings that were widely used in P/C circles. They were joined by pastoral counselors and professors David Seamands (1981, 1985, 1988) and Siang-Yang Tan (1992, 1996) whose writings helped to moved inner healing into some academic courses.

9. The healing testimonies provided by respondents were based on spontaneous experiences rather than the more structured practice of inner healing and deliverance that continued to be practiced outside renewal services in many if not most renewal congregations. Popular inner healing and deliverance teachers in TACF-like renewal churches include John and Paula Sanford, Chester and Betty Kylstra, and use of Ed Smith's Theophostic Ministries.

10. The testimony was given at St. Luke's Episcopal Church in Fairlawn, Ohio, on March 31, 1996. Excerpts taken from an audiotape of the service.

11. The Pearsonian correlation for spiritual healing and inner healing in the 1995 survey was .24; the correlation between spiritual healing and retaining the inner healing (in 1997) was .20. Both correlations were statistically significant, $p = .0000$.

12. The experience of a range of manifestations appears to demonstrate a small but significant correlation with having reported an emotional or inner healing. Those who reported a wider range of manifestations were more likely to report having experienced healing of memories ($r = .11$).

13. The revival at TACF was never quite as heterogeneous as Marcus implies in the video narrative. Although an average of twenty or more countries throughout the world were represented at each service, the pilgrims tended to be white and Protestant. See Poloma (1996; 1998a) for additional demographics.

14. Demographics from the two surveys do not reflect the diversity claimed by the video. Although pilgrims typically came from an average of twenty or more countries on a typical night during the first years of the revival, most were American or Canadian, already involved in the P/C movement (typically in an independent church), and white. Unlike the Azusa Street Revival that was known for its racial diversity, relatively few Blacks could be found in the meetings (see Poloma 1996, 1998a for statistics).

15. The uncritical acceptance, and reporting, of unchecked testimonies was noted by James Beverley (1995) after he sought to follow up three of the earliest reported cases of healing at TACF. It should be noted, however, that renewal leaders do not have the resources to pursue medical documentation (although they often encourage those who claim healings to do so). Not being in the medical profession themselves, they are more interested in faith building than in doing scientific research as they go about the day-to-day tasks of leading a revival. This focus seems to pay off for leaders and followers alike. Over the years I observed more reports of physical healing and watched some of the leaders hone their intuitive prophetic skills as they related to healing practices. In no cases have I witnessed physicians or medicine being disparaged.

16. I personally observed Arnott, TACF's pastor, devote more time to healing prayer while maintaining his low-key and nonintrusive style as renewal progressed. He began to get more "words of knowledge," calling for those with specific ailments to come forward for prayer. Being a regular observer at the renewal meetings, I came to know some who claimed healings and would ask about their medical situation from time to time. Some would continue to claim "full healing," while others would experience the problem returning. Two things seemed to be happening with healing conferences and a greater focus on healing: (1) leaders were "pushing the envelope" in seeking ways to improve their skills and (2) more people were claiming to be healed.

17. Companion pieces in this same issue of the TACF magazine provided testimonies from a pastor, Donna La Pierre of Lion of Judah Christian Center in Kingsbury, New York, who had been healed of pleurisy and from Alexander Crowley from Toronto who had been healed of pneumonia.

18. I am aware of a number of cases in which persons reported dramatic physical healing that turned out to be a temporary remission. Usually the person who was temporarily cured is left to work out an explanation or to derive meaning about the event outside renewal circles. In an attempt to provide a milieu for the exercise of faith healing, there is little solace provided to the victims of a theology that denies the possibility of what other traditions have called "redemptive suffering."

19. These associations held even when ritual, experience of bodily manifestations, and positive emotions were held constant (Poloma and Hoelter 1998, 269). In the model, spiritual healing was found to be an intervening variable with ritual participation, manifestations, and emotional response being used as independent variables.

20. The P/C approach to gaining control over consciousness differs somewhat from the more commonly known Eastern techniques, although some effects are quite similar. Yogi disciplines of India, the Taoist approach of China, and the Zen of Buddhism "all seek to free consciousness from the deterministic influences of outside forces—be they biological or social in nature." Systems and techniques have developed over the centuries to release kundalini and to move chi, but the P/C movement lacks similar accepted systematic theories that could explain or prepare believers. The focus tends to be on experiencing the presence of God with the faith that where God is, the "signs and wonders" will follow.

21. As someone who joined the prayer team at TACF and frequently prayed at the end of renewal services, I am at a loss to provide a scientific explanation for what frequently occurred. Often I could feel "heat" or "energy" in my hands, but that sensation was not new to me. What was new was to stand in front of a person in line for prayer, to extend my hand or gently take theirs, and to see seemingly violent physical responses. There appears to be similarities between the descriptions of chi (especially external chi gong) and yoga (especially kundalini) and my observations of somatic revival experiences.

22. Manifestations, it should be noted, are linked directly to only inner healing (and indirectly to physical and mental healing) in the Poloma and Hoelter P/C healing model.

23. The book jacket of *Waking the Tiger* (1989) describes Levine's work as offering "a new and hopeful vision of trauma. It views the human animal as a unique being, endowed with an instinctual capacity to heal as well as an intellectual spirit to harness this innate capacity. It asks and answers an intriguing question—why are animals in the wild, though threatened routinely, rarely traumatized? By understanding the dynamics that make wild animals virtually immune to traumatic symptoms, the mystery of human trauma is revealed."

24. This does not imply that all seemingly uncontrolled and uncontrollable physical responses have a positive effect on emotional response, healing, and self-identity. In other social contexts, seemingly bizarre physical manifestations might be linked with negative affect (for example, if

similar activity was to be demonstrated in a church that is opposed to or unfamiliar with the renewal). What is strongly suggested by these findings is a need to take the functioning of the instinctual brain into account when discussing healing and wholeness, particularly when addressing the topic of emotions.

25. Scheff (1979) has critiqued modern society for its poverty in the successful production of ritual. He asserts that most rituals in modern society are "over distanced, that is, they are too vicarious and therefore do not lead to catharsis." Successful catharsis reawakens collectively held distress, which is unresolved in everyday life. It appears that P/C revival rituals have been able not only to "reawaken distress" but also to successfully resolve it.

5

Hearing the Voice of God: Prophecy and the Mystical Self

In the last days, God says, I will pour out my Spirit on all people. Your sons and daughters will prophesy, your old men will dream dreams. Even on my servants both men and women, I will pour out my Spirit in those days, and they will prophesy.

—Joel 2:28–32; NIV

An appreciation of the meanings and functioning of prophecy is essential for an understanding of Pentecostal mysticism. According to the Pentecostal/Charismatic (P/C) worldview, prophecy is not a gift for only the spiritually elite; it is available to men as well as women, young as well as old, and children as well as adults. But prophecy is more than simply a personal mystical experience through which God speaks; it is also a corporate one, having meaning only as its content is shared with another person or a larger community. As such, prophecy can be likened to a bridge between the individual "mystical self" and the communal "mystical body."

A word of caution before we proceed with any discussion of P/C prophecy is in order. As Gerald Sheppard (2001, 48) has wisely noted, our "best efforts at *description*—in this case of something called 'prophecy'—are never timeless, innocent, or constant from one epoch to another." This is true for the functioning of prophecy within the varying streams of the P/C movement as well as for a comparison of prophecy with intuitive experiences outside the P/C movement. For example, Sheppard's (p. 48) description of prophecy as "public, impulsively spoken (rarely or temporarily written)" holds only in part for those in the revival waters. Public prophecy is "impulsively spoken" in renewal meetings, but it can be videotaped and audiotaped or printed in revival publications and on the Internet. While private prophecy exists in both traditional and revival P/C groups, it is rare in traditional Pentecostal gatherings but quite common in revival meetings, particularly during the prayer time that follows most meetings.[1]

Sheppard (2001) correctly notes that a wide range of activities can be described as "prophetic" by P/C adherents, a basic list holds for both traditional and revival streams of the P/C movement. Prophecy may "take the form of 'interpretation' by one person in a familiar language immediately following incomprehensible tongues (or glossolalia) delivered usually by another person." It can also include other variations, such as "'anointed preaching' when the preacher feels like a channel of the Holy Spirit and words seem to flow in an effortless manner"; the words of a "'healing evangelist' (who) might sense special prophetic insights accompanying the healing manifestations of the Spirit"; a "'word of knowledge' most pertinent to a single individual, delivered by one person to another." Both revival and traditional P/C groups share the belief that "prophecy does not typically predict the future, but gives assurance, confirmation, warning, or spiritual inducement" (p. 64).[2]

While many similarities can be seen in the expression of prophecy between revival meetings and the gatherings of their older traditional cousins, the manner of deliverance and importance ascribed to particular practices often differ. For example, the following colorful description of a prophetic moment by a Pentecostal scholar is a better reflection of the traditional Pentecostal and the 1970s charismatic stream of the P/C movement than of a contemporary revival service:

> The group may listen in hushed silence because the presence of God is felt as a special visitation, "speaking" directly and specifically to this group at this time. A love wave of weeping or consenting words by others in the group may swell in tune with the prophecy, then erupt in praise, glossolalia, and verbal interjections of gratitude at the end. All of these events may include physical gestures of grief and joy, a "holy dance" a "trembling" in the presence of God. (Sheppard 2001, 64)

Revival meetings do (increasingly) have times of "hushed silence," people may weep, others dance, there may be trembling; but the somatic and emotional responses are more likely described as being part of worship in which prophecy may or may not be given.

In sum, descriptions of the commonly accepted practice of prophecy will differ widely, thus sounding a note of caution about any simple definition of the phenomenon. *Definitions* of prophecy that attempt to capture its breadth prove to be vacuous, while those that simplistically limit it to foretelling are usually ill informed (Goldingay 2001). Long colorful *descriptions* can reflect the varied content, form, and style of prophecy, as well as the self-presentation of the prophet, but they do so at the expense of parsimony. One way to grab the horns of this dilemma is to approach prophecy with one eye on description and the other on definition by using Wittgenstein's conceptual framework of "family resemblances" (Goldingay 2001, 27). Prophecy's "characteristic profile" bears a strong family resemblance to other phenomena listed as "gifts of the Spirit" in New Testament writings (see especially 1 Cor. 12–13), including glossolalia ("tongues and interpretation"), discernment of spirits, words of wisdom, and words of knowledge as well as to the related practices of prophetic intercession, healing, and mime.[3] All require "hearing from God"—whether through an intuited impression, a vision, a dream, a divine coincidence (serendipity), or verbal proclamation—and then speaking forth God's word (cf. Ryle 1993, 1995; Dupont 1997; Cooke 1994; Jacobs 1995; Joyner 1996). All these forms are recognized as functioning to edify, encourage, and comfort; to provide correction and warning; to direct and guide; and to inspire intercessory prayer.

In sum, putting theological issues aside that seek the biblical boundaries of prophecy in order to distinguish it from its other spiritual relatives, a social scientific discussion of prophecy can best begin by placing the prophetic within the larger family of prayer forms. Whatever else prophecy may be, it is a form of prayer—more specifically, a form of revelatory prayer that assumes intimacy with a living God.

PROPHECY AS PRAYER

Research on forms of prayer (cf. Ladd and Spilka, 2002; Hood, Morris, and Harvey 1993; Poloma and Gallup 1991; Poloma and Pendleton 1989, 1991) suggests that spiritual writers who distinguished between "active prayer" and "contemplative prayer" have identified two major prayer forms that reflect common practice. Active prayer, including religious rituals, is grounded in an attempt by the "pray-er" to reach out to God—to connect in some meaningful way with God. It can stop with one-sided activity in which pray-ers, so to speak, do all the work—where they leave their messages at an unseen divine answering machine that may or may not return the call. While it may begin with an active soliloquy, contemplative prayer requires a more passive or receptive stance, with pray-ers being stilled as they wait for God to respond. Prayer often moves on to become a dialogue where God's activity increases and the pray-er's effort decreases.[4]

Research polls conducted in the United States have repeatedly shown that nearly 90 percent of Americans claim to pray. Of these pray-ers, the vast majority has reported different religious experiences during personal prayer. For example, 88 percent claimed they had (at least on occasion) experienced a deep sense of peace and well-being, 79 percent had felt the strong presence of God, 73 percent had received a definite answer to a specific prayer request, and 57 percent had felt divinely inspired or "led by God" to perform some specific action (Poloma and Gallup 1991). It is worth noting that evangelical or born-again pray-ers, a category of which P/C Christians are a subset, were more than twice as likely to report these experiences than were nonevangelicals. Prophecy, hearing and responding to the voice of God, may be regarded as an extension of simple prayer experiences commonly reported by the American public, experiences that are more common for P/C Christians and Evangelicals, than they are for nonevangelicals.

The British prophet Graham Cooke, who offers conferences internationally teaching P/C Christians how to unlock the prophetic charisma, makes the following statement about the relationship between prayer and prophecy: "In terms of preparation, prayer is absolutely vital to us. It's so important for everything but in particular with regard to the prophetic. Prayer and prophecy are inextricably linked in terms of their communication process; both involve listening before talking" (Cooke 1994, 50). Active prayer, usually forms of spontaneous or ritual prayers, often sets the stage for prophetic revelation.

STAGES OF SPIRITUAL ENCOUNTERS

In proposing a typology to describe revelation nearly forty years ago, sociologist Rodney Stark (1965, 99) suggested that religious experience can be conceptualized as a dyadic form of interaction—"the divinity and the individual as a pair of actors involved in a social encounter." Stark identified four possible configurations for such an encounter, the first three of which can be regarded as a prelude to the prophetic and the fourth providing a broad category that captures the heart of prophecy. These stages include sensing the divine presence; a mutual acknowledgment; affective response; and human participation in divine action.[5]

1. Sensing the divine presence

At this preliminary stage of revelation, the human actor somehow feels the existence or presence of the divine actor. Sensing deep peace and well-being in personal prayer may be an important first step toward the actualization of the prophetic charisma. This experience is relatively common among pray-ers. Findings from research polls (Poloma and Gallup 1991; Poloma and Pendleton 1991) report that nearly a third (32 percent) of those who pray claim to have this experience regularly, with only 12 percent saying they never have this experience of deep peace. Put another way, 88 percent of those who claimed to pray indicated that they had experienced the first stage of Stark's typology—at least on occasion. Prophecy has its roots in similar preliminary senses of God's immanence, particularly at religious gatherings where prophecies are usually given. P/C worship ritual and its attendant music (discussed in chapter 2) create a milieu in which many if not most in the gathering experience a sense of the divine.

2. Mutual acknowledgment

Not only do pray-ers sense a divine presence, but they may also sense the presence taking note of them. In private prayer this acknowledgment may come through a deeper insight into a spiritual or biblical truth or through an answer to a specific prayer request. Of the pray-ers studied by Margaret Poloma and George Gallup (1991), 39 percent said they had never received a spiritual insight during prayer and 27 percent said they had never received an answer to a specific prayer request, suggesting that perhaps a third of pray-ers never reached this second stage of Stark's revelatory typology. Most pray-ers, at least on occasion but many regularly, do appear to meet God in prayer and experience the encounter as an interactive one. For the P/C prophet this mutual acknowledgment may take the form of a sense that God is giving the prophet a "word" to speak, either to the entire congregation or to another person. The actual message at this point may be vague to nonexistent, but there is a sense of God's presence and possible call.

3. Affective response

According to Stark (1965) the awareness of mutual presence is replaced by an affective relationship akin to love or friendship. For those at P/C worship services during which prophecy is often generated, it may be impossible to distinguish between the second and third stages of revelation. Many of the worship songs (as discussed in chapter 2) focus on the love of God—some acknowledging God's love and others singing out love songs to the divine. As John Arnott stated unequivocally during the opening talk for *The Father Loves You Conference* (May 8, 2002), "The message of Father's love is foundational to what we believe." This foundational message can be heard wherever the revival winds have taken the Toronto Blessing, with many speakers joining Arnott in proclaiming this basic belief. Its proponents have contended that the loss of affectivity is what is wrong with the contemporary church and that the blessing of the revival has been to rekindle a divine romance. As Jack Deere (1993, 10) noted in a statement written several months before the Toronto outpouring:

> In my opinion, the greatest danger facing the church today does not come from without the church, but from within. It is not the New Age nor secular humanism that is crippling the effectiveness of the church today. It is the lack of love for God, the lukewarmness of the church, that is its greatest enemy today. A lukewarm, loveless version of Christianity may succeed in propagating a little religion here and there, but it will never capture the heart of a dying world.

It would appear that (for prophets and nonprophets alike) feelings of being loved and of loving God are heightened through revival worship and prayer. The prophetic impulse seems to be nestled in the receptive response to encounters with the divine experience. The initial sensing of the divine, mutual acknowledgment, and affective response appear to work in tandem to release the prophetic.

4. Human actor as confidant

The first three stages of Stark's typology are a prelude to engaging as a "fellow participant in action with the divine actor." This stage best describes the experience and activity of the prophet. What I have been suggesting is that prophecy is a particular type of prayer with experiences that are somewhat familiar to many pray-ers. One of the first encounters with the prophetic may be God offering personal guidance and direction, an issue that has been asked in surveys on prayer. Although praying for guidance in decision making appears to be a nearly universal request (with 92 percent of pray-ers asking for such guidance), only 9 percent of pray-ers in the Poloma–Gallup research claimed to receive regular "divine inspiration" or being led to perform some specific action.

While many others (48 percent) have this experience of divine guidance at least on occasion, 43 percent of praying respondents report that they have never had such an experience (Poloma and Gallup 1991, 56–58). Sensing divine instruction appears to be sought by the vast majority of pray-ers but is regularly experienced only by a much smaller minority. Being able to hear God and to respond to divine directives is at the heart of the prophetic act.

Those who prophesy learn the art of listening and responding over time, often under the tutelage of more established prophets. Cooke, a leading teacher on the prophetic in the recent renewal, introduces the prophetic to believers by describing his personal experience with prayer:

> Before the Lord called me into my current ministry, I was the business development manager for a large training and recruitment company. My life was a hectic round of business deals, management problems, employment, research, involvement with Government projects, taking training sessions, organizing events and overseeing the ongoing business strategy for the company. There were times in those busy days when I would indicate to my reception staff that I was taking ten minutes out and did not want to be disturbed. I would retreat into my office, close the door and sit quietly, thanking God and listening, praying, wanting his perspectives. Many right decisions came out of these short bursts of "time out in prayer." I can't honestly say I always heard God specifically speak in those moments (though sometimes I did!). However my track record at the company, together with continuous promotion amongst the staff, probably means that the Lord influenced me far more than I actually knew. Just as important was the fact that these short bursts of prayer kept my heart free from ungodly pressure. Prayer keeps the channel of communication open. (Cooke 1994, 51)

Religious experiences, often within the context of personal prayer, appear to open the pray-er to another way of knowing. It is often an experience, as suggested by the preceding quotation, in which a belief in the supernatural and natural ebb and flow together to produce and maintain an alternative worldview. The Poloma and Gallup study suggests that Stark's fourth stage of religious experience in which persons perceive themselves as co-actors with the divine, often receiving messages of leading and guidance, is not as rare as skeptics might assume. P/C Christians have taken this stage of religious experience and further developed it to provide a subculture in which hearing the voice of God is normal spirituality. It is a milieu in which the ministry of the prophetic is deemed normal and increasingly where the prophetic office is being restored. The P/C movement is not only part of a revealed religion known as Christianity, but it is a movement that professes a belief in, and practice of, ongoing revelation.

THE PROPHETIC AND STARK'S THEORY OF REVELATIONS

Although a belief in the prophetic is integral to the P/C worldview, as noted at the onset of this chapter, there are major differences in the intensity and nature of its practice. For many it has been somewhat routinized and limited to confirming existing religious reality, with perhaps only an occasional experience of prophecy as foretelling. As Stark (1991, 241–42) has proposed in his model of normal revelations, "Many common, ordinary, even mundane mental phenomena can be experienced as contact with the supernatural." Dreams, mental visions, impressions, and serendipitous occurrences are all regarded as common potential media for receiving prophecy. Although prophecy has continuously played a role in the one hundred years of P/C history, there has always been a corresponding need to control this explosive and institutionally disruptive experience.[6]

An important observation that Stark (1991, 242; see also 1999, 289–90) makes about revelatory experiences applies to our analysis of prophetic expressions in the current P/C revival: "Most episodes involving contact with the supernatural will merely confirm the conventional religious culture, even when the contact includes a specific communication, or revelation."[7] For many P/C believers the prophetic begins as a personal experience, often confirming some understanding of a biblical truth or some personal insight developed during prayer. Stark (1992, 244) has astutely noted, however, that "genius" often enters in the form of "creative individuals (who) will sometimes create profound revelations and will externalize the source of this new culture."

These persons are most likely to be of "deep religious concerns who perceive the shortcomings of conventional faith." It is among these men and women that what has come to be known as a prophetic ministry and later the status of prophet emerges. This structural process of creating and recreating prophetic ministries and roles has occurred within each new Pentecostal wave, including the Latter Rain, the Charismatic movement, the Third Wave, and the most recent 1990s revival. The prophetic is once again aroused, refashioned, and expanded by an increasingly vocal minority within the larger movement.

PROPHECY IN RENEWAL RITUAL

In renewal-type ritual, prophetic words may be accompanied with bodily actions (including jerking, violent shaking, and even animal sounds as described in chapter 3), but most prophetic words are delivered in a less dramatic style, often within the context of the prayer ministry offered at the end of the more formal renewal ritual. Prophets in the current renewal are generally discouraged against using the affected voice that often characterized traditional Pentecostal prophecy—forceful presentations that end with "thus saith the Lord"—although theatrics may be more acceptable for those who have established themselves with a ministry or status of a prophet. Prophecy is regarded as a "gift" that any Spirit-filled Christian should experience at least occasionally, but, as with all gifts, it is believed to be unequally distributed. Prophetic leader and teacher Cooke describes it as follows:

> Knowing that all spirit-filled Christians can prophesy does not make everyone who does a prophet. There are various levels and stages of prophetic anointing, beginning with the shallow end of basic prophecy, encouragement, edification, and comfort. However, moving through levels of prophetic ministry to the office of the prophet requires considerable training, experience, and development over a great many years. On average it takes approximately fifteen to twenty years to make a prophet, depending on the training, discipling, and mentoring one has received in that time. (Cooke 1994, 16)

Teachers on prophecy recognize the human dimension of this intuitive ability. John Paul Jackson compares the ability to receive supernatural messages to a satellite or receiving dish. Many people have operating dishes, but not all hear God. Intuited knowledge, according to Jackson, can come from God (prophecy), the human soul (mind, will, emotions) or from the devil. "Psychics and New Age practitioners may think they are hearing from God, but they are getting information disguised as revelation" (Jackson, 1999).

Prophecy, as already discussed, is a form of prayer—one that entails hearing from God and being able to speak for him. It can convey a word to the larger church (public) or to individuals (private).[8] It may originate in a sense to speak out (with or without knowing exactly what one will say as one begins to speak) as well as in dreams and visions (e.g., Cooke 1994; Ryle 1995). Although prayer team members, the most common carriers of private prophecy, are counseled against "mating or dating" in the words they speak to others (being encouraged rather to turn their questionable prophetic senses into prayers for the person), a number of respondents to the TACF surveys indicated that prophetic words given through leaders and prayer team members had a life-changing impact. In most cases seasoned listeners have been prepared for the prophetic word by their own sacred intuition or by a similar word having been given on different occasions by different prophets. One example of a prophetic word demonstrating a check and balance that is encouraged for interpreting private prophecy is provided by the account of a young German man who visited TACF:

> A few weeks before I went to Toronto, I visited a worship service in Germany. A young man I didn't know before had a vision for me. It was a vision for full-time ministry and a call for evangelism. After he told me this, he prayed prophetically for me. When I went to TACF I asked the Lord for confirmation of his call on my life. One evening a lady from the ministry team prayed for me. She prayed prophetically and exactly with the same words the young man used in Germany—but only in English. This was the confirmation for my call. Now my life changes and we move. Next year I will go to Bible college. (Case #178)

Such "divine coincidences" are quite commonplace for those who immerse themselves in the prophetic. A person is quietly seeking God for direction when another (often unknown) person approaches with a seeming answer.[9] This happening could occur two or more times before the recipient may finally take the seemingly proscribed action.

PROPHECY AND THE TRIUNE BRAIN
In order to cast another source of light on the common practice of private prophecy within the revival movement, I am going to indulge in a bit of playfulness. Using the "triune brain theory" as applied by Victor Turner to religious ritual (see chapter 3) as a frame, I will present an example of a personal experience with the prophetic. I have selected but one of numerous examples of personal prophecies I have received over the years to illustrate prophecy's psychological and interpersonal dynamics. Prophecy, both in giving and receiving an intuited "word from God," involves the whole multifaceted human brain, including the so-called *reptilian* or reptilian, *old mammalian* or emotional, and *new mammalian* or cognitive (left and right) sectors.

At a renewal meeting in a home fellowship I had attended during the early years of the renewal, a man who served as a pray-er came over to minister to me. Although he knew of the research I was doing, at that time we had done nothing more than exchange pleasantries. Some twenty people were gathered in a small living room where music was already playing when I arrived one Thursday evening. I made my way to an empty chair and assumed a quiet meditative stance. The gathering could be described as silent "Quaker worship plus music," during which there was no set ritual, with people coming and going as they pleased.

It was within this simple context that Rick came up to me and began to quietly pray. When I entered the room that night, Rick (who had just returned from the renewal meetings in Toronto) was lying on the floor, laughing and shaking. While praying for me, however, his manifestations were minimal, although on occasion he would jerk violently as if an electric current had just gone through his body. Both of us stood off to the side of the living room—I with my hands open and outstretched and eyes closed, and Rick, eyes closed, with his hands resting on my shoulders. As he silently prayed, I experienced an increase of the deep sense of peace that had begun to well up within me when I first entered the room.

After some time—perhaps five minutes or more—Rick began to speak simple phrases, repeating them again and again. With each one I easily "free associated" sensing I knew exactly what "God meant" in giving Rick the simple words and phrases to speak. I knew from past experience with prophecy that had I stopped Rick and asked for elaboration, he probably would not have been able to say anything meaningful. (In fact when I did try to raise some questions after the service, he indicated that he did not wish to talk. It was as if Rick did not want to deal with distinguishing what I might say from what he might intuitively speak to me.) According to my field notes, this process went on for three weeks in succession.

Rick did not ask me to "free associate"—he gave me no instructions. My mental response seemed to be automatic—a seeming subconscious response of the cognitive "right brain" to what was being said. Perhaps not surprisingly, the "right brain" intuitive response was quickly linked to existing left-brain assessments of a real situation. I was given over a dozen simple words or phrases by Rick during the first few weeks he prayed with me, and in each one I felt as if Rick was "reading my mail." I will give one illustration of a word that I free associated and the context in which it assumed meaning. It involved the tension I have always experienced in my role as an involved participant observer of the P/C movement.[10]

One of the words given to me the first night I attended the gathering was "lighten up." This immediately called to mind counsel I had received from a therapist about two and a half years earlier. She commented how serious I was about life and expressed concern that I did not "know how to play." I could hear her saying, "You will feel like you are going to an extreme when you 'lighten up,' but you will actually be on a middle ground." Rick kept repeating the phrase "lighten up," probably four or five times without any added commentary. Then there was more silent prayer, followed by "little Margaret, come to the party." This, too, he repeated slowly several times, and I immediately (without any seeming effort on the part of my reasoning skills) related it to the position I hold as a researcher of the renewal. Those who observe me would think I am able to enter in to revival ritual without difficulty (i.e., I can sing with enthusiasm, dance, laugh, weep, and assume meditative stances), but I know that I have *experienced* only a taste of what many others have reported.

What is significant, as I reflect on this prophetic moment, is that Rick could not have generated any of the implicit free associations by using his cognitive reasoning skills. Most who give prophetic words—be they "foretelling" or "forthtelling"—insist they are unable to perform on command. Rick claimed that he had been very hesitant to come over to pray with me (given my known position as a researcher in the renewal) and especially to speak the particular phrases he "felt led" to speak. Nor could Rick have done anything to elicit an emotional response from me—particularly the deep peace that has come to be a "sign" of God's presence in my life. That peace began as soon as I walked into the room and intensified as the evening went on. The words that were spoken and the free association that occurred through the workings of the right brain only deepened the peace I had already begun to experience.

Although the emotional responses I experienced were primarily ones of peace and being loved by God (rather than any of the more dramatic responses found in the renewal meetings), they do demonstrate the role the reptilian and emotional brain sectors may play in prophecy. I always felt an incredible sense of well-being as I left those small prayer gatherings. On occasion as Rick prayed, I felt an unexplainable warmth in my hands and then a sensation of energy—a kind of prickling sensation throughout my torso—that seemed to generate some involuntary twitching in my shoulders and upper back. I would then find my body doing repeated bends from the waist down, as my chin rested against my upper chest and my eyes remained closed.[11]

It was as if Rick's prayer had tapped into an unseen energy field that brought forth somatic responses through the activity of the reptilian brain. Although I was aware of the movement, I was interested neither in stopping them nor increasing the somatic responses. They seemed as normal as breathing.[12] Accompanying the manifestations was an incredible emotional sense of being loved and loving the Creator of the universe.

What has been demonstrated through this autobiographical description of prophecy is how a very simple unstructured ritual can provide a social context in which the whole brain is stimulated, including reflex responses, emotional reaction, as well as intuitive and rational cognition. The brain is the physical medium through which the unobservable Spirit and spirit seem to be dancing between work and play. The process described here reflects a "mystical consciousness"—one that involves "a different reality, considered from our ordinary point of view." As a form of mystical consciousness, it includes an "intuitive knowing, a type of perception that bypasses the usual sensory channels and rational intellect" (Deikman 1982, 21).

CAVEAT EMPTOR

While anyone is free to offer personal or public prophecy, parameters are quickly drawn to limit its misuse. "Guidelines" develop that become more defined and limiting with the passage of time. Eventually these guidelines can harden into well-known and accepted mores, often leaving (especially in well established P/C churches and organizations) the shell of prophetic belief without the experiential content. There is sound reason for this move toward the routinization of charisma. Although prophecy is an important factor in the revitalization of the P/C movement (as the chapters in part 2 will demonstrate), it also has undeniably proved to be one of the more problematic charismata. What is to be done about the person who disrupts religious drama and institutions in the name of being a spokesperson for the divine? How can the damage private prophecy potentially poses for the undiscerning believer be controlled by those more aware of its dysfunctional potential? What about its use to self-promote unscrupulous "prophets" to positions of power and prestige? And what to do about "heresies" that can be spoken by prophets who challenge religious doctrine and institutions?

Sufficient to say, many leaders (especially those who are prophetic themselves) are able to successfully control the damage that looms in the unscrupulous or naïve use of prophecy. Rules have been spelled out by teachers on the prophetic to caution believers about the dangers inherent in an uncritical acceptance of prophetic counsel and prognoses. New Testament prophecy, it is often said, is different from that of the Old Testament in its more limited role of being an instrument of edification and encouragement. Those who receive prophetic words or visions with a negative spin are commonly encouraged to use such words of knowledge for prayer rather than using them to disrupt others.

The teachings limiting prophecy are widely available through conferences, books, and videotapes as well as on Internet list serves and websites devoted to P/C prophetic activity. Experienced leaders seek to control potentially damaging prophecies that might be harmful to individuals and disruptive to communities, and their teachings do help to safeguard against the damage a half-crazed prophet can wrack on a community. Discernment is the rule of the day.

While anyone is in theory free to offer prophecy, some are more likely to be heard than others. Those who are given the status of (or succeed in promoting themselves as) a prophet sometimes do not model the widely accepted norms that they themselves may teach.[13] A widely accepted four-level prophetic hierarchy has been offered by Mike Bickle and Jim Goll (1997), both noted for their prophetic ministries, to describe the major differences among prophets. These levels (in ascending order) are (1) simple prophecy; (2) prophetic gifting; (3) prophetic ministry; and (4) prophetic office.

Simple prophecy is the label that best fits much of the prophetic activity described in this chapter. It is the ability to use what others might call *intuition,* which can also be found in spiritually oriented persons of varying religious persuasions, as a means of blessing others. We have seen how it can be described as an extension of prayer experiences commonly found among pray-ers. It includes thoughts that come to mind that seem to be divine in origin and (less frequently) visions, pictures, or prophetic dreams. Simple prophecy functions to strengthen, to encourage, and to comfort.

Prophetic gifting has the same function as simple prophecy but with the intuitive abilities refined and turned up a notch or two. The visions will be sharper, words will be more definitive, pictures will be clearer, and dreams will be more relevant. It is only with the third level of *prophetic ministry* that prophets are encouraged to give direction and correction to others. Bickle and Goll (1997, 33) describe such experiences as more regularly receiving words, dreams, and visions; having "open visions" (angelic visitations, audible voices, etc.); and as often including detailed information, such as names, faces, dates, and future events. It is at the fourth level—that of *the prophet*—that we find the "most powerful" prophetic activity, although the prophets do have "less authority than those who wrote the scriptures."

The prophet functions "to provide direction and correction to those in church government, and often leaders in the secular world as well." Prophets allegedly have "a constant flow of divine revelation," with many "open visions." Increasingly they are the ones who produce the long prophecies that many found on the Internet and the book-length prophetic manuscripts available at conferences and Christian bookstores. While not all who are in the P/C movement would subscribe to this particular four-level hierarchical model that peaks with the office of the prophet, most would agree that some prophets are more gifted than are others.

THE RISE OF THE PROPHETIC OFFICE

There has been a proliferation of materials on prophecy in the P/C movement beginning in the 1990s and continuing into the new millennium, reflecting a rise in the number of prophets and new prophetic ministries. Leaders of these ministries often use a restorationist eschatology to legitimate the "office of prophet." For many who are on the prophetic cutting edge, the rise of prophets is a sign of the end-time church; the development of the office of the prophet signals that the church is being restored to its pristine condition with the fivefold ministries listed in Eph. 4:12–13. Three of the ministries (that of evangelist, pastor, and teacher) have already reportedly been restored to the Christian church; the other two, that of prophet and apostle, are in the process of emerging. In the words of Bill Hamon, whose forty-year career has influenced many P/C leaders:

> The whole world will be affected when the apostles and prophets are fully restored. Their supernatural prophetic and apostolic words will signal the rise and fall of many nations and people. They will be instrumental in determining goat and sheep nations so that when Jesus Christ comes He can put the sheep nations on His right and the goat nations on His left. It will not be long until Christians realize the tremendous ways the restoration of the prophets and apostles will affect them and the corporate Church. (Hamon 1997, 2)

While *simple prophecy* is the subject of many teachings and appropriate warnings, potential problems stemming from emerging prophetic leaders are less likely to be controlled. Those who intentionally or unintentionally aspire to the office of prophet must continually demonstrate their powers in order to retain a following.[14] The stakes are high for those with prophetic ministries, who are supported by biblically derived doctrine that promotes a divinely mandated restoration of the fivefold ministry for the entire church. Institutionally speaking, some prophets and apostles (sometimes with one person wearing both mantles) are seeking places in the P/C movement that parallel ecclesiastic bishops in historic traditions. With personal charisma yet to be institutionalized, the pressures of prophetic performance are never far removed.

This move toward routinization of the prophetic charisma is a path familiar to historians of the early church. Cecil Robeck (1988, 735–37) has described how the early church "was no stranger to prophetic activity," with room being made within the church structure for prophets to work on both the itinerant and local levels. By the Middle Ages, prophetic activity was more likely to be confined to practices well within the bounds of the official church structure. Prophecy as a charisma became routinized within ecclesiastical office. The Protestant Reformation opened the door for a resurgence of prophecy in some independent sectors, but prophetic activity was more likely to be limited to God speaking through the preacher. With Pentecostalism and then the larger P/C movement came the restoration of prophecy as practiced by early Christianity. The problem, as Robeck (p. 238) points out is twofold: "There is the question of (1) how to distinguish genuine oracles from false ones and (2) what authority contemporary oracles have in light of a closed canon of Scripture."

The second problem has been partially resolved. Most will agree that contemporary prophecy cannot add to or detract from the Bible (although there is plenty of room to prophesy with creative interpretations of the sacred text). The first problem, however, still begs a solution. As P/C history continues to unfold, the difficulty of resolving the first problem identified by Robeck has resulted in a purposive silencing of many would-be prophets. Especially in traditional Pentecostal denominations, some pastors and leaders have taken a de facto cessationist position that relegates prophecy to a pastor's Sunday sermon. While prophecy may be given creedal importance, in fact it is often no more likely to find expression in institutionalized Pentecostalism than in historic denominational churches (Poloma n.d.). While routinization of charisma has clipped prophetic wings in some P/C sectors, a new prophetic movement has taken hold as an integral part of the worldwide P/C revival renewal.[15] It is within the revival streams of the P/C movement that the problem of distinguishing "genuine oracles from false ones" has yet to find a resolution.

Eddie Hyatt (2002b), a scholar of historic Christian revivals, has recently presented some "warning signs" for prophetic ministries gone astray. These include (1) when prophecy is used to enhance the status of a movement and its leaders; (2) when prophecy becomes a means for determining the will of God; (3) when prophecy is preoccupied with images, numbers, and symbols; (4) when those prophesying are not open to testing or correction or both; and (5) when prophecy becomes a replacement for the scriptures and common sense. While aspiring prophets are taught to judge simple prophecy, it is not clear exactly how such guidelines are being applied to those who claim a special prophetic mantle.

AND YOUR DAUGHTERS SHALL PROPHESY

"There are not many female prophets in biblical literature," writes Pentecostal biblical scholar Lilly Nortje'-Meyer (2001, 138). And there are few female prophets in the P/C revival movement. Women can and do prophesy, but less than a handful have prophetic ministries or are graced with the mantle of prophecy.[16] The prophesying daughters are limited largely to giving "simple prophecy" while serving on prayer teams and do "prophetic intercession" where they pray behind the scenes of many churches and ministries.[17] While the Spirit is believed to descend on both sons and daughters, the sons have a decided advantage in climbing the P/C hierarchical ladder. Only the most creative and gifted (or those married to male P/C leaders) are given P/C renewal platforms, allowing their voices to be heard beyond a private prophetic role.

The dearth of women prophets reflects the lack of female leadership that has always been found in the P/C movement where the role of women has been a paradoxical one—one of liberation and empowerment that simultaneously restrains all but a handful of women from positions of leadership.[18] As Marie Griffith (1997, 199) reported in her excellent study of P/C women in Women's Aglow Fellowship International:

> God calls his daughters to perform mighty acts and inaugurate prodigious transformations through their prayers, rendering Christian women vital instruments of regeneration and healing to a broken and dying world. Believing that

power issues from vulnerability—or, paradoxically, that vulnerability recreates itself as power—these women avow their capacity to remake all creation.

Women involved in the P/C revival, like their sisters in Aglow studied by Griffith (1997, 210), may pepper their salted "celebrations of the male-dominated status quo" with some "accompanying critique, yet the robust note of the final triumph may well disarm whatever challenges reside there." Griffith goes on to conclude:

> If, in certain ways, prayer and testimony seem to create possibilities for the liberation and transformation worshipers claim to experience, they may just as readily work to opposite ends, further institutionalizing the roles and boundaries that constrict women's space. From that angle, one consequence of a fervently charismatic, biblically oriented piety for women may be blindness to their own sociopolitical, religious, and domestic disempowerment, the hazardous result of seeing the world only through Jesus-colored glasses. (p. 210)

Griffith's findings reflecting the marginalization of American charismatic women are reinforced through a British study of charismatic prophecy. Cartledge (2001) observed that although "Pentecostal women play a significant role in testifying, prophesying, healing, counseling and teaching within the church," this encouragement may actually function "as a means of both inclusion and exclusion." Cartledge (pp. 99, 109) briefly describes this paradox, raising both a question and a problematic concern:

> It includes women and affirms their prophetic activity and ministry but also appears to contain them within this realm. Does it, paradoxically, exclude them from an institutional ministry since they are not affirmed at this level? If this is the case, it suggests that charismatic authority also carries the capacity to threaten the institutional order. Women, of course, may prefer the freedom of cultural authority and charisma over and against the restriction of institutional order. Nevertheless for those women who feel called both to a charismatic and an institutional ministry there is a tension in a way that perhaps does not exist for men.

This "disempowerment" will become even more evident to the astute reader in part II. Reflecting the evangelical and fundamentalist proscriptions that have been placed on women ministers rather than the expressed belief in Christian equality, the major actors in the P/C drama of revival in North America tend to be white, nondenominational Protestant males.

NOTES

1. Little attention has been paid to prophecy in social scientific discussions of religious experience. It is significant that in the 599 pages of text used to present twenty-four scholarly articles in the *Handbook of Religious Experience* (Hood 1995) only three passing references were made to prophecy, two of them in an article submitted by me.

2. There are noteworthy differences even in this list of common practices. Revival speakers are more likely to adopt a teaching style—one conveying more "ordinariness" than the "special anointing" of the colorful preaching style of traditional Pentecostals. Reflecting the fact that newer streams of revival have a range of external manifestations, followers of this stream are less likely to single out glossolalia as a "litmus test" of Spirit baptism. And they are much more likely to deliver prophetic words without a glossolaic prelude than are traditional Pentecostals.

3. Some unusual manifestations (especially the animal sounds) discussed in chapter 3 were interpreted as prophetic. John Arnott (1995, 170) observed in a chapter devoted to the "prophetic animal sounds" how these "sounds are often made in the context of prophecy, vision, and revelation."

4. While it is impossible to demonstrate that the divine does in fact communicate directly to humans using the methodological tools of social science, it is equally impossible to prove that the divine does not do so. What is possible to demonstrate through the social scientific perspective is that many people believe they are in dialogue and interaction with God—and that this definition of the situation has real social consequences.

5. Philip Richter (1996) provided a sociological account of the Toronto Blessing in the U.K. in which he utilizes Glock and Stark's (1965) well-known typology of religious experience to introduce the phenomenon. The typology (upon which Stark's [1965] article builds) includes confirming, responsive, ecstatic, and revelational categories. Richter observes that the ecstatic and revelational categories are only infrequently found within mainstream religion. Richter (p. 101) states, "The Toronto Blessing stands out from ordinary religious experience in being predominantly ecstatic [intimate relationship with the divine], and in some cases, revelational [messages or commission by the divine], in form." Revelation was probably more prevalent than Richter suggests, and as the years have gone by, both revelation and ecstasy are sought by those who are still swimming in the revival river.

6. By the 1940s many of the unique Pentecostal expressions had become somewhat routinized. A fresh restorationist movement, known as the Latter Rain (Durrand and Shupe 1983; Synan 1984; Riss 1987), arose to revive Pentecostalism but was soon condemned by the leaders of the stronger Pentecostal sects. The Latter Rain did have an impact on the Charismatic movement of the 1960s and 1970s, reviving the prophetic during this new wave of P/C activity. McGuire (1982) offers an excellent discussion of the routinization of prophecy among Catholic neo-Pentecostals that could be applied to Pentecostal groups as well.

7. The cultural confirmatory nature of the prophetic can be illustrated through differing assumptions about intuitive gifting between adherents of P/C Christianity and the so-called New Age movement. For P/C Christians prophecy is a gift of the Holy Spirit, coming from a divine source outside of person to empower for service. For many in the New Age movement, intuitive gifting resides inside the person as an extension of a benevolent universe or Spirit. New Age adherents are likely to root their experiences in Eastern non-Christian or in Native American worldviews while those of the P/C movement take the Judeo-Christians scriptures as their guiding script. P/C Christians would label New Age practices as pagan, idolatrous, and even demonic. This has not kept some innovative P/C adherents from New Age fairs where they have set up booths (with appropriately New Age labels) to pray for healing, offer opportunities for dream analysis, and prophesy. At least one group has been conducting dream workshops through programs offered at a local Borders Book Store in Texas.

8. Those men and women who are deemed to have a ministry of prophecy are the ones most likely to speak a prophetic word to a larger church congregation, although on occasion a simple prophet may give the message. Those who are acknowledged as having or who may be seeking the prophetic office are more likely to speak to the larger P/C movement with some success. In its earliest stage, renewal teachings on prophecy seemed to focus on simple prophecy. As it continues its path toward routinization, teachings become more complex and the institution more structured. The Internet has provided another forum for a widespread dissemination of both prophecies and teachings about prophecies.

9. This happened to the writer at a prophetic conference she was attending in 1998. At the time I had completed two surveys at TACF and attended dozens of conferences since I began the research in late 1994. I was ready to move on! At a conference I was finding particularly tedious, I sat off to the side with my head in my hands praying, "Lord, what is it that you want? You know how I feel, but I need to know your will." Just then a woman came over to me, taking both of my hands before she began to repeat over and over again: "Don't stop now. . . . Don't stop now. . . . Don't stop now." After repeating this phrase at least a dozen times, she left as quietly and quickly as she came. I never opened my eyes (to this day I have no idea who she was), but my anxiety was changed to amusement as I continued in prayer.

I can cite dozens of similar instances, including a time just before I began working earnestly on writing this book in 2001. Having published a number of articles and given seemingly countless presentations on the revival, I was again ready to move on. As I took this impulse to prayer, my "writer's block" seemed to lift allowing me to prepare an outline for the manuscript. Not long after this personal experience, a man (who did not know I was researching the renewal) was praying for me. Suddenly he said, "I see a book—are you an author?" Without an aye or nay response, I told him to continue, and he provided words of encouragement and affirmation that were a welcome confirmation.

10. Receiving prophecies relating to my research endeavors is not a new experience. When I was collecting data for my first book on the P/C movement in the late 1970s, I had a related experience. I was interviewing a Presbyterian minister with a gift of healing who prophetically spoke a word about seeing "a battle going on between my intellect and my emotions" in the middle of an interview I was doing with him. That prophetic encounter has never been far from my mind over my years as a researcher. Rick's freestanding words had a similar effect as the minister's prophecy and prayer had on me some twenty years earlier.

11. Deep bends done from the waist in rapid succession were a common response to prayer at TACF, often interpreted to be a form of worship—a bowing before God. I was struck from the onset about the striking similarity between this seemingly spontaneous practice and the somatic motion found in orthodox Jewish ritual prayer.

12. While physical responses during prophecy seem to vary greatly, the overwhelming sense of peace and love of God that I felt during such times of prayer seem to be emotions shared by others. When the TACF survey respondents were asked to identify the emotions they experienced during the "physical manifestation that left the greatest impact on them," the two most often cited were peace (82 percent) and love of God (83 percent).

13. On occasion I have seen a main itinerating speaker "prophesy" to a physically impaired seeker that he or she is being healed although there is no sign of the person's healing at the time of the prophet's departure. Or a prophet may be foretelling a particular event with a seeming political agenda (or claim foreknowledge for an event), wrapping the "prophetic" word with passages from Revelations or other eschatological scriptures. This lack of accountability leaves any problems engendered by the itinerant prophet for the local pastor to resolve.

14. Earlier works on the charismatic stream of the P/C movement suggest that prophecy was often used in intentional communities to provide norms for the community and to control the personal behavior of individual members (see Poloma 1982; McGuire 1982). Prophecy was thus both empowering and (at times) a manipulative means of control. Possibly because of a widespread awareness of the abuse of prophecy during earlier eras of the movement, most present-day leaders appear less likely to attempt direct control of individual behavior or activity through prophetic words.

15. This new prophetic movement quietly began in the 1980s in North America during a plateau following the mainstreaming of Pentecostalism into mainline Protestant and Catholic churches. It gathered momentum in the so-called Third Wave where the vitality of the P/C worldview was restored in independent and newly emerging churches and parachurch ministries. It was used to launch and spread (as will be discussed in the next chapter) revivals at TACF as well as its American counterpart in Pensacola, Florida. It has played an important role in the development of new churches and parachurch ministries.

16. Cindy Jacobs, the founder of Generals of Intercession (an international intercessorary prayer ministry) and a member of the international board of Women's Aglow, is probably the best known of the prophets. Others include Jill Austin founder of Potter's House and Trish Bootsma who joined the pastoral staff at TACF in the late 1990s.

17. Cartledge (2001) reports in his empirical study of prophecy (defined broadly in terms of "family resemblance") that women (61 percent of his sample) were less likely to give an interpretation of tongues ($r = -.09$), prophesy ($r = -.19$), give a word of wisdom/knowledge ($r = .14$), and to prophesy privately ($r = .11$). (All the correlations in parentheses are statistically significant at the .01 level, except for interpreting tongues, which is significant at the .05 level.) It is interesting to note that women were more likely to report being slain in the Spirit than were men ($r = .11$), an experience that in effect silences the voice.

18. An early issue of *Spread the Fire* (October 1997) tackled the controversial issue of women in the ministry presenting TACF's position of encouraging "spiritually gifted" women. From the beginning of the revival, Mary Audrey Racroft has been on TACF's pastoral staff, providing a model and ray of hope for women aspiring to public ministry. More recently Trish Bootsma has become TACF's "prophetic pastor" and A. J. Mallett, one of the revival's iterating ministers. As modeled by Carol and John Arnott, spouses of the pastoral staff are (if they wish) regarded as part of the pastoral team and can be involved in pastoral ministry. Although TACF has provided room for women pastors, this practice seems to be the exception rather than the rule in revival churches.

Interlude: Turner's Collective Overbrain and Revival Experiences

It seems to me that religion may be partly the product of humanity's intuitions of its dual interiority and the fruitful creative Spirit generated by the interplay of the gene pool, as the Ancient of Days, and the upper brain as Logos, to use the intuitive language of one historical religion, Christianity. The Filioque principle (the Spirit proceeding from the Father and the Son), Western Christians might say! Since culture is in one sense, to paraphrase Wilhelm Dilthey, objectivated and crystallized mentality (Geist), *it may well be that some cultures reinforce one or another semiautonomous cerebral system at the expense of others through education and other modes of conditioning. This results in conflict between them or repression of one by another, instead of free interplay and mutual support—what is sometimes called love.* (Turner 1993, 104; italics in original.)

In the closing pages of this first part, I would like to return to Victor Turner's exploratory dialogue between neurology and "culturology." In it Turner treats ritual, in the words of one commentator, as "a special kind of performance in the cultural arena where the reptilian and old-mammalian brain meet the neocortex" (Schechner 1986, 13). Renewal ritual provides a context for this "special kind of performance" where the mystical self in all its complexity is nurtured in religious community.

The discussion of the mystical self, the central focus for the first part of the book, has been framed in part by the model developed by Victor Turner in which neurology has been coupled with culturology. The model provides a heuristic device for presenting a description of renewal/revival activity without losing sight of the rich experience and affective responses of the participants.

It serves as a medium for the discussion of revival experiences that permits so-cial scientifically inclined readers, at least on some level, to comprehend the in-ner workings of the revitalization of the Pentecostal/Charismatic (P/C) movement. Turner (1993, 104), it is important to note, had no intention of "re-ducing ritual to cerebral neurology," nor was he claiming that "ritual is nothing but the structure and functioning of the brain writ large." Hopefully the trap of reducing religious experience to some peculiar wiring of the human brain has been sidestepped by stressing the dynamic interaction of mind, body, and spirit in the development and presentation of the mystical self.

Turner's thesis can also be used to provide a transitional link to the second section of this work on institutional expressions of revival. He not only regarded the human brain and nervous system as being represented by various strata, but also suggested the possibility of a Jungian-inspired "collective overbrain." The *collective overbrain* was said to be a "global population of brains [. . .] whose members are incessantly communicating with one another through every phys-ical and mental instrumentality." Whether there is such an overarching mental structure, be it Jung's "overbrain," Dilthey's "Geist," or Durkheim's "collective conscious," has been subject to much debate. The concept of an overbrain can, however, serve as a metaphor for a collective sense of the mystical out of which creative structural forms emerge. For Turner the overbrain is reflected in both ritual and *communitas* where there can be found "free interplay and mutual sup-port—what is sometimes called love" (Turner 1993, 104).

LOVE AND REVIVAL

The heart of the renewal experience, as already discussed, is love—a tangible experience of being loved by God, which in turn beckons the beloved to ex-tend this love to others. As we have demonstrated in chapter 2, love is a cen-tral theme of revival music, metaphor, and myth. Furthermore, love is interpreted as the source of somatic revival responses discussed in chapter 3 as "Father God plays with His children" and Jesus "romancing his bride." Being loved by God bears tangible fruit in the various forms of healing illus-trated in chapter 4. And it is God's love that is heralded through the prophets whose voices continue to speak into the revival, be they "simple prophets" or those given the mantle of a "prophetic office" presented in chapter 5.

Of particular significance for this closing discussion of the love and the overbrain is how prophecy intersects with healing in the P/C culture.

Prophetic words are often given at conferences to signal prayer for select medical maladies. Private prophecy may similarly include prophetic prayer or proclamation for the healing of mind, body, and spirit. Healing is sought not only for personal well-being but for a range of broken relationships that include healing racial hatred, the battle between the sexes, divisions among religious denominations, and enmity among nations and nationalities.

Two selected inserts attached to the Toronto Airport Christian Fellowship (TACF) questionnaires will be used to illustrate how personal feelings of enmity and strife can be "healed" during revival rituals.[1] The first is a brief testimonial submitted by a young Chinese American woman. Uncomfortable with her marginal status, she described a healing she received after being prayed with by a Chinese missionary as follows:

> I felt a separation from other Chinese people because, as a first generation Chinese, I am not accepted by people born in China since I do not speak Chinese. I am also separate from Americans because I am Chinese in their eyes. I am a minority in a never-never-land. Anna [the missionary] immediately accepted me. I knew this—and it was important for me to experience this kind of acceptance. It was a real demonstration of God's power to break dividing walls. (Case #752)

Other reported "healings" reflected divisions within geographic areas that have experienced centuries of mistrust and warfare. A British man expressed a common feeling of being moved by the many nationalities and cultures commonly found at TACF services:

> I was moved many times in Toronto by our fellowship at breakfast amongst Brits, Germans, French, and Dutch. As a European languages teacher, the delight in sharing our unity was very significant to me. So I pray that the blessing will be known literally at national levels as people return to Europe from Toronto with love and reconciliation in their hearts. . . . The Lord gave me a vision in the hotel room in Canada—a clear stream of thousands of individual lights and fire, like burning torches, combined and united, forming a huge bridge or arch of flame across the Atlantic, and then diversifying throughout Europe. It was healing the hates and conflicts of the past and restoring His love to these nations which were the first to spread His light across the world. (Case #584)

Testimonies of this type—reflecting personal examples of "healings" between men and women, blacks and whites, English and Irish, Koreans and

Japanese—are commonly presented at TACF-like renewal conferences that are held around the globe. People report being empowered to "let go" of past hurts and hatreds and to love as they have experienced divine love.

Social scientists are reluctant to speak of love.[2] Yet it is love—experiences of divine love that in turn affect human love—that is at the heart of the renewal. The problem here (as in the past) is that a movement's charismatic moment is often fleeting, spawning factional groups that fuel divisiveness and destruction. The history of the P/C movement during this century is no exception. In fact it could be argued that despite the repeated call to reconciliation, encouraging testimonials and the positive survey self-reports, little significant change has been effected outside the P/C parameters by the present revival. Critics might note that few people of color participate in renewal meetings held throughout North America, prophetic daughters still play more limited roles than prophetic sons, and religious unity is limited largely to a subset of Evangelical Christendom. Yet the evidence suggests that the fragile liminal and playful moment of this latest outpouring of charisma has offered renewed hope of a coming kingdom of God to millions around the world.

Many, if not most, pilgrims found themselves empowered by the revival services—an empowerment that was accompanied by claims of greater love and service to others.[3] As selves are renewed and made whole, perhaps the foundations are being laid for healthy interpersonal relations that will actually bring about changes in the larger world. At present the thought of the P/C movement being a significant force for facilitating peace and harmony might seem improbable. However, maybe—just maybe—it can be a catalyst for Turner's "free interplay and mutual support—that we sometimes call love."

I would like to conclude this first section with a narrative from a Toronto pilgrim. He will remain anonymous because I believe his story represents an important interpersonal dimension that is integral to revival mysticism. While such stories may not be as commonplace as the laughing and shaking, experiences of healing, or declarations of prophecy, this experience is not totally unique. "Phil" (not his real name) is a local renewal leader who had been engaged in some street ministry. What follows is an account provided to me (December 2002) by Phil during an interview conducted in Cleveland, Ohio:

> As I walked an area under the bridge of a large city where the homeless slept one winter night, I noted movement under some tattered blankets that lay to the side of the street. As I approached, I sensed God directing me, "Go, lie down

with that man and hold him." I balked at the word I thought I was hearing. What would the man think? I looked down again to see a pair of eyes peering out of the blanket. Once more I sensed the divine command.

Although still reluctant, I looked into the homeless man's eyes, and said, "I would like to hold you. Would that be ok?" As I stooped over and took the emaciated figure covered with dirt and vomit into my arms, I realized the man was burning with fever. I told him that I needed to take him immediately to a shelter or to a hospital. The man replied, "No, it's too late for that. But I found a Bible in the trash container yesterday and was reading it. I prayed, 'Jesus, if you are real, hold me.' You are Jesus, aren't you?"

I kept saying, "No, I am Phil," but the man acted as if he had not heard me. He continued to call me "Jesus" as I held him, offered words of comfort and wiped his brow. It wasn't long before the death rattle grew louder, and the man died in my arms.

The love experienced during the renewal is empowering, for mission and ministry is seen to be the love of Jesus himself—the divine loving the human. It is the Spirit of Jesus who is asserted to move through the believer as he or she responds to a call to proclaim and build the kingdom of God. In the next section the spotlight will move away from the many who have been called into the refreshing waters of revival to the chosen who have sought to harness its energy to revitalize Christendom. With the narrative of the mystical self as background, the account will now shift to the corporate dimension of P/C revival as told through the voice of prophecy.

NOTES

1. One testimony was previously cited in chapter 4 where a white South African woman who was featured in the video *Go Inside the Toronto Blessing* (Marcus 1997) exclaimed: "I want to love everyone. I do love everyone—white or black, it makes no difference. I want to love with a passion."

2. My discipline of sociology has never come to grips with Pitirim Sorokin (one of its masters of social theory) and his research affair with altruistic love (see Sorokin 1954; Matter 1975). Sorokin's Lilly Endowment funded center, the Harvard Research Center in Creative Altruism, was a seeming embarrassment to a discipline seeking scientific standing and has seemingly been forgotten by all but a few contemporary sociologists. Sorokin's path-breaking work is experiencing a renaissance through the efforts of Stephen Post as president of the Templeton Funded Institute for Research on Unlimited Love (IRUL) at Case Western Reserve University.

3. Support for the relationship between the experience of the prophetic and empowerment for service could also be found in the TACF follow-up survey data, where 62 percent reported an increase in "receiving prophetic words"; 47 percent in "receiving words of knowledge"; 48 percent in being used in "prophetic intercession"; and 42 percent in "receiving prophetic dreams." There was a statistically significant correlation ($r = .32$; $p = .0001$) between an increase in prophetic empowerment and an increase in service to others (including reaching out to the poor, almsgiving, giving to missions, and assisting families and friends in need).

II

The Mystical Body

Water, Wind, and Fire: Prophetic Narrative and Revival

Other things being equal, failed prophecies are harmful for religious movements. Although prophecies may arouse a great deal of excitement and attract many new followers beforehand, the subsequent disappointment usually more than offsets these benefits.

—*Rodney Stark*

Man's resourcefulness goes simply beyond protecting a belief. Suppose an individual believes something with his whole heart; suppose further that he has a commitment to this belief, but he has taken irrevocable actions because of it; finally suppose that he is presented with evidence, unequivocal and undeniable evidence, that his belief is wrong: What will happen? The individual will frequently emerge, not only unshaken but even more convinced of the truth of his beliefs than ever before. Indeed, he may even show new fervor about convincing and converting other people to his view.

—*L. H. Festinger, H. W. Riecken, and S. Schacter*

The role that prophecy has played in revival movements and institution building has been of minimal interest to social psychologists and sociologists. Analyses of the relationship between the prophetic and social consequences that do exist have focused primarily on failed prophecy, producing somewhat contradictory conclusions. Leon Festinger, Henry Riecken, and Stanley Schacter's (1956, 3) study of prophecy, a selection of which has been cited in the preceding, has been critiqued as being "too narrow," as being "too positivistic," and as "treating subjects as irrational and driven by forces beyond their comprehension" (Dein 2001,

385). Some would see Rodney Stark's (1996, 137) assessment of prophecy (see the preceding), presented in terms of a cost-benefit analysis and the level of tension the religious group has with the larger culture, as an improvement over the earlier thesis advanced by Festinger et al., but it, too, is inadequate for depicting the functioning of prophecy in Pentecostal/Charismatic (P/C) revival.

In light of the democratization and common use of prophecy within P/C revival communities described in the last chapter, both models would appear to suffer from similar limitations. While making important contributions to a neglected topic, the focus of Festinger and Stark tends to be one-sided. By limiting discussion to "failed prophecy," these scholars have failed to capture the social drama produced by prophetic narrative with perceived "successes" as well as "failures."

The limited focus on studies on the prophetic can be traced to a narrow definition of "prophecy" as a foretelling of a cataclysmic event (cf. Cohn 1962; Zygmunt 1972; Bader 1999). Few prophecies of the P/C movement are of this genre, although they are the type that has most often captured the attention of scholars. Prophecy, as will be demonstrated in this and subsequent chapters, reflects a kind of "alternate consciousness" that characterizes the P/C worldview. In the P/C movement, prophecy can be used to provide a social history far broader than the "failed prophecies" discussed in the social science literature.

Undoubtedly, there is tension in any movement where prophecy is practiced, but fulfilled prophecy often has been catalytic in both launching and revitalizing religious movements. No account of the Toronto Blessing and its related revival movements would be complete without including an analysis of the prophetic. This chapter will focus on the role prophecy has played in the launching and directing of the ongoing revival, with subsequent chapters providing some accounts of institutional effects of the prophetic in reshaping the contemporary P/C movement.

PROPHETIC SAFETY VALVES

Prophecies can and do fail, but in the P/C movement there are common safety valves for damage control. Believers are regularly instructed that prophetic words spoken privately to a person and prophetic proclamations given in an assembly are both channeled through fallible human agents. As Marc Dupont (2000, 9), the leading prophet for the Toronto Airport Christian Fellowship (TACF) revival, notes: "No one except the Lord is infallible. The Holy Spirit speaks perfectly while we hear imperfectly. But, someone with a recognized prophetic ministry should prophesy accurately rather than give what amounts to a 'false prophecy' that never comes to pass." While prophets must strive to hear divine messages correctly and listeners must discern, both are reminded of the possibility of error and distortion.

Dupont warns further about another kind of "false prophecy"—given by prophets "who sensationalize words of judgment, destruction, and gloom but without giving any hope and encouragement to the church." Reflecting the emphasis of TACF revival on God's love, Dupont insists that "true prophecy always produces peace, hope and comfort in knowing that God is good!" New Testament prophecy, for the most part, is believed to edify, exhort, and build up those who hear it. Messages generally have a positive spin, and there is little encouragement given to prophetic proclamations of hellfire and brimstone.

Another safety valve against aberrant prophecy is that prophetic messages are subservient to the prayerful understanding of the scriptures. Believers are often reminded (particularly in local churches where aberrant prophecy is apt to do the most damage) to examine and discern prophetic words, especially in light of their understanding of biblical teachings. Recipients of prophecy are encouraged to check for resonance between their interior sense about a matter and what the prophecy claims. In a teaching on "Overcoming Prophetic Pitfalls," TACF pastor John Arnott (2000, 7) reminds the reader of the importance of having a personal relationship with God over a dependence on prophetic words:

> If you have your own intimate relationship with God, receiving prophecies from other gifted people will become secondary and will then take a confirming role. This way we avoid becoming too vulnerable to being led by someone else's prophetic words. When you hear a prophetic word, you should have an inner witness, a "yes" of agreement inside, even through it may seem out of reach and impossible.

Prophetic proclamations seem to be on the rise during this renewal (especially since would-be prophets can readily disseminate their visions and dreams over the Internet), but even prophecies by established prophets tend to be held lightly.[1] "Wait and see" is a stance commonly taken even in those communities where the prophetic has been woven into the organizational fabric.[2]

Prophetic proclamations, sometimes in the form of prediction but more often as counsel and encouragement, have played a significant role in the rise of P/C movement organizations and church structure. Any narrative of the recent revival that seeks to capture its spirit must include prophecies that have revitalized and changed the shape of this religious movement. The prophetic, especially prophecy as foretelling, provides an important strand in the folk history of the contemporary revival in accounting the revival's beginnings and its spread around the globe. Multiple prophecies, both public and private, have been given, as we shall see, to pinpoint revival sites, projecting both events and anticipated outcome. Successful predictions are told and retold in religious conferences and meetings to narrate revival history and direction, while "failed" prophecies are left either to whither by the wayside or to be revived through events yet to unfold.

PROPHETIC PATHS TO REVIVAL

Although TACF remains the center of this revival account, it has been birthed and nurtured by what has come before, especially in the Association of Vineyard Churches (AVC). Other streams of renewal, most notably the ministry of Rodney Howard-Browne (early 1990s) and the Argentine revival (1985–1995), had indirect effects on the unfolding of the TACF outpouring, but the Toronto Blessing is a direct effect of early 1990s AVC style and values. As such it can be distinguished from the face of revival presented in classical Pentecostalism (best illustrated by the Brownsville Revival in Pensacola) and independent parachurch ministries (most notably that of Howard-Browne).

Early TACF history and the origins of its revival were greatly influenced by John Wimber and the AVC's experiment with the prophetic. As an institutional newcomer to the P/C movement in the early 1980s, the AVC was marked by an openness to free expression of charisma, even in the face of criticism. Virtually all practices and experiences of the early TACF outpouring had occurred within the AVC previously, although the momentum for these minirevivals tended to be short lived. The AVC was birthed out of followers of the Jesus Movement in Southern California and nurtured in the Calvary Chapel (Costa Mesa, California) until Chuck Smith (Calvary Chapel) and Wimber (AVC) went their separate ways in 1983 (Jackson, W. 1999). One alleged reason for the split between Wimber and Smith can be traced to their respective differences in public display of what Wimber called the "signs and wonders." Wimber, a charismatic leader (in both the sociological and the religious sense), tended to push the spiritual envelope as far as his understanding of biblical practices would allow. One of his daring ventures in the late 1980s brought the AVC into contact with a radical understanding of the prophetic found in a group that came to be known as the "Kansas City prophets."[3]

THE AVC AND THE KANSAS CITY PROPHETS

The story of the Kansas City prophets begins with Mike Bickle, a church he founded (Kansas City Fellowship), and the prophets who gathered around him during the 1980s. Bickle's first real experience with more direct and radical prophecies than he had previously encountered came in June of 1982. A prophetic word was delivered by an itinerant minister (Augustine Alcala), who spoke a public prophecy in Bickle's church in St. Louis. Alcala prophesied that Bickle would be leaving St. Louis for Kansas City where he would establish another church. Other predictions were made by Alcala, but at that time Bickle was not entirely convinced about the prophetic words that had been spoken to him (Jackson, W. 1999; Bickle 1997).

During a tour of Cairo, Egypt, a few months earlier, Bickle had a religious experience in which he felt the Lord was giving him a "four fold plan for the end-time revival church." In time the acronym IHOP came to be applied to Bickle's ministry, representing these "four essentials" on which the new church was to be built: Intercessory prayer (with unceasing prayer and fasting), Holiness through which men and women became "lovers of God," Offerings (extravagant giving) to the poor of the world, and Prophetic ministry (Bickle 1997).[4] Bickle described his experience of personal prophecy as the "internal audible voice of God"—a voice that was echoed through the prophetic words given later by Alcala. Being more radical than the repetition of Christian truisms under a prophetic mantle (i.e., "My children, know that the Father loves you" or "My people, I inhabit your praise") practiced widely in the 1960s and 1970s in the P/C movement, prophecy as foretelling was to become an important part of Bickle's ministry.

In late 1982 Bickle left St. Louis for Kansas City to plant his new church as directed by Bickle's personal prayer experience of the "inner audible voice of God" and reinforced by the voice of the prophet Alcala.[5] He soon met another prophet in spring of 1983—one who said he had been "waiting for his coming." For some ten years, Bob Jones had been telling anyone who would listen that God was "going to raise up a group of young people in the south of Kansas City." William Jackson (1999, 196) summarizes the word that was given to Jones as follows:

> While he was out of his body, he says the Lord spoke to him and said, "You go back and teach the leaders of the latter-day church that the old leadership is coming to an end. A new quality of leadership across the earth with a deep commitment to the Word of God, a passion for Jesus, and a burden for holiness is coming into being to bring forth the bride of Christ.
>
> After his full recovery, the Lord spoke to him again saying that He was going to raise up a group of young people in the south of Kansas City who would not reject him nor God. They would be there by the spring of 1983 and before the snow melted on the first day of spring they would accept him. They would be on the south side of the city; they would be speaking about intercession and revival and would be led by a twenty-seven year old man.

Bickle seemed to be a good match for Jones's prophetic expectation. He was twenty-seven years old when he arrived in Kansas City in 1982 preaching the need for unceasing prayer, fasting, and holiness. He also began nightly intercessory prayer meetings for revival that attracted a youthful following.[6] Bob Jones arranged through a mutual friend to meet with a somewhat skeptical Bickle in the spring of 1983. After more experience with Jones' prophetic abilities (including "signs" in nature involving an unannounced comet, an unanticipated spring snowfall, and a reiteration of much of Alcala's original prophecy), Bickle embraced Jones as a "prophet of God."[7]

In early 1988 Jones predicted that Wimber would phone Bickle and that "this would open up a door for future ministry with John and the Vineyard" (Jackson, W. 1999, 179). Wimber did call five days later, beginning a brief but close association with both Bickle and Paul Cain. Cain discovered his prophetic abilities as a young man during the Post-War Healing Revival of the 1950s as he traveled with a well-known healer of the time, William Branham. "In 1958 Cain grew disillusioned with the healing movement, some of whose leaders had by then been damaged by allegations of pride, competition and immorality" (Hilborn 2001, 139). He believed God was telling him that there was a "new breed" of Christians emerging who would not fall prey to such shortcomings. Until then, he was to remain in the "desert." After meeting Bickle in 1987, Cain felt the old prophecy was about to come to pass, and he joined John Paul Jackson, Jack Deere, and Bob Jones to become the best known of the Kansas City prophets.

With repeated serendipitous experiences, a more radical form of prophecy common to the earlier Latter Rain movement found a new home in the AVC. In 1990 (a time when the Kansas City prophets were being accused of "heresy" by some outspoken critics), Wimber not only stood by Bickle and Cain but also began to travel extensively with them. Despite the accusations of "false prophecy and misconduct" directed at Bickle, Wimber stood by the Kansas City prophets and encouraged Bickle to bring his church into the AVC.[8] Like Bickle, Wimber was learning through Cain, Jones, and other so-called Kansas City prophets that prophecy can take on a more exciting form than simple forthtelling or affirmation—it can also foretell and predict.

Shortly after the Kansas City Fellowship joined the AVC, the relationship between Wimber and the Kansas City prophets began to deteriorate.[9] The emphasis of the Kansas City prophets on revival, end-times church, and prophecy proved to be somewhat incompatible with that of Wimber's Evangelical Quaker and Reformed thought. In his history of the AVC, William Jackson (1999, 230–31) noted the tension that existed from the beginning of the relationship between the AVC and Kansas City prophets as one stemming from the Vineyard's Reformed foundation and the Arminian emphasis of the Kansas City prophets on fasting, intercession, holiness, and revival.[10] This same tension would be a major contributor to Wimber's ousting of the Toronto Airport Vineyard (TAV) from the AVC in December of 1995.

Although the older AVC pastors were more reluctant to embrace the radical prophetic, the Kansas City prophets had a strong following among many newer members of the AVC. Perhaps recognizing that even during its heyday, the radical prophetic was embraced by only a minority (albeit a significant one), Wimber began to distance himself from Bickle and Cain. Despite the reported "power" experienced at many of the AVC conferences and churches in 1991, the gap between those who accepted the prophecies about revival coming to pass and those who did not seemed to widen.

By 1992 Wimber no longer traveled with Cain and eventually became quite critical "about his own naiveté" on the prophetic (Beverley 1997, 79). Wimber's separation from Cain and the Kansas City prophets was not enough, however, to silence sounds of prophecy within the AVC. Less radical forms of prophecy had always played a role in the Vineyard, and not everyone saw the "new course" taken by the AVC to back away from the prophetic drama as a step forward (Jackson, W. 1999, 276). The prophetic and revival seemed somehow to be intricately linked together.[11] Other prophecies joined those of the Kansas City prophets, and new prophets began to arise within the ranks of the AVC, including the voices of some non-American prophets predicting a soon-to-come revival in Toronto.

PROPHETIC PREDICTIONS AND REVIVAL FIRE
According to Beverley (1995), the 1994 Toronto Blessing associated with the AVC had been predicted at various times and by different prophets "during the last forty years." Two such incidents of prophetic proclamation for which she was an eyewitness were provided by prophetess Cindy Jacobs in her discussion of the 1990s revival:

> Many of the moves of God we are seeing in the 1990s were prophesied in the 1980s. I remember two gatherings of prayer leaders held in 1986—one in Tulsa, Oklahoma, the other in Pasadena, California—in which almost identical prophecies were given about a sweeping revival that would begin in Canada. As I write, sparks of revival are already leaping into the United States from Toronto. (Jacobs 1995, 16)

In fact "sparks of revival" were experienced in countless places during the 1980s and early 1990s, particularly through Wimber and other ministries affiliated with the AVC. It was not until Toronto, however, that the sparks became a blazing fire setting off hot spots around the globe.

As a Vineyard pastor, Arnott had seen and tasted the kinds of religious experiences that later characterized the revival, but they were never as enduring or as intense as those that came after Randy Clark's visit in January 1994.[12] Moreover, Arnott reportedly saw no way for a revival to occur in a huge metropolitan area like Toronto. He shared his response to the prophecies given to him and his subsequent "empowering" as follows:

> In spite of these apparent obstacles, several prophetic words had come our way through three of our friends, Marc Dupont, Stacey Campbell and Larry Randolph. They all promised that "More" was on the way. As I look back I see now how dull my heart was toward believing that God would move in a new way. Their words seemed to speak of days a long way off, days I had almost given up believing for.

In November of 1993, Carol and I went to Argentina to see the effects of the revival there. The nation was and is still being profoundly changed by the power of the Holy Spirit. Our experience in Argentina left me with a profound impartation of faith to "go for it" and a new power for ministry greater than what I had previously known. When Claudio Freidzon prayed for me I began to believe for God to move, even in our church. But it never entered my heart to imagine the wonderful events that were about to unfold. (Arnott 1999, 6)

When a public prophecy comes to pass as it seemingly did at the small TAV (now TACF) in January 1994, it becomes both a source of hope and a model for increased prophetic activity.[13] In May 1992—almost two years before the Toronto Blessing began—Dupont, a member of the pastoral team at TAV, reported a lengthy prophetic vision that seemed to anticipate the Toronto Blessing. Roberts (1994, 16) succinctly summarizes the vision as follows:

In the vision he sees water falling over and onto an extremely large rock. There is a huge volume of water. He believes God is telling him that "Toronto shall be a place where much living water will be flowing with great power, even though at the present time both the church and the city are like big rocks, cold and hard against God's love and his Spirit." He sees this water flow out over the plains of Canada and ignite revival.

Part of Dupont's (1995) lengthy prophecy predicted a new revival in Toronto that would intersect with revivals already going on in other parts of the world:[14]

When the winds of the Spirit begin to blow, there will be elements [influencing revival] from all four corners of the earth . . . but the makeup of what will happen will not be like revival that has happened anywhere else in the world. I believe that Toronto will be affected by what is currently happening in Asia, South America, the Soviet countries, Britain and Europe, but it will still be highly unique.

In July 1993 while on a visit to Vancouver, Dupont was again given a prophetic vision. "He foresees 'power and authority' coming on the church in the Toronto area. There is going to be a move of the Spirit of God on that city that is going to include the powerful signs and wonders, such as in the early days of the church in Jerusalem" (Roberts 1994, 17). In December 1993, John Arnott, pastor of TACF, received a confirming prophesy about the revival that was yet to unfold when a stranger visited him at his office and told Arnott that "he's been running with the footmen, but he's going to ride with the horse-men" (Roberts 1994, 20). A visiting prophet and visiting speaker at TAV, Larry Randolf, also offered confirmation when he told the church "that a great anointing is coming and that it's almost here."

Dupont was not the first or the only prophet to predict that something was about to happen in Canada that would have an impact on the larger Christian world. Although Dupont's prophecy was the first public proclamation to single out Toronto as the chosen city, famed pastor and prophet David Yonggi Cho of Korea prophesied nearly five years earlier (April 24, 1987) that "the last great move of the Spirit will originate in Canada, and . . . will be brought to the 210 nations of the Earth before Jesus returns" (Riss 1987). Four years later in 1991, Cho gave a prophecy in Seattle said to foretell the revival that would begin eighteen months after that of TACF in Pensacola, Florida.[15] John Kilpatrick, pastor of Brownsville Assembly of God in Pensacola, reported the event as follows:

> In 1991, David Yonggi Cho gave a prophecy in Seattle. He was praying, and said, "Lord, you have segregated America for Judgment? Or are you going to pour out your Spirit?" . . . And in his motel room, the Holy Spirit spoke to him and said, "Take a world atlas." And he took out his atlas, and the Holy Spirit told him to point. And his finger went right to Pensacola, Florida. When he did that, the Lord spoke to him and said, "I will start revival in America, in this seaside city. It will burn like a match, to all the way over to the Mississippi River. It will fan up the East Coast. It will come back down through the North and Midwest. Down in the Southwest and up through the Northwest. And all of America will be ablaze with the glory of God." (new-wine@grmi.org, June 27, 1996)

Personal prophecies at times complemented these public proclamations, often with the consequence of moving players to new strategic locations. Renee DeLoriea (1997, 15) provides a detailed account about the personal prophetic word that led her to relocate from the Seattle area to Pensacola in 1989:

> All around me in that airport in Wichita, Kansas, people were looking at me strangely, but I knew the force backing me into that wall was the power of God. I had been walking down the corridor, minding my own business, when an incredible force pushed me backward—like a feather being swept by a strong wind. I had to obey. . . .

As I was pushed farther and farther to the floor, God spoke to my spirit in an almost audible voice, clearly saying, "Azusa Street: Pensacola, Florida. Azusa Street: Pensacola, Florida." That day in January, 1989, I knew that God was going to send revival to Pensacola, Florida. I realized even then that this revival would somehow touch the world just as the Azusa Street Revival in Los Angeles had changed the course of Church history in the early 1900s. (DeLoriea 1997, 15)

Accounts of private prophecy being linked with subsequent outbreaks of renewal/revival are commonly woven into revival narrative. Howard-Browne, the evangelist through whom revival sparks began flying in the late 1980s, had emigrated to Orlando, Florida, from South Africa in 1987. Howard-Browne describes his move to the United States as a call from God—"God called us to see revival come to America" (Brookes 2000, 19). Beginning in April 1989 in Albany, New York, Howard-Browne began to "experience continued revival during his meetings," including the pre-Toronto meetings held at Karl Strader's Carpenter's Home Church (Assemblies of God) in Lakeland, Florida, in 1993. Hilborn (2001, 143) reported the following on Howard-Browne in his chronological account of the Toronto Blessing:

As with the "Happy Hunters" and John Wimber in the previous decade, while conducting the Lakeland meetings, Howard-Browne presides over notable outbreaks of "holy laughter." Indeed, this phenomenon not only featured in his call to ministry in 1979, it has been a prominent aspect of his public meetings since 1989. Following his stint at Lakeland, the laughter spreads, as those who have attended return to their own congregations. Among those radically affected are Paul and Mona Johnian's Boston-based Christian Teaching and Worship Centre, the Episcopal Church of Christ the King in Lakeland itself; Oral Roberts University and Rhema Bible College—both in Tulsa, Oklahoma.

In August 1993 a reluctant, skeptical, and reportedly "burned out" Vineyard pastor by the name of Randy Clark decided to check out Howard-Browne at a meeting held at Kenneth Hagin's Rhema Bible Church in Tulsa, Oklahoma (Riss 2002; Hilborn 2001). Clark, self-described as nearly having had a "nervous breakdown" after a tough but unfruitful ministry at Vineyard Christian Fellowship in St. Louis, Missouri, found both his skepticism and heaviness lift as he ended up on the floor laughing. In a subsequent meeting at Lakeland, Florida, Clark felt a tremendous power come into his hands as

Howard-Browne tells him: "This is the fire of God in your hands—go home and pray for everybody in your church." Clark does as directed and an estimated 95 percent of the congregation "fell under the power" (Hilborn 2001, 145). Word spread quickly through the AVC about Clark's new anointing, and in November 1993 John Arnott invited him to conduct services at his Vineyard in Toronto the following January.

Although Clark was somewhat apprehensive, he felt the Holy Spirit spoke to him as he embarked on the mission. Clark (2001, 23) relates the prophetic incident that took him "from fear and doubt that God might not use me in Toronto into faith and certainty that He was [going to use him]":

> The day we left St. Louis to fly to Toronto, I knew that something was going to happen. The night before, my friend from Texas, Richard Holcomb, had called to give me a word of prophecy. It was January 19, 1994, the night before I was to begin preaching a series of meetings in Toronto. I will never forget that word.
>
> "Randy, the Lord has given me the second clearest word for you that I have ever had." "What is it?" I asked.
>
> The Lord says, "Test me now, test me now, test me now. Do not be afraid, I will back you up. I just want your eyes to be opened to see My resources for you in the heavenlies just as Elijah prayed that Gehazi's eyes would be opened. And do not become anxious, because when you become anxious, you can't hear Me."

It was Clark, as discussed in chapter 3, who was used to torch the revival fires at TAV on January 20, 1994.

Prophecies and prophets, as demonstrated by this small sampling of stories, have played a significant role in foretelling events and in directing prophetic players during the revival of the 1990s—a role that continues to operate at both the personal and corporate levels within revival churches and ministries. Prophecies given publicly prior to the Toronto Blessing, the Pensacola (Florida) Revival, and other Spirit outpourings were often bolstered with private or personal prophecies and matched with serendipitous events, creating a postmodern narrative of the supernatural that seems almost surreal.

YET ANOTHER WAVE?

The revival that began at TAV on January 20, 1994, was originally scheduled as a four-night series. Hilborn (2001, 152) reported:

This is Thursday, and has been designated as a family night. Friday is set for a children's meeting, Saturday for youth and adults, and Sunday for the regular Vineyard worship service. At the end of this first meeting, Clark invites people forward for prayer. Virtually the whole congregation responds. This results in their exhibiting a range of manifestations including laughter, falling, prostration, and various apparent weakenings of bodily control, which will soon collectively be dubbed "drunkenness in the Spirit." Several of the 80% or so of those who find themselves on the carpet report seeing visions and undergoing intense conviction and spiritual transformation. Deeply impressed by all this, Arnott persuades Clark to stay on, and he continues to lead what become daily meetings through to mid-March, when he is obliged to return to his home church in St. Louis. During this period, testimonies to conversions and healings among family and friends of the TAV congregation become commonplace.

Following Clark's departure guest speakers (many of whom were then "nameless and faceless" for the larger P/C movement) and team leadership stepped in to develop a pattern of daily ministry described earlier that continues to the time of this writing. Tens of thousands came to the meetings at TACF (TAV) as word about the renewal spread, with many carrying the "anointing" back to their home churches around the globe. Sometime during 1996 or early 1997, however, the renewal seemed to have crested, with both survey results and prophecies reflecting this change from seeming playful chaos to more predictable renewal ritual.

In the 1997 follow-up survey conducted with TACF pilgrims first surveyed in 1995, some ambivalence could be detected about the state of the revival that was now in its fourth year. Although the survey revealed that 82 percent of the respondents were involved in the renewal at a local site and 94 percent were "more certain than ever that their experiences of God are real," opinions were divided about the revival's efficacy. A slim majority asserted that the "renewal is at least as strong as it was in 1995" (56 percent) and that the renewal "has impacted the larger church" (51 percent). Almost half of the respondents (45 percent) agreed with the statement that "the critics have played a significant role in preventing the spread of the revival," with 55 percent in disagreement or having no opinion. Only half the respondents were able to claim that the renewal was "the most important thing" in their lives. At the same time, the vast majority of these respondents seemed to be looking toward another wave of renewal, with 82 percent indicating that "the best was yet to come" (Poloma 1998a).[16]

The survey respondents were not alone in their evaluation that the revival had peaked. Dupont (1996, 4) reported on "the next wave" in an article in TACF's publication *Spread the Fire*. Dupont shared how in late May 1995 he had "contemplated the impact of the current renewal," noting how "wonderful" it was but how he hesitated to call this period of refreshing a genuine "revival." During the summer of 1996, Dupont preached "a great deal on the transition and the coming new anointing." He also received a prophecy that summer that a fresh outpouring would begin in September: "This increase would manifest in two ways: in authority for healings and miracles and also in authority for preaching the gospel" (p. 7). Dupont predicted more "exciting news" that pointed to further democratization of the gifts of the Spirit: "This unveiling of authority and outpouring of increased anointing is no longer for a Christian elite of select leaders. It is for the whole Church" (p. 8).

During this period of prophetic proclamations about yet another move of the Holy Spirit, a 1987 prophecy given by an Assemblies of God minister (David Minor) was widely circulated with the contemporary renewal prophets providing fresh interpretations that resonated with Minor's predictions of blessing, judgment, and increased anointing. "I cannot tolerate My church in its present form," God reportedly spoke through Minor's pre-TACF prophecy, "nor will I tolerate it. Ministries and organizations will shake and fall in the face of this wind." Although the original prophecy fit well in the "time of shaking" that brought down popular televangelists who were affiliated with the Assemblies of God in the late 1980s, the exact nature of the "shaking" in the 1990s was left to the hearer's interpretation. More significant, however, was the use of Minor's prophecy reprinted in a 1996 issue of *Spread the Fire* that promised another wave of revival (a forecast of "two winds") as well as a prediction of the end times:

> Know this also. There will be those who shall seek to hide from this present wind and they will try to flow with the second wind, but they will again be blown away by it. Only those who have turned their faces into the present wind shall be allowed to be propelled by the second wind. You have longed for revival and a return to the miraculous and the supernatural. You and your generation shall see it, but it shall only come by My processes, saith the Lord. The Church of this nation cannot contain My power in its present form. But as it turns to the wind of the Holiness of God, it shall be purged and changed to contain my

glory. This is judgment that has begun with the house of God, but it is not the end. When the second wind has come and brought in My harvest then shall the end come. (Minor 1996)

The expectation of "two waves" or "a second wind" became widespread as the spontaneity and abandon reflected in the intense physical manifestations (discussed in chapter 3) gave way to talk about end-time harvests and prophetic productions that seemed staged and inauthentic.[17] A new wave was coming, believers were promised, but those who had resisted the earlier one or had stepped away from the renewal would not be surfing it.

While Minor's prophecy was being disseminated and reprinted, Bickle (1996, 9) also spoke of a new move of God, using the metaphors of wine, fire, and wind. He defended the first wave of the revival, often criticized for not winning enough converts, as being "mostly for the Body of Christ." This move was about healing and restoring the Church to its "first love." The fire, claimed Bickle, came next through the old Pentecostal-style revival that began on Father's Day 1995, at Brownsville Assembly of God in Pensacola, Florida. The "hellfire and brimstone" style of evangelist Stephen Hill emphasized human sinfulness and the call to repentance while TACF tended toward a depiction of a "nice" God who is pouring out love and mercy rather than judgment. Bickle prophesied that the new wind/wave was now to be unleashed: "The wind of God will usher hundreds of thousands into the kingdom of God in huge cities and perhaps a billion world-wide. The wind is the 'big one,' and we're headed into it!"[18]

On September 14,1996, Cain gave his prophetic message to John and Carol Arnott about the things yet to come. John Arnott reported the essence of the prophecy as follows:

> The Lord has initiated the Toronto Blessing, not man. . . . He has refreshed His people in order to prepare them for the next level of visitation. . . . We are now at the place of the Lord's threshing floor. . . . The Toronto Blessing has gathered the wheat and the chaff during this visitation. God is preparing the wheat to go on to the next level. . . . Others (the chaff) will be blown away by the next wind, or fall. . . . You are to rise and stand to the occasion. . . . You are to lead the people on to the next level, from appetizer to the main course. . . . The days ahead should be employed for preparation for the next thing God will do. (Arnott 1999, 4)

It is noteworthy that in the earliest days of the Toronto Blessing (January 1994 through early 1996) public prophecies were minimal, although personal prophecies were abundant during personal ministry and prayer. Occasionally, a public prophecy on the renewal would appear on the early list serves developed to promote the renewal, but it was not until 1996 that a special list serve was developed by New-Wine (the then leading Internet promoter of the revival) specifically to share prophetic words. The expanded interest in the prophetic was also reflected in the rise of special conferences to teach renewal participants about the gift of prophecy. In some sectors of the renewal, freeflowing prophecy was about to become institutionalized

Prophecy, Charisma, and Institutionalization of the Renewal

The encouragement, the democratization, and use of prophecy have played a prominent role in the revival of the 1990s. The classic P/C emphasis on glossolalia, or speaking in tongues, was eclipsed by both public and private prophetic expressions that became commonplace renewal experiences. Prophetic proclamations that began in the 1980s seemed to bear fruit in the events of the mid-1990s, with scores of prophets rising to prominence within the movement, offering books and conferences to teach others to "move in the prophetic." These men (and occasionally women) were regarded by many as holding the office of prophet (in principle, if not in name), complementing the positions of pastors, teachers, and evangelists already found in churches.

From its inception, the prophets and the prophetic were central features of the revival. The voice of prophets not only foretold the recent American revivals but also provided redirection, reassurance, and promise when the early wave crested. Well-known prophets became part of the itinerating conference circuit, stoking cooling revival coals with words of encouragement and exhortation. Although it is not possible to detect a causal relationship between the predictive prophecies proclaiming religious revitalization and the events that followed, it is possible to note the correlative relationship between prophetic words and revival activities. To paraphrase the famous social psychologist W. I. Thomas's "definition of the situation," if people define the prophetic words as being of divine origin, these prophecies can have real institutional consequences. Prophecies about the rise of prophets and apostles for the "end-time" church set the stage for some to be offered the label of prophet or apostle and for others to claim the position for themselves. The prophetic assumed a public face.

While all can prophesy, not all can be prophets with established parachurch ministries to promote their prophetic status. The label of prophet was adopted and adapted for select persons, usually male leaders who assumed prophetic mantels. The nameless and faceless characteristic of the earliest days of the renewal where leaders (and prophets) were neither widely known nor promoted soon gave way to the masses flocking to conferences (including prophetic conferences) to be ministered to (and to receive prophecies from) the "men of God" (see Poloma 1997). Some of the recognized prophets were men who predicted and pioneered the rise of the prophetic in the 1980s—men whose narratives are included in this chapter. Other prophets had emerged out of the larger Spirit movement of the 1980s and 1990s, often establishing ministries or promoting existing ministries in which they itinerated to teach about and demonstrate the prophetic. A few, like Cain, were prophets in an earlier revival and were given a new voice and a new audience with the revival of the 1990s.

The institutionalization of the prophetic also seemed to accompany a subtle emergence of two faces of ethnocentrism. One was directed toward those who were once involved in the renewal and were now inactive, illustrated by the references to those who abandoned the "river of renewal" after only a brief walk in its waters. The prophetic vision reported in Ezek. 47: 3–5 of a river flowing from the temple was commonly used to describe those who stayed in the revival river just long enough to get their ankles wet and to encourage the faithful to press on. True revivalists had to wade through the knee-deep and waist-deep waters until the river's current picked them up and carried them off. The faithful remnant and those who join this remnant were promised to see even greater feats of revival.

The prophecies also reflected a more common division in North America's Christendom—the tension between those who cling to more traditional religion versus the entrepreneurs of nondenominational revival. Reportedly, the "old wineskins" of religion were of no use in this age of the Spirit, and "new wineskins" and "new wine" were replacing them. As we have seen in prophecies already presented, there was to be a falling away of the "chaff" during this second wind. Recognizing the plateau or even denouement in the movement (which continues at the time of this writing), prophetic leaders were assuring the faithful who were still drawn to the river that more was on the way. This second face of the prophetic can be seen in Dupont's (May 31) 1996 prophecy.

Behold I am doing a new thing. The former things have come to pass. I am sending a tidal wave of my Spirit. There is a wave of My Spirit coming upon this
world that the world has never seen yet before. . . . Much of my church has been
in an arrogance of their own understanding. They have been standing before
My people and saying, God does this, God does this, and God doesn't do that. I
have not been speaking to them. . . . But I say to you, the winds of my Spirit are
blowing against the church and I will destroy the apathy. . . . And I am going to
break the complacency and apathy towards Me. There is a false spirit. There is a
false spirit that has been working amongst much of the church. It is the spirit of
the anti-christ. It is the spirit of religion. (www.tacf.org/proph96 [accessed December 1996])

The prophecies about the second wind, deeper river, or bigger wave also
took note of the change in the affect in the post-1996 renewal meetings. The
manifestations still occurred, but not with the same intensity, spontaneity, and
variety that had been seen in the earliest years. There was a noticeable shift
away from the dramatic "party" manifestations, with less reports of laughter,
being drunk in the Spirit, and resting in the Spirit. There was a reported increase, however, in other somatic and more somber manifestations, particularly those associated with the prophetic and prophetic intercession (Poloma
1998a). While "party days" still happen, the rituals (particularly during non-
conference times) were much more subdued even at TACF. Many churches
that once experienced TACF-like revivals went back to business as usual. This
change (and exhortation) was reflected in another Dupont prophecy widely
circulated over the Internet:

I have told you that I would do a new thing in your time. Not a new thing from
what you have known in the past, but a new thing that you have not seen before. I have told you that when My Spirit is poured out on all of mankind that
your men and women would prophesy, that your old ones would dream
dreams, and that your young men would see visions. I say to you that I save
the best for last. The last days outpouring of my Spirit began with a party of
My disciples becoming intoxicated with My presence. So has this installment
of the last days outpouring of my Spirit. It has begun with a party. A party in
which all have been invited to but few have chosen to respond to, because they
prefer the old wine to the new. (www.revivalnow.com [accessed November
1999])

In many ways 1996 was a watershed for TACF revival. It had reached a plateau after having had its impact confined largely to nondenominational and select Pentecostal communities. Revivals in Pensacola, Florida, Smithton, Missouri, and other less enduring sites all reflecting somewhat different P/C flavors had begun to draw some of the same pilgrims who once flocked to Toronto. And many pilgrims took a "been there and done that" stance, returning to Christian expressions that required less "emotion work" and less of the "living on the edge" that revival spirituality demands. Names and faces have changed as new leaders of the revival and first-time visitors who had not participated in the 1990s refreshing occupy seats in a less full auditorium in anticipation of the next wave.[19] Prophecies from leading prophetic voices continue to proclaim that "more" is on the way. Pastor John Arnott (2003a, 7) raises the question, "Will there be more?" in a recent issue of *Spread the Fire*, and responds: "We have received many prophetic words that much more is coming and that the next wave will be even greater." He then goes on to share his vision:

> Our hope is that revival will increase in such a way that the culture around us will awaken to the good news of Christ and that millions will be saved. We not only want to see people saved but also see them get connected to a local church, discipled, healed and released into the fullness of their callings. We want to continue Christ-centered preaching and see powerful outpourings of the Holy Spirit with miraculous signs and wonders. We are looking for spectacular healings for hopeless wheelchair cases and people on deathbeds to be miraculously raised up. . . . We have seen and heard to many wonderful things already, but I believe it is only the beginning. If there is one thing I have learned in the last 9 years, it is that God is an excellent God, always advancing and increasing. He wants the "more" even more than we do. He wants to see His power manifested through healings, signs and wonders even more than we do."

REVIVAL ESCHATOLOGY

Revival has commonly signaled prophecies about the end times descending on humankind. Like the followers of earlier P/C revivals, many of those influenced by this latest increased activity of the Spirit interpret it as a sure sign that Jesus is soon returning with an evangelical emphasis on the mandate to gather in the harvest of souls before He returns (Wilson 2002). Although this very basic eschatological belief sounds a simple muted note in the present revival when compared with the rhetoric and actions of the founding fathers and mothers of classical Pentecostalism, it can be heard clearly in contemporary prophecies, even if most refrain from presenting a systematic theology to defend the belief.

Despite the frequent eschatological interjections found in prophetic heralding of the Second Coming, prophets appear cautious. Most if not all leaders, for example, refuse to place a date on the Second Coming of Jesus. They also appear to astutely avoid a divisive point among Pentecostal believers about whether this return of Jesus will precede the great tribulation or will come after it. Although Armageddon is believed to correlate with the Second Coming, the emphasis of the prophets and their prophecies tends to rest on the hope Christians have in knowing that God's kingdom is at hand. Many P/C Christians share implicitly the eschatological theology of Fundamentalism, but the perceived presence of the Spirit tends to mute the doom and gloom in presenting eschatological messages.[20]

Rick Joyner, a contemporary prophet best known for his books on the future of the church, has provided some of the most widespread descriptive eschatological prophecies reflected in titles like *Overcoming Evil in the Last Days* (2003), *Shadows of Things to Come* (2001), *A Prophetic Vision for the 21st Century* (1999), *The Quest* (1996) and its sequel, *The Call* (1999). His books and newsletter (*Morning Star Prophetic Bulletin)* contain ongoing accounts of detailed prophetic dreams and visions that demonstrate wariness about "easy Christianity" and predictions about the coming "end times." In one of his earliest books (*The World Aflame,* published in 1993), Joyner profiled the 1904 Welsh Revival, which he claimed to be "the world's greatest revival." This pre-Toronto publication predicts that more revivals are coming—that "God will do it again"—but that believers must "prepare or perish" as the end times approach. As with most contemporary prophets, Joyner issued a warning about timing:

> To properly understand this vision you must keep in mind that it represents a GRADUAL unfolding which takes place over a period of time, possibly many years. Though I do not know the timing of these events, it is obvious that some are already beginning to take place. I do not know whether the complete un-

folding takes five years or fifty. I do know that they will come as travail does upon a woman in labor. That is, they will come in waves with relative calm in between. As we get closer to the birth, these "contractions" will become both more frequent and more intense until they are constant. I also perceive that the timing of these events will not be the same for all parts of the body of Christ." (Joyner, 1993, 147)

According to Joyner, God revealed, "that there will soon be a great outpouring of His Spirit" and the coming "revival will be greater than all those preceding it." Shadowing this good news, however, loomed a dark cloud. Joyner wrote:

Wars will increase. There will even be some nuclear exchanges but on a limited basis, mostly between third world nations. Far more will perish by plagues and natural disasters than by wars during the period of this vision. The very foundations of civilization will shake and erode. Even the world's most stable governments will be melting like wax, losing authority and control over their populations. Eventually it will be hard to find anyone with the courage to assume authority. This will cause sweeping paranoia throughout the entire earth. (Joyner 1993, 153)

The scenario, detailed by Joyner and implied in other eschatological renewal prophecies, focuses first on deeper intimacy with the divine, empowerment for evangelism, a "harvest" of new converts, Armageddon, and then the return of Jesus.

Eschatology, Revival, and 9-11

Although end-times eschatology has been a resounding historical note in Pentecostalism, it was surprisingly mute during the aftermath of the American tragedy of September 11, 2001. The terrorist destruction of the World Trade Center seemed to have caught the prophets by surprise, and little attempt was made to rewrite prophetic history. Although at least one major renewal prophet claimed to have had a vision that (in retrospect) was related to the tragedy, most prophetic voices sounded words of comfort and encouragement rather than cries of Armageddon.

The case of Jim Goll, Founder of Ministry to the Nations, provides one illustration of the ambiguity often found in prophetic visions, dreams, and insights. The recipient may believe a vision is "prophetic," but the interpretation may come only over time and often in retrospect of the event. The following is an account reported by Goll in the issue of *Spread the Fire* devoted to 9-11:

> In the late 1980's I spent hundreds of hours in prayer and intercession doing prayer walks with other prophetic intercessors in Manhattan, New York City. During that time I had a vision in which I saw lower Manhattan in smoldering rubble. I did not understand what I was seeing at that time. As I watched the vision unfold, I saw small green shoots springing forth from out of the midst of destruction. More and more plants started bursting forth until eventually the whole scene was covered like a beautiful green pasture.
>
> I asked the Lord, "What is this?" I heard the following, "Out of the midst of a time of turmoil and destruction, My triumphant church shall spring forth like a tender shoot out of dryground." Though I did not understand the reality of the vision those 12 years ago, the understanding is clearer today. Lower Manhattan lies in ruin. It has devastated us all. This is not just a U.S. tragedy—it is a global event of massive proportions. We have crossed a threshold in the Spirit from one period of time into another. (Goll 2001, 24)

Goll's words joined those of other prophets who spoke words of edification, encouragement, and hope rather than visions of the future. There were reminders that God is in charge and believers are encouraged to trust Him. Most prophets agreed that the tragedy was not God's doing—it was not an act of divine wrath and judgment. There were many calls for fervent prayer as the only weapon that Christians have in what they believe is a spiritual battle. "Let us seize the moment and turn tragedy into an opportunity for the Lord's grace and glory to come shining through," proclaimed Jim Goll after reporting his earlier vision. "Now is the time! Prayer is the hinge of history!" Some reminded their listeners of the importance of forgiveness, even reaching out to local Muslim communities and reminding believers that terrorism is a fringe activity.

All in all, the comments coming from the prophets sounded more pastoral than prophetic and much in line with the words of other religious leaders throughout North America. Arnott spoke on behalf of the renewal movement when he wrote that "peace-loving Muslims are ashamed and embarrassed about what has happened." Arnott's attention then turned toward relating the tragedy to the heart of the renewal, namely, experiencing "God's felt presence":

This wonderful River of God's presence, which has continually been poured out upon us for eight years now, is surely more relevant than ever before. When the presence of God is with you in a present reality, you are much more aware of His power and ability to protect and deliver you. The realities of His kingdom are close at hand. Love, joy and peace are not mere theological precepts, but desperately needed realities that strengthen and heal the inner man. His presence brings us His eternal kingdom as the temporal becomes obviously insignificant. (Arnott 2001, 5)

PROPHETIC SYMBOLISM AND REVIVAL GOLD

Beginning in 1998, a new prophetic sign began sweeping through American renewal churches in the form of gold dust and dental "miracles." The miracles could be viewed on video presentations, read about in secular and Christian publications, discussed on the Internet, and personally witnessed in churches throughout the country.[21] According to some accounts, the American experience of revival gold (which had been commonly reported in Argentina during the 1980s) surfaced in 1998 when a popular revivalist's associate reported "golden glitter" on a cancer patient who just experienced a miraculous cure. As the American revivalist, Ruth Ward Helfin, was watching the video of the service where Silvania Machado had been healed, dust appeared on Helfin's own body.[22] Within a few months gold dust was being reported everywhere. According to Helfin, "We're seeing gold not only here but in Jerusalem— where I keep a home—and in Belgium, Denmark, France, Asia and all over the United States. It's everywhere we go" (Shiflett 2000).

"Gold" glitter (which often seemed to "fade" soon after falling) was soon eclipsed by "dental miracles" where amalgam fillings were reported to turn into gold or silver or gold caps appeared on the teeth of believers. After seeing "dental miracles" in South Africa, Arnott showed the three thousand people gathered for an Intercession Conference at TACF in March 1999 pictures "of people with new gold fillings." Arnott then began to pray that the same thing would happen in Toronto, and instantly people began to report changes in their dental work. According to a survey taken by TACF of some 150 people who reported receiving gold fillings "or other miraculous changes in their mouths" during this conference, about one-third of the respondents reported going to see their dentists. Of those who sought and received a dental evaluation, about

5 percent "found that their dental records conflicted with what appeared in their mouths, but the dentist was skeptical or fearful and simply said than an error must have been made on the records or that the records were too old to be accurate (Janzen and Fish 1999, 4).

Despite attempts to secure factual information by TACF, the data that exists would fail to move a skeptic from nonbelief.[23] Many followers reportedly were not interested in "proving" whether or not these "miracles" (which they believe they saw with their own eyes) had occurred. They *knew* that *something* was happening and that *something* took on the mantle of the prophetic in the order of the "prophetic mime" discussed in chapter 3. God was moving in their midst and believers tried to discern the meaning of the sign that was being given by the golden miracles.

Leaders seemed to concur that the gold phenomenon was a sign of God's lavish love, of the glorious Divine Presence, of purification from sin, of the infinite riches that God wishes to bestow on believers, and of a challenge to the skepticism of the Western worldview (Riss 1999). For many involved in the renewal, experiencing the Divine beyond the symbol was far more important than the gold phenomenon.[24]

The prophetic—in its broadest sense, the process through which God speaks to people—has played a major role in the renewal movement in foretelling its Canadian arrival, in providing fresh coals for cooling revival fires, and in birthing churches and ministries that embody the alternative worldview that characterizes the P/C movement. In the next chapter we will take a closer look at the role the prophetic has played in the origins and development of a Southern California church and its attendant ministries. Continuing to use the lenses that prophecy provides, we will present a prophetic narrative of the founding of Harvest Rock Church in Pasadena, California, and the impact it is having on revitalizing American Pentecostalism.

NOTES

1. The disposable and selective nature of prophetic words can be illustrated by my inability to access some of the prophecies once readily found on websites devoted to renewal prophecies as this book went to press. Fortunately, I made hard copies of hundreds of prophecies including all prophecies used in this chapter. Their content is important for telling the evolving revival story, and they are being presented here even though some are not accessible (or at least not easily accessible) at this time.

2. It should be noted that not all streams of the P/C movement equally embrace prophetic activity, although it has been practiced since the earliest days of the movement. Prophecy can be institutionally dangerous, and it appears to be one of the spiritual gifts that is readily tamed into insipid proclamations (when it is practiced at all). Predictive prophecy experienced resurgence in the P/C movement during the Latter Rain revival (1948)—a revival described as "powerful but short-lived" (Jackson, W. 1999, 183). Despite its failure as an institutional presence, the Latter Rain had a decisive influence on the Charismatic movement in the 1960s and 1970s, the Third Wave, and the ongoing revival of the new millennium.

3. Based on his investigation of the Kansas City prophets and the Toronto Blessing, Beverley opines, "One cannot understand the modern prophetic movement of the 1990s without some scrutiny of the controversy that erupted in 1990 over the Kansas City prophets" (Beverley 1995, 121). The Kansas City prophets not only pointed to a Toronto-like revival, but its members have continued to influence and shape streams of this movement.

4. Paul Cain, whose prophetic activities are central to the story of the Kansas City prophets, confirmed Bickle's sense of ministry and this fourfold plan through a prophecy he gave to Bickle some years later. It was the prophet Paul Cain, perhaps the best-known Kansas City prophet, who provided the acronym of IHOP (Beverly 1995) for the four essentials of intercession, holiness, offerings, and prophetic ministry.

5. Bickle (1997) insisted that he did not go to Kansas City because a prophet told him to do so, but rather because the voice of God instructed him to begin a ministry in that city. Bickle's testimony to the importance of hearing God for oneself over taking action based on prophetic proclamations reflects the teaching of John Arnott noted earlier.

6. Bickle resigned as the pastor of Kansas City Fellowship in January 2000 to direct the International House of Prayer (IHOP) in Kansas City, where prayer by hundreds of young "missionary" volunteers takes place twenty-four hours a day. Bickle also directs other ministries related to his IHOP commission involving prayer, outreach to the poor, and prophecy reflecting the prophecies he received in the 1980s.

7. Bickle, a once outspoken cessationist who believed the "gifts" of the Spirit were not for contemporary times, had by this time embraced the other major gifts but remained reluctant to accept the prophetic. According to his account, he was skeptical of the first prophecy given to him by Augustine Alcala, yet ironically kept recalling Alcala's warning that he would encounter a "false prophet." Bickle was fearful that Jones might be that "false prophet" about whom he had been warned (Bickle 1997).

8. In his investigative reporting of the controversy, Beverley provides "four explanations for the ministry of Bob Jones, Paul Cain, and other prophets connected with Kansas City," ranging from total skepticism to uncritical acceptance. The one he promotes after his investigation is a

cautious and partial acceptance that "prophetic gifting in KCF was real but often abused, authentic but often careless." Beverley (1995, 128) goes on to say, "After considerable investigation, I am convinced that God has given specific, accurate, and dramatic words of knowledge to both Jones and Cain. However, some caveats are in order. I remain almost totally skeptical of the alleged prophetic messages given to Bob Jones. . . . I believe that Paul Cain has made significant errors in both prophecy and words of knowledge."

9. Wimber's association with the Kansas City prophets seemed out of step with many of his followers. The problem came to a head when confusion developed over Cain's prophecy that "revival, tokens of revival" would break out in London in October 1990—an event which some saw fulfilled in the "new level of power" experienced by those who were present at the U.K. conferences and others questioning whether this increase in power was really "revival" (Jackson, W. 1999, 224–25; see also Hilborn 2001, 141–42).

10. William Jackson (1999, 227) reports that approximately 25 percent were for the prophetic and 25 percent were against it, with 50 percent appearing neutral toward it.

11. While revival prophecies and promises were flowing in the 1980s and early 1990s, Bickle's Kansas City Fellowship was believed to be in the midst of a spiritual drought. In 1988 Bickle (1997) received a prophecy that his church would experience a ten-year drought after which "new wine would begin to flow" in the spring of 1994. The Toronto Blessing, beginning as it did in January 1994 and quickly spreading around the globe, has been regarded as a fulfillment of this prophetic word.

12. Hilborn (2001, 132–47) has detailed some of the revival influences that have been part of Arnott's life since the late 1960s, including the late Katherine Kuhlman, Benny Hinn, Claudio Freidzon, and Rodney Howard-Browne. Arnott's original church in Stratford, Ontario, joined the AVC in 1987.

13. It is interesting to note TACF pastor John Arnott's (2000, 7) reflection on the relationship between his own personal "sense" and the prophetic words spoken by Dupont: "Carol and I never dreamed that we would be ministering as we are today, yet inside both of us there was an inner love for the power and presence of the Holy Spirit. When that prophetic word came through Marc Dupont, we were able to hear the word and receive encouragement from it while at the same time holding it in our hearts until God would bring it to pass in His time."

14. Beverley (1995) divides this long prophecy into eighteen parts, examining each of them with guidelines he established for the purpose. He concluded, "On the bottom line, fifteen of the eighteen prophecies are either general, vague, or have yet to be fulfilled. This is not a great track record on which to build certainty" (p. 142). While this may be true, the fact that Dupont undisputedly received a word of major significance—one that he published well in advance of the event—provided an important element for a narrative history of the Toronto Blessing.

15. For a comparison of and connecting links between the revivals at the Toronto Airport Christian Fellowship (TACF) and at Brownsville Assembly of God, see Poloma (1998b). See also Barnes (2002) for a succinct discussion of the Pensacola Revival.

16. The follow-up survey was carried out shortly after the publication of Hank Hanegraaff's critical work *Counterfeit Revival* in 1997. For a critique of Hanegraaff's scathing book, see Beverley (1997).

17. At this time it appeared that new rituals were in the process of emerging under the prophetic rubric. At one service, a woman dressed as a bride but wearing combat boots delivered a word about the "warring bride." Another more widely performed prophecy was based on a prophetic dream of Carol Arnott where others would join her in waving imaginary "golden swords." As the sense of charisma seemed to wane, there seemed to be an almost innate need to develop primitive forms of ritual to capture the past while simultaneously proclaiming that more was yet to come.

18. Bickle (1997) reported how neither he, nor Bob Jones, nor Jack Deare, nor Paul Cain originally felt comfortable about the form the Toronto revival took and were even somewhat critical about it. Paul Cain received a prophecy that it was the work of God—but it was only the "hors d'oeuvres." "I am pouring out the wine of the Spirit—but it is only the 'hors d'oeuvres.' . . . I am pouring out the wine of the Spirit to awaken a hunger for the main meal—the fire of the Spirit and a fresh revelation of Jesus." Cain prophesied that the largest group would reject the appetizer, while another group would stay so focused on the hors d'oeuvres—"they are going to fill up on them and will have no appetite for the main meal." Bob Jones added that the Toronto Blessing was the "beginning of what God had said" to the Kansas City prophets about revival.

19. My last visit to TACF was in March 2002 to attend "The Father Loves You" conference. Over 1,500 persons from over a dozen countries registered for this conference, with more coming to the free evening sessions. Approximately one-third were first-time visitors, a figure that TACF leaders report as consistent with all their monthly conferences. Although the numbers are down from the height of the renewal, the conference sites for various streams of the revival have increased in number since 1994, providing opportunities for local experiences similar to those at TACF. Facts such as these support those in leadership who contend the revival lives on.

20. Even at the turn of the new millennium, there was relatively little doomsday talk in revival circles despite the secular media's search for it. J. Lee Grady (1999, 6), columnist for the popular *Charisma* magazine, spoke for many in the movement with an editorial on "Silly Rumors, Crazy Fears": "Preachers and publishers are fueling doomsday hysteria with videos and books that make outlandish claims about when and how the book of Revelation will be fulfilled or how the Y2K computer bug will trigger the Great Tribulation. It's all nonsense, and most of these 'prophecy experts' will have egg on their faces in six months. Don't be gullible enough to believe them."

21. My first experience with a testimony about "golden fillings" came from one of my students at Vanguard University of Southern California in 1998. Nothing more was heard until I attended a service at Harvest Rock Church in Pasadena where several people claimed they now had gold fillings on March 28, 1999. The following Sunday "gold dust" fell at St. Luke's Episcopal Church in Akron, Ohio, where I was attending Easter worship. No attempt will be made to "explain" the gold phenomenon (although it would be interesting to explore its connection to medieval alchemy through the eyes of a Jungean). Rather the focus here is on the prophetic dimension of the "gold rush" and the interpretation given to the experience by leaders of the renewal.

22. Machado, a Brazilian minister, soon began to speak in churches on the renewal circuit. John Arnott, pastor of TACF, cancelled Machado's scheduled appearance at the revival center after a geochemist from the University of Toronto concluded following testing that the specks did not contain any gold or platinum but were some type of plastic film.

23. Golden miracles during revivals are not limited to the P/C movement. The Marian apparitions during the 1980s that occurred around the globe found Catholic pilgrims (including my friends) attesting to rosaries and crosses having turned to gold. When giving a paper at a professional meeting in 2001 in which I talked briefly about gold and the revival at TACF, another sociologist approached me after the presentation asking if she could talk with me privately. A practicing Catholic, she prefaced her comments by saying that if I told her story, she would deny it. It seemed that she had an experience of a porcelain crown turning to gold some ten years ago (allegedly verified by her dentist) while she was watching a Christian television program. She claimed that, not knowing what to make of the experience, she put the incident behind her. She seemed to be seeking any additional insights I might have had.

24. The Father's House (formerly Grace Fellowship), an Assemblies of God congregation in Barberton, Ohio, experienced the "golden blessing" in October 2000, after the pastor Mike Guarnieri accompanied a group from his church to TACF. During that visit, the music minister and his wife reported that their fillings had turned to gold. The "anointing" accompanied them to Barberton where Guarnieri reported to me that they stopped trying to check out accounts of gold outpouring and dental transformations after they reached one hundred. Guarnieri believes that the gold is simply a gift of God to His bride, the church. "People give gold to their loved ones all the time and the response is joy, appreciation and love. So, why shouldn't God give His children gold?" (Jenkins 2001).

7

Digging the Local Wells of Revival: The Los Angeles Story

God is saying, "I want to rebuild the walls of Los Angeles. I want to nurse Los Angeles like when Amy Semple Mcpherson healed and fed the city and shook it from end to end." God began to deal with me about His covenant of love with Los Angeles. . . . This city has been the cradle of revivals. When God looks on Los Angeles, He doesn't just look at the devastation. He remembers the covenant of those who loved Him and were poured out for Him. He remembers William Seymour. He remembers Frank Bartleman. He remembers these guys—and He will not easily give up. He bound Himself in a love covenant with people and with a city.

—*Lou Engle*

Whatever other form they may take, such as Lou Engle prophesying in a Sunday morning service at Harvest Rock Church in Pasadena on January 25, 1998, in the preceding, the accounts of the Pentecostal/Charismatic (P/C) movement have always included the surreal, serendipitous, and the supernatural. As one longtime Pentecostal recently commented to me, "Virtual reality has always been part of our history!" The illusive and the empirically real often blend together, providing ample illustration of the postmodern observation that reality is not what it first appears to be. What better setting for P/C narrative than Southern California? God seemed to be expressing a sense of divine humor in birthing worldwide Pentecostalism in an area that would soon become the movie capital of the world!

The Southern California production of the P/C movement has included a wide array of internationally known actors, including William Semour (the black evangelist who launched the revival that launched the movement on Azusa Street in Los Angeles), Frank Bartleman (the reporter who faithfully recorded the events at Azusa Street in the first decade of the twentieth century), and Amy Semple McPherson (founder of the International Church of the Foursquare Gospel). Later players included Kathryn Kuhlman (the famous Pentecostal evangelist who began her California healing ministry in Pasadena before moving it to Los Angeles); Demos Shakarian (founder of the International Full Gospel Businessman's Association); Dennis Bennett (the Episcopal priest whose experience of glossolalia in Van Nuys, California, helped to bring Pentecostalism to mainstream denominations); John Wimber (whose populist teachings and worship style brought another generation into the movement); and Jan and Paul Crouch (founders of international Trinity Broadcasting Network). These and others starred in scenes that ranged from the first Pentecostal revival at Azusa Street to the founding of denominations and parachurch organizations, to the launching of the charismatic stream of the movement, and to establishing international Christian television via satellite.

A leading role in the 1990s revival in Southern California has been played by the Harvest Rock Church (HRC), located at Mott Auditorium in Pasadena on the campus of the U.S. Center for World Mission. (Ironically, the church meets on the site of the former Nazarene campus where early Nazarenes prayed for revival—and rejected it when it came in the form of Azusa Street.) HRC, a multiethnic, Spirit-filled congregation of one thousand members founded in April 1994, has launched (according to the list on its website) a network of nearly 150 affiliated churches with a strong institutional base that continues to play a major role in P/C revitalization. Its story is one that includes prophecy and foresight, seeming miracles and wise choices, and divine invitation and human responses. Its major players will be placed within a P/C narrative that allows for the supernatural to blend with the natural that is so integral to the P/C worldview.

HOW IT ALL BEGAN: DREAMING DREAMS, SEEING VISIONS
The story of Harvest Rock Church begins in Maryland in 1982 with the unusual friendship of Ché Ahn and Lou Engle. Even then they must at times have seemed like an odd couple—a talented, somewhat reserved Korean American who eventually would earn a doctorate at Fuller Theological Seminary and a passionate Californian of German heritage who loved to pray and fast. Years later Ahn would write about his attraction to Engle:

When I first met Lou back in the early '80s, he was a seminary drop out, mowing lawns for a living. His life, however, was not just about pushing a lawn mower—Lou knew how to push through prayer. I had never met a person whose life was more reflective of Jesus's example in prayer and fasting than Lou's. . . . . Lou wasn't gifted as a pastor, evangelist, or administrator, the typical gifts one might look for when building a church planting team; he didn't even have a marketable skill to rely on for financial support. But Lou was and is a prophet, and that is why I said, "Lou, I believe God wants to provide for you to be in full-time ministry in California. Your primary job will be to pray and fast. I'll do the eating—you do the fasting!" (Ahn and Engle 2001, 13–14)

The draw between the two men was mutual. Challenged by Ahn's vision of a future revival, Engle (personal interview by the author, Pasadena, Calif., April 1996) agreed to return to his native California. Engle recalled Ahn's vision and subsequent confirming events that was a catalyst for bonding the two men:

The year is 1982. I am in Maryland and Ché is pastor of a church. Ché has a dream. In the dream a black man is saying, "Come to Los Angeles. There is going to be a great revival. There is going to be a great harvest." Then he woke up—and the Holy Spirit was upon him. Ché began to seek confirmation and to seek council from the leadership of People of Destiny International [PDI].

Ahn prayed that Larry Tomzak, cofounder of People of Destiny International (PDI) would commission him to plant a new church as a confirmation of that dream. Six months passed before Tomzak asked him to lunch—a lunch during which Ahn was certain that Tomzak would send him out to establish a new congregation. And so it came to pass that Ahn was chosen for a PDI church plant (although Tomzak would have preferred that the new congregation be closer to Maryland than the site of Ahn's dream).

The elders of PDI were open to Ahn's request that the church be established in California, but they asked him to seek further divine confirmation. It was for the purpose of "seeking God" that Ahn spent a few days in a condominium in Ocean City, Maryland. At one point, Ahn had an "impression" to turn on the television to see if Pat Robertson's "700 Club" was on the air. Ahn surfed the channels and came to Robertson's show just as he was giving a word of knowledge: "There is a pastor who is asking God for a confirmation about planting a church. The Lord says this of him. 'And if you go out in unity and harmony, the Lord will give you great success'" (Ahn 1998).[1]

In 1984 twelve persons from PDI, including Ahn and Engle, left for Los Angeles as the black man in the dream instructed. They had been reading a book by Frank Bartleman, the reporter who made Pentecostal history with his firsthand account of the Azusa Street Revival, and they "felt called" to settle in Pasadena to await the fresh move of the Spirit in the greater Los Angeles area. Engle (personal interview by the author, Pasadena, Calif., April 1996) reported the connection between Bartleman and Pasadena as follows:

> In that book, he [Bartleman] was claiming Pasadena for God. We had been cry-ing out to God about where we should go, and this book seemed to be instruct-ing us to come to Pasadena. . . . Phineas Bresee [founder of the Church of the Nazarene] had come into the city and said, "By the grace of God I am going to light a fire that reaches the heavens in Pasadena." Now when the Pentecostal outpouring came, Frank Bartleman and Bresee were worlds apart on it. Bresee said basically that the Pentecostal thing would be just a little ripple in what God was doing. Bartleman was a better prophet than Bresee.

The next ten years were difficult ones for the visionaries who settled into Pasadena in 1984. The cold brass heavens seemed to reflect the widespread charismatic "spiritual drought" of the 1980s during which the rapid growth the P/C movement experienced in the 1970s was fast becoming but a mem-ory. Despite prayer, fasting, active evangelism, there was no sign of the ex-pected revival. Over the years Ahn's church grew to about five hundred people, but it was not the revival of the founder's dreams. As Ahn (1998, 10) described the situation:

> On other fronts, we did everything possible to evangelize during that decade. We did open air preaching at California State of Los Angeles. We went door to door witnessing. We did street theater. We went into the ghettos. We held spe-cial meetings. We brought in special speakers. Yet we saw little fruit. Evangeli-cally the church started to grow, and God started to add some wonderful people—but it was a far cry from revival.

Prophetic light sometimes came through the brass ceiling, as when Engle heard a promise that the mantle of Frank Bartleman would be his. In the midst of the struggles and crises that caused Ahn to describe the period as "the eight-ies from Hades," Engle (personal interview by the author, Pasadena, Calif., April 1996) received what he regarded as a major prophetic breakthrough:

During this season, I picked up this book by Bartleman again, and the Lord began stirring in my heart that this is what he wanted to do in Los Angeles again. One night—I think I had been fasting and praying—I just cried out to God. I cried, "Give me the mantle of Frank Bartleman. I want to see revival—I want to see revival in Pasadena."

The next day a brother comes up to me—someone with whom I had covenanted and with whom my heart is knit. He didn't know what I had been praying for, but he said, "I had a dream of you last night, and in the dream I saw a black book. On it I read the word 'revival' on the cover. I turned on the inside and saw the picture of a guy's face, and it said 'Frank Bartleman'. I was looking at his face, and it turned into your face."

The prayer and its seeming confirmation, coupled with still other serendipitous encounters, helped to keep Engle's vision alive as he continued to encourage and support his friend, Ahn.[2]

Ahn received his own faith boost when he met the black man of his prophetic dream. It was during a clergy gathering in 1992 that Ahn spotted the man who in a dream a decade earlier had said, "Come to Los Angeles. There is going to be a great revival. There is going to be a great harvest." Ahn approached him and asked if he had been praying for revival. The man replied that he had begun praying for revival in Los Angeles in 1982 (the year of Ahn's dream) when he heard a Korean (probably David [Paul] Yonggi Cho) speak about how he had prayed for revival in Korea. This encounter provided fresh encouragement for both Ahn and Engle. As the latter noted of this spiritual watershed, "We felt this was a sign that Azusa Street still lives."

Problems between Ahn's church in Pasadena and the parent People of Destiny International were brewing during the years of the drought and finally came to a head in 1993. It was during this time that the renewal prophetess Cindy Jacobs called Ahn and told him that 1993 would be the hardest year of his life and that he would be leaving the church he had founded in Pasadena—but "not until 1994." He resigned as pastor in 1993 but did not leave the church until 1994, breaking his nineteen-year relationship with PDI. This move left him in a marginal position within the church he founded, without a personal ministry and struggling financially. Ahn (1998, 15) describes his situation as follows:

The leaders accepted my resignation as senior pastor, but asked for me to stay on for a one-year transition period. I agreed. I stepped down as senior pastor and became a staff evangelist. A pastor whom I had raised up became the new senior pastor. Now the young man to whom I was a pastor while he was in seminary became my new pastor and my boss. My salary was drastically reduced, and to say the least, so was my pride. Yet the real pain I was facing was deep confusion and personal disillusionment. . . . I didn't realize it then, but God was breaking me and preparing me for 1994, the year that God would begin to fulfill the dream of the promised revival.

Relief from the deep depression that had engulfed Ahn came with the outbreak of the renewal in Anaheim, California, early in 1994. Just weeks after the Toronto Airport Christian Fellowship (TACF) experienced its first touch of renewal, the Anaheim Vineyard Christian Fellowship held a "Let the Fire Fall" conference where Ahn had his first taste of holy laughter. Ahn was in a self-described "deep depression" from the events of 1993 and his departure from the church he had founded; but at the Anaheim Vineyard conference, he experienced an unexpected refreshing. Although he had been skeptical about the manifestations associated with TACF revival, Ahn says his doubts vanished when he experienced holy laughter at the conference. Ahn reported: "I couldn't stop laughing. It lasted at least 20 minutes. The result was immediate fruit in my life. I was excited about ministry again. More important, I was once again in love with Jesus. I felt His presence and knew something incredible had happened in my life (Kilpatrick 1999, 50). In March, Ahn and Engle invited fifteen people who were unchurched to join them for a prayer meeting in Ahn's home. Thirty people showed up for this initial gathering that led to the founding of Harvest Rock Church on April 4, 1994.[3]

THE SOUTHERN CALIFORNIA REVIVAL

It was not until October 1994 that Ahn and Engle made their first trip to TACF for the first "Catch the Fire" conference. They both received what Engle (personal interview by the author, Pasadena, Calif., April 1996) had described as "another explosion," an experience of empowerment together with the physical manifestations that often accompanied the renewal blessing.[4] Ahn then asked Arnott, TACF's pastor, if he would be willing to come to Pasadena to speak and minister. When Arnott came to the rented facilities at Mott Auditorium on January 2, 1995, more than two thousand people showed up. This event led to HRC's debut on the Internet as a renewal "hot spot"—an American extension of the Toronto Blessing that by this time had attracted international attention. It was around this event that Rick Wright, a Vineyard pastor from nearby Glendale, California, joined the Ahn and Engle team.

Rick Wright's vision for the revival of the Los Angeles area began in 1981 when he was pastor of a small charismatic church that he had founded in Glendale. As Rick Wright told the author in a personal interview (Pasadena, Calif., March 1998): "The Lord gave me a word that we would see more people saved than we had buildings for them. All I knew is that we were going to have an incredible revival. That word had become a passion, as my vision moved beyond Glendale to expand to the greater Los Angeles area." Rick Wright's passion was fueled by prophecies given in the mid to late 1980s by prophets Bob Jones and Rick Joyner as they began to speak of visions they had received about Los Angeles. As Wright noted, "We knew our vision would fit right in." But it took more than a decade for Wright to experience a taste of the revival he believed was forthcoming. In the early 1990s, Wright began to pray, "Lord, where is this revival?" He sensed the Lord responding, "Continue to knock for two and a half more years and I will begin to answer your prayer." Based on this personal word of knowledge, Wright said he expected something major to happen at the end of 1993 or the beginning of 1994. When he heard about the Toronto experience, he became convinced that a similar development was soon to happen in Southern California. As Wright (personal interview by the author, Pasadena, Calif., March 1998) reports:

> Bob Jones told us the revival would "start in the northeast in the land of the chickadee." I asked him, "What does that mean?" He replied that he did not know. So when the renewal started in Toronto, I called and asked the secretary, "Do you know what a 'chickadee' is?" She said yes—"they are the little birds that fly around up here." I thought, "Praise God! This is it!"

Rick Wright visited Toronto in the summer of 1994 and on returning experienced a minirevival in his church in Glendale for several months. He returned to Toronto again in October and ran into Ahn. Ahn reported that he had invited Arnott to come to Harvest Rock and asked if he would be willing to help. Wright responded affirmatively: "Whatever it is, I want to be involved."

When Arnott came to Pasadena several months later, Rick Wright received what he believed was another "word from the Lord" about the upcoming revival. During a minivision, Wright reported he heard God saying, "I am opening the heavens over Los Angeles; go tell Ché to pray for strategy." When he did as instructed, Ahn replied that the Lord told him, "I am putting you and Rick together for a revival."[5] It was at this point that Wright began prayerfully exploring a merger with Ahn's church.

Rick Wright's Glendale Vineyard church joined with HRC, a merger that coincided with the beginning of the nightly renewal meetings in March 1995. Their new meeting place was the John R. Mott Auditorium.[6] At first Ahn was reluctant to locate his church on the same campus where his old PDI church still met. It took a prophetic dream by Jim Goll, a Kansas City prophet, to precipitate the move. Goll telephoned Ahn in March 1998 to say: "Ché, I had a dream about you last night. I saw you holding a bottle of Motts applesauce. Does this mean anything to you?" Ahn responded by telling him that HRC was considering a move to the Mott Auditorium. Goll then went on to offer a prophetic interpretation: "Now I know what the dream means. You are holding Mott in your hands. I believe God wants you to possess Mott Auditorium. The applesauce means that you will bear fruit as you do."

The new church joined the Association of Vineyard Churches (AVC), changing its name to the Vineyard Christian Fellowship of Greater Pasadena, but it resigned from the AVC immediately after the Toronto church was ousted in December 1995. Another of Goll's prophetic words was used to frame the church's brief nine-month affiliation with the Vineyard. Just about the time Ahn had joined the Vineyard, Goll telephoned him in March 1998 saying: "Ché, I had an open vision as I was leaving my living room. I heard a cork popping, and saw you with a bottle of rose wine. On the front of the bottle was written 'nine months'. The bottle had been shaken, and the cork popped out. The wine had changed in the bottle. You were now holding another substance." At the time Ahn did not know the meaning of the vision, although Goll did. Just after Ahn's church left the Vineyard, Goll phoned to remind Ahn of the vision and the nine-month label on the bottle in the vision. He went on to explain:

> The wine bottle represents your church. You were a Vineyard, and after nine months (by the time the Rose Parade would take place in Pasadena—hence the rose on the label), the cork popped open. I saw the wine had changed and you became a new substance. You were no longer a Vineyard.

Two other congregations soon joined the newly formed Pasadena church under the leadership of Ahn. Jim Johnson, with his administrative skills, brought in the Cornerstore Christian Fellowship, and Karl Malouf, with his pastoral gifts, brought in the former Community Bible Church. Ahn, the senior pastor and itinerant evangelist, soon came to be described as an "apostle" and as one having an "apostolic ministry" to the nations. Engle was most likely to be described in terms of his being a "prophetic revivalist" and a "prayer warrior." Rick Wright wore a prophetic mantle (shared with his wife, Pam).[7] Malouf was widely regarded as the de facto pastor, while Jim Johnson was acclaimed as the pastoral administrator.

With these four senior pastors merging their congregations into the newly formed church, HRC's membership grew rapidly to approximately one thousand people. The church provided an institutional context for revival fires to burn briefly in Pasadena, clearing the way for new institutions to develop with an impact beyond the Los Angeles area.[8] These included Ahn and Rick Wright's establishment of Harvest International Ministries, a nascent postmodern international denomination; Engle's founding of Elijah Revolution, a ministry for youth; and Ahn and Engle's related ministry known as The Call.

INSTITUTIONALIZING THE REVIVAL
Despite the alleged "spiritual drought" of the 1980s and early 1990s, there did seem to be an unprecedented flurry of prophetic activity that pointed toward a revival and revival fruits. "Something" did happen at Toronto, and that "something" was imparted to pilgrims who carried it to the ends of the globe. As we saw in the last chapter, by 1996 some began to question whether the revival had peaked and whether that which had been experienced was *really* revival. Where was the "harvest" of souls? Where were the cities and countries that were on fire for the spread of Christianity? Where were the supernatural signs that would convince the most hardened skeptic that God was alive and well on Planet Earth? What happened in the churches through which the river of revival had freely flowed but where the water was now reduced to a trickle? These functional questions were being raised as the charismatic moment showed signs of lifting.

Although revival "hot spots" had developed from coast to coast throughout North America during the early years of the Toronto revival, most of them were short lived. By 1996 even the best known of the revival sites were seeing fewer visitors at their nightly meetings.[9] The movement seemed to have reached a plateau. For the next two years, prophecies and teachings were given regularly about "another wave"—one that would usher in the great harvest of new converts to the faith. This interlude was broken by the so-called golden blessing with its "dental miracles" and "gold flakes." Many believed a new wave was coming, one that would be different yet more powerful than that which came before it. There was little subsequent evidence, however, that the wind, wave, or fire as experienced in the earliest days of the renewal would be returning any time soon or that untold numbers of the unchurched would be finding their way to revival centers. Charisma was in the process of becoming institutionalized with the development of more predictable ritual in place of spontaneity; the emergence of recognized leaders from the mass of nameless and faceless workers, theme conferences, and programs designed to fill the empty meeting halls; and the creation of new organizational matrices to replace older affiliations (see Poloma 1996).

Grant Wacker (2001) has brilliantly described the P/C movement as being a curious blend of primitivism (supernaturalism) and pragmatism even during its early history. The movement seems to thrive in a milieu that welcomes not only divine activity but also an entrepreneurial spirit. While the supernatural is always playing in the background much like a hidden Windows program, the computer screen tells of operations that are aptly described as both pragmatic and entrepreneurial. The emergence of renewal networks positioned to become the denominations of tomorrow provides an important illustration of the revitalization process underway in the P/C movement at the turn of the twenty-first century that speaks of this blend of supernatural and pragmatic influences.

Partners in Harvest and Harvest International Ministries

It was in early 1996, just after the Toronto Airport Vineyard (TAV) had been severed from the Association of Vineyard Churches (AVC), that Arnott was approached by pastors of churches influenced by the Toronto Blessing for spiritual "covering." Some were new church plants; others were existing churches looking for affiliation with others of like revival mind. Partners in Harvest (PIH)—"a family of churches and ministries pursuing renewal and revival"—was developed by Arnott to meet such requests. As Arnott wrote in an open letter to pastors:

> I realized after talking to several leaders in the Body of Christ that all of us have a need for our churches and ministries to have an identity as well as a desire to belong to something bigger than ourselves. . . . We are discovering this to be true in terms of our own network of churches, Partners in Harvest. We are able to

share resources with one another and strengthen each other's hand, in many and varied ways. We want to present to you what we believe is a very effective and efficient "new wine skin" for both growing and networking a renewal church that has a high value on wholeness, and a desire for outreach, evangelism and harvest. (Partners in Harvest 1996)

By the spring of 2002, PIH had 94 churches/ministries who identify as Partners in Harvest and another 248 (most of whom are members of other denominations or networks) who represent Friends in Harvest (FIH) and affiliate more loosely with PIH. The network is served by "Family Days," gatherings held approximately eight times a year at TACF just prior to major renewal conferences, allowing pastors and ministry leaders of PIH churches to be "encouraged and blessed" at the Toronto church. An elaborate website and periodic e-mails provide the electronic means for this "relational network."

The emphasis on an organizational structure that promotes personal relationships is a theme that Arnott and Fred Wright (International Coordinator of PIH/FIH) have borrowed from the AVC. Both Arnott and Fred Wright had served in leadership roles within the AVC before it severed ties with the revival church—Arnott in Canada and Fred Wright in the United States. Like Wimber and the AVC, the leaders of this new network questioned its organizational status. Whether to call PIH/FIH a "denomination" had been addressed early on the FAQ of the network's website. "If a denomination means an identifying name for a specific family in the broader church, then we are. If denomination refers to conformity to a tight pattern of insisting on firm control, they we are not."

The primary expressed purpose of PIH/FIH is to keep the coals of renewal burning by encouraging and empowering leaders of churches committed to P/C Christianity. While attendance at nightly renewal meetings at TACF has tapered off and most local churches have been unable to maintain the momentum of local renewal gatherings, TACF conferences remain a time and place where charisma freely flows and new visitors (typically about one-third of the conference) still experience the Toronto Blessing for the first time. Through the holistic healing and empowering of its leaders, it is assumed that evangelism and the development of new church congregations will follow.[10]

Ahn had given some brief consideration to joining PIH when it was first formed, eventually deciding instead on forming his own network of renewal churches. The prophetess Cindy Jacobs (2000, 111) shares how she addresses the issue in a conversation with Ahn:

> I hadn't talked to Ché for a while and didn't really know much of what was going on in his life. I also didn't have his phone number, so I had to do some homework to find it. After a time I was able to connect with him, and he shared with me that he was seriously considering joining with a certain apostolic movement. The movement was a wonderful one that, personally, I loved. All of a sudden the Holy Spirit started to speak to me, telling me that Ché was *not* to join the new apostolic movement that was forming because he was going to be the head of a whole movement himself. Ché sounded a little surprised; but as he started to think, he realized that there were already beginning signs that other churches and pastors had a desire to align with the work he was doing at Harvest Rock Church in Pasadena, California.

Although cordial relational and professional ties persist between Arnott and Ahn, their respective networks have somewhat different tacks. Having its roots in the Toronto Blessing did not prevent HRC from shifting its identity away from being the "Renewal Center for the West Coast of the United States" (as indicated on its website in 1998) toward being a "new apostolic church." This restorationist approach is more characteristic of the denomination with which Ahn had been a part for so many years than the Vineyard model that he encountered during the Toronto revival. Ahn is being proclaimed as one of the new apostles as well as president of the restorationist network, Harvest International Ministries (HIM).

Harvest International Ministries

Although both PIH and HIM play on the word "harvest," demonstrating a shared concern for evangelism, Ahn's organization bears the marks of his longtime vision of an international ministry with a focus on missions and an eye on the prophesied "last days."[11] While PIH places its emphasis on the "Great Commandment" in preaching the love of the Father (trusting that evangelism will somehow flow from a deeper awareness of God's love), the focus of HIM is clearly on the "Great Commission" of evangelism, with its correlative call to old revival-style repentance.

By mid-2002, there were 141 churches listed on the HIM website, with nearly one-third being located outside North America and another one-third in California. Approximately half of the churches and ministries outside North America are based in Asia, particularly in South Korea (reflecting Ahn's evangelizing in Asia), with another 20 percent in Africa (reflecting years of Rick Wright's ministry on that continent). HIM is a self-described "voluntary association of churches, ministries, and missionaries seeking to influence nations." It reports to "gladly welcome(s) affiliation with local and international churches that demonstrate a heart for missions, a hunger for revival and renewal and a fervency for sharing the Gospel with the lost" (Harvest Rock Church, 2003).[12]

HIM differs somewhat from PIH in its structural model and articulation of its strategies and goals. Ahn's passion for world missions is the spirit of HIM that takes flesh in a model provided by C. Peter Wagner, particularly in the development known as a "new apostolic reformation." Wagner, one of Ahn's professors at Fuller Theological Seminary where Ahn earned a doctorate in World Mission, is one of several leaders involved in promoting a restoration of the "apostolic age" through "apostolic equipping."[13] Seeking out those with an "apostolic anointing," HIM endeavors to encourage, train, and help support their ministries.

As the revival movement reached a plateau, in some sectors the search for another wind or wave had the prophets taking a backseat to make room for the apostles (or a merging of the prophetic and apostolic roles). There was a subtle but noticeable shift underway from prophecy as a dynamic democratic process to lifting up apostles who would either have the prophetic gifting themselves or link closely with a prophet or prophets. In a personal interview (Pasadena, Calif., March 1998) Ahn emphasized that the fivefold biblical offices of pastor, teacher, evangelist, prophet, and apostle, with the apostolic being the last to be restored. Rick Wright (personal interview by the author, Pasadena, Calif., March 1998), the vice president of HIM and pastor of the newly planted Hollywood Harvest Rock Church, professes a similar belief about the immanence of apostolic restoration. Like Ahn, he believes he may have an apostolic calling and is convinced about the important role the apostles will play in these last days:

I long to see again the signs and wonders accompany the apostolic—to see the dead raised and watch whole cities get saved. That's what I want to see. It is my cry and my prayer. "Lord, restore apostolic ministry, apostolic purity, apostolic anointing." In some groups the prophetic has been pretty much restored, but we don't yet understand the apostolic role.

Whether these new apostles will function as miracle workers governing large groups of churches remains to be seen, but they are playing a role in revitalizing and restructuring the P/C movement.

The Call

On June 29, 2002, an estimated 85,000 to 100,000 persons gathered in New York's Flushing Meadows-Corona Park, allegedly the largest gathering at that site since the World's Fair in 1964 (WebCoordinator@thecallrevolution.com). They were part of The Call NYC. Organized by Ahn and Engle, The Call was described as "a solemn assembly of worship, prayer, fasting, and repentance, to launch a worldwide spiritual revolution and societal transformation of all the nations of the world." It is "about reconciliation between generations" and a "response to the groundswell of desperation in today's youth" (The Call Revolution, July 2002). The June 22 gathering, one of many already held and yet to be held worldwide, was a culmination of a week of worship and "spiritual warfare" in New York City, particularly aimed at the youth. International Revival Network (ron@openheaven.com, e-mail message received June 30, 2002) described the event as follows:

> On Saturday June 29, 85,000 youth and their families gathered in the face of soaring temperatures and overwhelming humidity to storm heaven. Not a festival, but a fast, participants from around the nation and the world worshipped and prayed from 6 a.m. to 6 p.m., drinking only water as they entreated God on behalf of the greater New York City area, as well as for the state, the nation, and the world.

Thousands of volunteers participated in mobilizing and working for the gathering for a full year at the cost of one million dollars, financed through gifts and donations. In addition to the prayer gathering, June 23 to July 7 saw about four thousand youth and adults ministering in "Operation Blessing International" that included eight service projects of community revitalization.

The initial gathering of The Call was in the District of Columbia on the Washington Mall in September of 2000 and followed by two others in 2001, one in Boston (September) and another in the Philippines (November). Some two dozen more gatherings are in varying stages of planning at other national and international sites, including California (San Diego, Pasadena, and the Bay Area), Missouri, Texas, Seattle, Atlanta, Minneapolis, Nashville, Colorado, Korea, Argentina, Germany, Ireland, Poland, Colombia, Nigeria, Jerusalem, Wales, Scotland, England, and Australia.

The reported vision behind The Call is "nothing less than turning a nation back to God." Although it denies being political, its expression in the United States reflects the religio-political agenda of the religious right in the so-called religious culture wars. Ahn and Engle (2001, 35–36) describe its purpose as one of leading the way in repentance from sin:

> The purpose of The Call is to cause individuals, the Church, and the nation to return to God. It's about refusing to tolerate sin! It's about turning over the tables in places where kids, parents, and governments have allowed the money changers to move in and steal our values! It's about reestablishing purity and humility by repenting for our personal sins, the sins of the Church and the sins of our nation.[14]

In reviewing the "sins" that capture the imagination of its leaders, it appears that The Call comes down on the conservative side of the religious culture wars. Its cry is to reclaim the land and to actively do spiritual battle against a select group of sins with revolutionary fervor:

> God never handed the earth to the Evil One. The earth is the Lord's. Nazirites are being called to storm and seize the gates of this Philistine culture by herald-ing a call to extreme love, extreme purity, and extreme prayer and fasting. Who will lead the parade of history on politics, the arts and media, education, sci-ence, and music? Will you? A demonic decree has been unleashed upon your generation! Arise, Nazirites, arise! It's time for a revolution—a revolution of righteousness and love!

A particular focus on the front lines of the religio-political battlefield is prayer in schools, abortion, and the decree outlawing the Ten Commandments in public schools.

Like the other activities of HRC and HIM, The Call has a prophetic narra-tive that describes its unfolding. Ahn and Engle (2001, 14–15) describe "the beginning" as follows:

> Lou has always envisioned stadiums filled to capacity with young people gath-ering for a solemn assembly, specifically praying and fasting for revival. But shortly after the renowned Promise Keepers' *Stand In the Gap* event held in Washington D.C. on October 3, 1997, Lou received a prophetic vision of a youth counterpart gathering on the Washington D.C. mall. Soon he was preaching the vision in youth conferences throughout the nation. In Phoenix, Arizona, the

spirit of prayer fell so profoundly upon the young people that they began to cry out for the vision to be fulfilled. Finally, in the spring of 1999, a woman—one who had never heard him preach—asked, "Have you ever considered organizing a massive gathering of youth in Washington D.C. to pray for America?"

This turned out to be more than a speculative question. The woman gave him a check for $100,000 as seed money to launch the vision.

Engle was in need of an "administrator" to implement his prophetic vision, a role better filled by someone with Ahn's talents than Engle's. Although Ahn was supportive, he explained to Engle that he was unable to become personally involved in The Call, save for an advisory role. Little did Ahn know that he was about to become the CEO and chairman of the board while Engle served The Call as president of the organization.

In a particularly moving prayer service, Ahn reported weeping as he "gave God afresh my family, Harvest Rock Church, and Harvest International Ministry" (Ahn and Engle 2001, 15). During the night, Ahn reported that "the Lord awoke me with a startling question: 'Son, are you willing to drop everything to help your brother, Lou?'" (p. 16). Recalling his recommitment of the previous evening and after securing the support of his family and church staff, Ahn accepted the challenge. The initial fruit was The Call D.C. on September 2, 2000, in which a reported 350,000–400,000 youth and adults gathered for twelve hours to worship, repent, pray, and listen to religious speakers.

Despite the large crowds of young people drawn to The Call, the gatherings have attracted little attention outside renewal circles. They are unlikely to fulfill the goal of ushering in worldwide revival, but they do function to bring a freshly packaged P/C movement to thousands of young people who may have never experienced the previous waves of revival. As the late David du Plessis, the famous "Mr. Pentecost" of the Charismatic movement of the 1970s, commonly would say: "God has no grandchildren." Each generation has to experience the reality of the P/C movement for itself. The Call is an important medium through which many young people are committing themselves to the faith of a graying movement.

PROPHECY IN NARRATIVE: A POSTSCRIPT

There are different perspectives or lenses through which an account can be given. What has been done in this chapter is to use a prophetic lens to describe

the rise of a church and its attendant ministries that has been quietly revitalizing the P/C movement. The vision of a major revival of Los Angeles has not
(yet?) come to pass as expected. Most residents of Pasadena (much less Los
Angeles) are unaware of HRC's presence or purpose. Not all has unfolded
according to plan—or prophecy. Despite seemingly "failed" or unfulfilled
expectations, however, the spirit of prophecy lives on and continues to instill
life into HRC's institutional life and activities.

In the next chapter we will move across the country from California to the
Ohio Valley where a so-called city church is working for revival in the greater
Cleveland area. In it we find Pentecostal, mainline charismatic, and "third
wave" churches coming together into a single network to revitalize the P/C
movement within a larger community. Once again prophetic voices can be
heard clearly in its unfolding history.

NOTES

1. Ahn reported his astonishment and hoped the program would be rerun later in the evening
so that he could tape it as the requested confirmation for his perceived divine call. He set up a
portable tape recorder, and, sure enough, the program aired again later that evening. When he
played the take for the pastors and elders the following week, all were convinced that Ahn had
heard from God.

2. Some years later while still in the midst of a spiritual drought where there was little sign of
the revival, Engle encountered a black lady who came up to him saying she had no idea who he
was. She then said, "Well in 1906 there was this black lady praying with a guy named Frank
Bartleman. I feel I'm that black lady looking for that Bartleman." Engle (personal interview by
the author, Pasadena, Calif., April 1996) was amazed and asked if he could come to her church.
There he found other women praying and fasting seven days a week, twenty-four hours a day,
for revival.

3. The April 4 date was one that emerged over the years of narrative history as HRC's
"official" founding date. Engle once shared with an audience that "the church really got
started in January 1994 when the Spirit of God was poured out on a gathering of Asian kids
at the U.S. Center for World Mission." Following this minirevival, Engle's young son had a
dream that included a premonition of the nightly revival meetings that would take place at
Mott Auditorium. This all occurred reportedly before the outpouring of the Toronto Blessing
on January 24, 1994, before the first home meeting of the church in March 1994, and before
Arnott's visit in January 1995 (personal interview with Lou Engle by the author, Pasadena,
Calif., April 1996).

4. Ahn's experience in Toronto was emotionally quite different from that of his earlier revival experience in Anaheim. Instead of joy and laughter, Ahn (2000, 217) reported "the Holy Spirit uncovered hurts I had suppressed" and which had developed into "damaging bitter roots." Tears of repentance and inner healing brought changes in Ahn's personal life and the way he ministered that he attributes to that visit.

5. Some time later Ché Ahn and Rick Wright received what they believed was a prophetic sign affirming this call to work together. As they were riding in a car together, Ahn just finished saying, "At least we know that God has brought us together for this work." Just then they spotted a black Mercedes with the license plate that read RICK CHE.

6. Engle (1998, 99) was convinced Mott was a special place because of its Nazarene roots, reporting that God had instructed him to "move next door. Get close to this building because something's going to happen here."

7. In early 2002 Pam and Rick Wright left the Pasadena church to plant an HRC in Hollywood. Wright's church is a member of Harvest International Ministries, and he continues as vice president of the church network he helped Ahn to found. In the fall of that same year, Jim Johnson suddenly left HRC, and the publication he edited for HRC (*Harvest Times*) was temporarily suspended.

8. Despite the many prophecies and visions, HRC has failed to have any noticeable impact on Pasadena much less the Los Angeles area. When I asked about this in an interview with Rick Wright in 1998, Wright responded: "I don't think it is yet time. I had a dream a few weeks ago in which the Lord told me '98 is not the year we have been waiting for. I feel we are getting close. Maybe it is '99. I felt as if I was being told, 'You have one more year to prepare for something you have been working all your life for.' From all indications, this local impact is still an unfulfilled prophecy at the time of this writing.

9. For the first six months after Arnott's visit to HRC and the launching of the nightly revival meetings, gatherings were held six nights a week. In June 1995 they were scaled back to five nights, attracting a range from a low of 100 people to an excess of 1,200, with an average of approximately 250 (an August 1995 personal e-mail from Mike Nardi, an HRC member). When I began to visit HRC in January of 1996, the attendance of the nightly meetings was more likely to read thirty or forty people, save for special conferences or special speakers. Both the number of conferences and the special speakers have decreased, and the nightly renewal meetings are but a memory.

10. More recently (since 2000) the mission of PIH became more focused for Coordinator Fred Wright. In a personal interview (Toronto, Canada, May 2002) with the author, he shared the angst that had developed within him about his ability to lead, saying "I didn't know what the

route was (to renewal); I only had a bus." Through a time of focused prayer he concluded: "I believe if there is any reason God did what He did for us (the revival), It Is for us to know Him as Father. Keeping the revival relevant means realizing that the Father really loves us and wants us to experientially know His love."

11. The emphasis on an international ministry, particularly to Asian countries, was one of the alleged reasons for Ahn's break with Larry Tomzak and the People of Destiny before the renewal began. The breach between Tomzak and Ahn has been healed, with Tomzak serving on the board of directors for HIM.

12. Figures on HIM's membership mentioned in sermons and at conferences have always been higher than the ministries listed on the official website. It would appear that HIM is operating on two levels. One is a group of independent renewal churches (primarily on the U.S. West Coast) that have come together under Ahn's leadership. These are usually small independent churches that utilize the opportunities for networking, to receive counsel and encouragement and for opportunities to attend conferences in exchange for a contribution of 3 percent to 10 percent of the ministry's annual income to support HIM. On another level there are "apostles" in other countries who (like Ahn) have other ministries turning to them for HIM-like support. These apostles from other nations may join HIM and in joining bring their churches with them under the HIM umbrella.

13. In a personal interview by the author with Ahn (Pasadena, Calif., March 1998), he explained to me how the last of the fivefold biblical ministries was being restored. The 1970s saw the restoration of the office of the evangelist, the 1980s marked the rise of the prophetic office, and the 1990s ushered in the restoration of the apostolic. Although Ahn does not generally proclaim himself to be an apostle, he is frequently referred to as an apostle or as having an "apostolic ministry."

14. The twenty major targeted sins (in alphabetical order and not according to "weightiness) are: abortion; emotional, physical and sexual abuse; adultery, bitterness (self hatred and hatred of others), divorce, drug abuse, fornication, greed (materialism), homosexuality, idolatry (anything that comes before Jesus in one's life), injustice (focused on abortion and removing prayer from schools), legalism (law is put before love), lying, murder, pornography, pride, the occult, racism, and rebellion (make voice heard through the polls).

8

One in the Spirit:
The Rise of the City Church

You are a city on a hill that will give light to the entire nation and the nations. You are a city that was once the butt of other people's jokes. You were the place of ridicule from many other cities across the nation who would point to you and laugh and snicker behind your back and say things against you. But now, says the Lord, you are a city set on a hill. And you shall be a light to the nations.

And in this place I will pioneer and I will build a radical new type of church. And know, says the Lord, that the church of my dreams will be built in this city. And this place will take over, spiritually, the place of Philadelphia of the founding fathers where there will be brotherly love in this place. And the divide between Evangelical and Charismatic will be healed in this place. There will be togetherness. And in this place my "fathers" will live who have a father's heart for the nation. And I will establish in this city a prophetic tower and raise up watchmen to watch over the nations. Intercession will be born in this place and will go to a higher dimension.

In this place it will have a new prototype of church and the church of my dreams will be birthed here and its on the drawing board even now, says the Lord, for have I not put it into the hearts of men in this place? Have I not drawn men together in this place to build this new church, to build a prototype, to build a church that is the first in the series, a prototype?

—*U.K. Prophet Graham Cook; April 1998 at a Prophetic Conference sponsored by Metro Church South; text provided in Jim Wies's Weekly Article #141, September 4, 2000*

Some twenty years has passed since the denouement of the Charismatic movement that swept through the mainline traditions with its promise to usher in Christian unity. In the end, the charismatic flow in mainline denominations left only vestiges of pneumatic experiences and somewhat weak institutional structures. Some Pentecostal denominations reaped the exodus of the disenchanted flock leaving denominational organizations, but it was the nondenominational and neodenominational churches with their promise of new wineskin for the new wine of revival that made the greater gain. Despite the talk about unity, however, cooperative ventures remained the exception rather than the rule for different streams of the Pentecostal/Charismatic (P/C) movement, save perhaps for discussions about ecumenism initiated by academics and some church leaders. Unity in spirit and cooperative outreach for P/C Christians, for the most part, were as illusive at the end of the twentieth century as it was at its beginning.

After the charismatic drought of the 1980s, the revival of the 1990s provided much-needed spiritual refreshment for those who plunged into its river. Out of these experiences, new tributaries were forced on P/C terrain. Some, like Partners in Harvest (PIH), the church network established by TACF, and Harvest International Ministries (HIM), the network founded by HRC, suggest the emergence of new denominations to consciously promote the supernatural gifts found in times of "refreshing." These interchurch networks bear striking similarities to the denominations that emerged out of the initial American Pentecostal revival during the first quarter of the twentieth century. The P/C movement is rife with historical examples of a struggle against "dead" institutional forces that threaten its vibrant charismatic spirit, only to find these new structures falling into the same organizational traps as the old (see Poloma 1989; 2002).

The early days of Azusa Street blurred the lines of gender, color, class, and denomination, but soon gave way to legalistic Pentecostal structures that mirrored the sexism, racism, classism, and religious divide of the larger culture. Historic Pentecostalism succumbed to the rigors of law over the freedom of spirit, with sects and emerging denominations often doing battle with each other. The outbreak of the Latter Rain, followed by the Charismatic movement in the mainline churches and the Jesus movement in the global counterculture all provide examples from the second half of the twentieth century of the hostility or at least the indifference of descendents of the early Pentecostals (who were by now enjoying limited respectability) toward new revivals.

The revival of the 1990s that swept across nations offered the same promise of revitalization that earlier revivals provided—and the same threat of further fragmenting the P/C movement. Many of those who found themselves leading the revival had drunk from more than one stream of the movement and were aware of the old pitfalls. As did the founders of Pentecostalism at the beginning of the twentieth century, those leaders tasting of fresh revival waters wanted structures that were malleable and adaptable, ones built on "relationships" rather than rules. This can be observed in both PIH and HIM, two of the neodenominational networks to develop out of the revival. Both PIH and HIM allow for full membership status as well as the status of "friend," permitting a church or ministry to maintain dual denominational affiliation.

Yet another form of cooperative structure has emerged, aimed at bringing revival to a locality in northeastern Ohio. It is a form that some believe is on the forefront of a restructuring of the P/C movement. Its leaders call it the city church, "a visible, functional expression of 'one church' and many congregations," having to do more with a common vision than structure. (Personal interview with Tom Hare by the author, Cleveland, Ohio, September 27, 2002.)

PROPHECY AND THE CITY CHURCH

Cleveland: The City of God's Dreams

For Clevelanders, used to hearing their city described as "the mistake on the lake" or "the armpit of the nation," the prophetic word given in the 1990s (part of which has been used to open this chapter) that Cleveland was the "city of God's dreams" seemed unbelievable. Some, however, heard and believed the prophecies about the greater Cleveland area, compiling them to eventually write a "new report"—"a good report, one of rebirth, renewal, and revival" (Metro Church South n.d., 2).

At the time that prophets were hearing promises of revival, some of the same prophets were singling out northeastern Ohio as one of the sites for fresh fire. In 1984, Marc Dupont (who later prophesied the spiritual outpouring at Toronto) proclaimed: "The Ohio Valley will be the first region in the United States to experience wholesale, end-time revival!" (Metro Church South n.d, 32.).[1] In September 1989, three of the Kansas City prophets (Bob Jones, Jim Goll, and Francis Frangipane) met a "group of pastors, wives, and others" from northeastern Ohio at a "spiritual warfare conference" held in Kansas City—a conference described as "one of prophecy, exhortation and inquiring of the Lord regarding the city" (Metro Church South n.d., 42). During this meeting "key insights" were prophetically provided that would bring revival to the area, including the formation of a "Cleveland brotherhood," God's raising up an "Apostolic City," and instructions to pray for an "anointing" that God was promising to Cleveland (Metro Church South n.d., 34). An eyewitness to this prophetic word further describes it as follows:

> The Holy Spirit gave these men many revelatory insights into certain situations in the city, insights that were quite miraculous and which attested to the veracity of the whole prophecy. The sense was that this Psalm (18) was an inspired curriculum or training manual for the metropolitan Cleveland area, like a spiritual treasure map that would help the city church in finding the treasures of her inheritance. In a symbolic way what was received in that room on that day was received for the whole church in Cleveland. Not only that, but it was revealed that to fulfill this word it was God's plan to bring other prepared vessels into the city, and that God would fulfill His wonderful promises to all of us together. (Gonzales, 2000)

Jim Goll, one of the former Kansas City prophets now living in Tennessee, returned to renewal meetings in Cleveland in 1996 and 1997. Some of the prophetic highlights of these meetings were presented as follows:

- Shiloh (Restoration prayer center in Kansas City) comes forth; Cleveland will come forth (a reference to two works emerging at the same time).[2] Transition—Something new emerging in the city.
- Fathers [sic] being raised up to carry government.
- Release your authority or it will shrivel up.
- A spotlight will come out of Cleveland.
- A second chance for Cleveland to fulfill prophetic destiny.
- Connection between Cleveland and Akron.
- An anointing of ministry to youth (Metro Church South n.d., 36).

In March of 1997, Tom Hare, former pastor of Church of the King (COTK), a nondenominational Cleveland area church that had become the local site for the Toronto Blessing, initiated a call for a region-wide forty-day fast that is believed to be the seedbed to the forming of HarvestNet (over 120 churches registered as participating in the fast). The new organization was launched when Tom Hare and two other independent church pastors (Steve Witt and

Steve Neptune, both of whom continue to play a major role in HarvestNet) met in a chain restaurant in the west Cleveland suburb of Strongsville and launched the endeavor. HarvestNet soon began to provide "regional training for worldwide harvest" and "to become a model of practical interchurch cooperation which was felt to be a key value necessary for the emerging of the anticipated city-wide church" (personal interview with Tom Hare by the author, Cleveland, Ohio, September 27, 2002).

The Rise of HarvestNet

This is not a little thing that God is doing with HarvestNet. It's not an experiment; it's not insignificant. The concepts and the realities that are embraced in this vision . . . will be replicated in a hundred cities. And I believe that representatives from HarvestNet will go to cities, sometimes with me, and we will present this to pastors as a real antidote for the whole striving and confusion that exists in training people. There is something that you guys have received from the Lord that is absolutely essential to the rest of the body of Christ to obtain. . . . This is only the beginning of a conceptual ministry breakthrough that is going to be replicated and the Lord is going to have pleasure in what it produces. (Francis Frangipane 2002)

Some began to identify with the seedling vision of a Cleveland citywide church that would transcend old and new denominational and congregational barriers. After prayer and fasting, a group of pastors began to gather regularly for corporate prayer and for lunch. This eclectic and relational gathering that came to be known as the Christian Leadership Alliance sought to involve other church leaders by bringing in speakers and prophets from outside the community. As Tom Hare (personal interview by the author, Cleveland, Ohio, September 2000) commented: "These individuals were sowing God's vision into the spiritual genetic code of the Church in this region."

When the Toronto Blessing broke out in early 1994, Tom Hare was pastor of COTK, a nondenominational congregation in one of the eastern Cleveland suburbs. As early as June 1994, COTK experienced a minor outbreak of the Toronto Blessing, with its signs and wonders. In October of that year, the church began to host monthly refreshing meetings patterned after those of the Toronto Airport Christian Fellowship (TACF). In March 1995, a team from TACF came to minister to an overflowing crowd in the church's rented facilities. This event marked the beginning of COTK's hosting renewal meetings four nights a week, becoming for a short time the "Toronto" of northeast Ohio. By late 1995 Hare began to feel that people were "missing the point" about the renewal. As he noted during a personal interview with me in 2000: "People were perceiving it only as a rain of refreshing. It is refreshing, but the purpose is to water the crop. It needed to grow in depth, purpose, and magnitude."

Hare was one of a growing number of leaders who agreed that it was time to "get off the carpet" and prepare for evangelism. By late 1995, as the renewal began to experience the first signs of cooling, in some sectors there was less talk about personally experiencing intimacy with God and more about gathering the soon-to-come "harvest of souls" during a "new wave of revival." The renewal at TACF was becoming old news as P/C Christians began flocking to newer well-publicized sites with a different temper, especially the Brownsville Assembly of God (BAOG) in Pensacola, Florida. As a southern old Pentecostal church, the language of the meetings at BAOG has more to do with "turn or burn" than Toronto's message that "God is nice." What emerged over the following couple of years was a synthesis of BAOG's call for "soul saving" together with TACF's invitation to a "deeper intimacy" with the Father.

It was out of a desire to model the value of "relational unity in a practical fashion" as well as to search for structure and plans of action that would prepare for the end-time harvest that HarvestNet emerged in 1997. Pastors of six churches initially joined together, including COTK, St. Luke's Episcopal Church in the Akron area, and Metro Church South in the Cleveland area (the latter two will be discussed later in this chapter). Over the next five years, twenty-two other churches would join the venture, including the Akron City Vineyard, another church whose brief narrative will also be included as part of this narrative.

HarvestNet describes its mission as the training of workers for the harvest of souls that are prophesied to be coming to the area—a mission that would be pursued through HarvestNet Institute (2003). A brochure describes HarvestNet as "a training center based in Northeast Ohio . . . to equip the next generation of leaders and workers for the massive harvest of souls that is coming, not only to the greater Cleveland area, but to the nation and the world." HarvestNet leaders believe that local congregations must work together as a citywide church to accomplish the task that is coming. Its brochure on HarvestNet Institute of northeast Ohio offers the following explanation:

The city-wide church is a formidable force of talent, diversity, gifting and anointing. In fact, it is within the city-wide church, throughout its local expression, that
God has given "some to be apostles, some to be prophets, some to be evangelists,
and some to be pastors and teachers, to prepare God's people for works of
service . . . " (Ephesians 4:11). It is in unity that the church has strength. . . . It is
this common vision of Unity, strength and anointing which birthed HarvestNet:
A broad range of area churches representing thousands of people, coming
together to meet the challenge to train workers in this region. (HarvestNet
Institute 2003)

HarvestNet Institute is similar to other training schools (including those at
TACF and Harvest Rock Church [HRC] mentioned in the last chapter) that
have developed around the country as alternatives to traditional seminaries.
They are shaped by Fuller Theological Seminary Professor C. Peter Wagner's
call for a "new paradigm" for training ministers for what Wagner (1999) calls
"New Apostolic Reformation Churches." These institutes offer on-site training
as well as academic instruction about the range of so-called fivefold ministries
(pastors, teachers, evangelists, as well as the more controversial prophetic, and
apostolic ministries). The twenty-eight regional pastors who now make up
HarvestNet appear to agree that the Institute is one vehicle to express their
Christian unity, despite the racial, socioeconomic, and denominational differences among their congregations.

More focused and inclusive training programs, including the Pioneer
Ministry Path and the Ministry Adventure Program (MAP), are now underway under the auspices of HarvestNet. Whereas the Pioneer Ministries
Path is "designed to identify and equip entrepreneurial individuals who
could launch new churches and other ministries both in the U.S. and
abroad," the MAP provides personal discipleship for young people in helping them to develop a "spiritual map" for their lives through academic
training, self-assessment tools (personal-style inventory, personality types,
developing goals, assessing strengths and weaknesses, etc.), and internships
at local churches or ministries. The emphasis for both programs is not simply on academic learning but on personal growth and praxis, including the
development and use of "spiritual gifts" that will prepare a new generation
of leaders for the P/C movement.[3] Like The Call (discussed in the last chapter), MAP is directed at bringing the next generation into P/C leadership
and mission.

The composite of HarvestNet is largely white and suburban, although attempts are being made to broaden the base.[4] Perhaps one of the most creative developments is the soon-to-be established HarvestNet Resource Team, designed to "function like an army" with talented and skilled persons responding to church needs throughout the community as they are able. It may involve sending a musician or music director, providing a Sunday school leader, or offering a skilled artisan to a church in need. The emphasis is on helping to distribute resources throughout the city church; its ideology is to build the "kingdom of God" rather than enhance a few privileged churches. Assistance is not to be limited to HarvestNet churches but rather is to be shared as freely as the resources allow with any church that requests it.

Other cooperative ministries have already developed with HarvestNet support, including the Healing Rooms, an International House of Prayer, and a Restoration Arts Conservatory. Each has a specific focus to further the kingdom of God as seen through the eyes of the P/C worldview in the greater Cleveland area.

The Healing Rooms of Greater Cleveland is the area's response to a trend toward a democratization of divine healing and a move away from the emphasis on healing evangelists as discussed in chapter 4. Tracing their history to the healing rooms established by John G. Lake who started healing centers in the northwestern United States in the 1920s, once again places of concentrated prayer for divine healing are being established throughout the country. Some 120 volunteers from forty Cleveland area churches serve regularly in the healing prayer ministry located in the rented facilities of a medical building in a western Cleveland suburb. Prayer teams can spend as much as an hour with visitors, praying with them and offering encouragement, although they refrain from offering medical advice. "We're here, purely, totally, on a spiritual level," says Jim White, the founder of The Healing Rooms of Greater Cleveland (Briggs 2002).[5] Prayer for healing is available free of charge to anyone seeking it.

Another interchurch ministry that aligns with HarvestNet is patterned after Mike Bickle's prayer ministry in Kansas City. A form letter that I received from Mike Noble (August 2002), director of the International House of Prayer (IHOP)—Cleveland, describes its mission as follows:

> The vision of the International House of Prayer is to establish day and night prayer and worship that continues seven days a week, 365 days a year until

Jesus returns. We are modeling this after the House of Prayer in Kansas City, which has been doing day and night prayer and worship for over two and a half years. There are approximately 100 other cities in the United States and the world raising up 24-hour prayer houses. We are working toward this objective by gathering and scheduling prayer teams from all around Greater Cleveland to pray in two-hour prayer increments. We have already established 76 hours per week of worship and prayer.

At present there are over forty churches involved in the ongoing prayer gatherings taking place in the lobby of an old theater on Cleveland's west side. "Our vision," reports Noble, "is to build a strong unified voice of diverse congregations who are crying out day and night for God's presence and power to come into our city."

As descendants of early Pentecostal believers who cared little about architecture, stained glass, or classical church music, followers of the P/C movement have rarely been promoters of liturgical arts. Restoration Arts Conservatory (RAC), "another new cross-denominational ministry working in partnership with HarvestNet," attempts to bring the largely neglected performing arts into worship and evangelism. Classes are being offered for the first time in the fall of 2002 through HarvestNet Institute in dance, music, and theater with the purpose of providing "an opportunity to "raise the bar for performance in the Body of Christ and to bring a new level of excellence to the calling we have in the Arts." Its brochure states further, "We assist students in understanding the times, developing their artistic skills, preparing for performances, concerts, and various outreach venues and offering a world view centered on Jesus and grounded in the Holy Scriptures."

Cooperative ventures among regional churches such as those presented briefly here have been largely unknown in P/C culture where resources have been used primarily for the benefit of the local congregation and secondarily for foreign missions. HarvestNet and those with a vision for city church are seeking new structures and ministries that creatively foster interchurch cooperation by providing spiritual resources and services for the community. In their prophetic interpretation of events, there is a sense that the foundations for this venture have been divinely established. A short visit to three of the member churches will demonstrate why many believe God has already brought important players to the area who are making possible Cleveland's heavenly restoration.

Tales of Three Churches

The flames from the Toronto revival fires leapt across Lake Erie from Toronto to blaze for a time at COTK in Cleveland's eastern suburbs where the now director of HarvestNet had been the pastor. Although COTK was the first renewal star to shine in the area and is one of the charter members of HarvestNet, other churches have risen to play more salient roles in sponsoring renewal conferences and providing resources and leadership in ministries discussed briefly in this chapter. These churches have their own accounts of the impact that the Toronto Blessing had either in revitalizing or in establishing their congregations. Three narratives will be briefly presented here to demonstrate the role the revival of the 1990s played in other area congregations who share the vision of a city church for the greater Cleveland area.

St. Luke's Episcopal Church

St. Luke's Episcopal Church (formerly of Bath and now Fairlawn, Ohio, both Akron suburbs) has been a flagship for the P/C movement in the mainline churches for over thirty years. Its founding pastor, Charles Irish, had received the baptism of the Holy Spirit (and the gift of tongues) in the late 1960s during the height of the Charismatic movement. Irish, who had served in the Marines and enjoyed a successful career as a businessman before his ordination, became disillusioned when he found himself lacking the ability to pastor his small but divided church. Irish was about to leave the ministry and begin training as a psychotherapist when he learned that his high school-age daughter had come under the influence of a Methodist couple who spoke in tongues! When Irish set out to confront them, he had a religious experience through their prayer that proved to shatter his stereotypes about charismatics and brought new life to his ministry. Shortly after leaving the meeting with this couple, Irish began to speak in tongues. He describes the effects of his experience as follows:

> My confusion began to wear off. Now the peace of God descended and I knew, for the first time, He was part of my life. He was part of my life, not just in concept and hope, but in reality and power. For the first time, I knew Him! That evening I awoke in the middle of the night praising Him! God had broken through into my life. (Irish 1993, 16)

Under his adept leadership, the church became a center for charismatic worship and training, with a particular ministry of inner healing. Unlike many mainline churches whose touch of charisma soon evaporated or was deliberately quenched by dissenters, St. Luke's remained a vital charismatic congregation that grew steadily over the years. Although the waves of the spirit sometimes ebbed, the church regularly sponsored charismatic conferences that generated a fresh flow of renewal experiences throughout St. Luke's history. The church became a flagship for the charismatic movement in the Episcopal Church, and Irish left to head the national movement. Roger Ames, a charismatic priest who had experienced his own "paradigm shift" in part through the ministry of John Wimber, came in as the church's new rector in the early 1980s, building on the foundations that Irish had laid. St. Luke's remains the site for regular renewal conferences, under its own sponsorship or co-sponsored with Metro Church South as well as those sponsored by HarvestNet.

At the time of the outbreak of the Toronto Blessing, St. Luke's was planning a fund-raising campaign for a new building to accommodate growth in a congregation that had already outgrown its facilities. Although it had distanced itself from the larger Episcopal Charismatic movement when Irish returned to St. Luke's to serve as an associate rector, the leadership appeared resolved in its efforts to bring renewal to the larger Anglican community. Unlike small nondenominational or independent churches that are more fluid and better able to move with a renewal like Toronto's, alignment with this new controversial movement was not without risk for this affluent suburban denominational church.

In first hearing parishioner reports about the Toronto revival in mid-1994, Father Roger Ames reply was, "You don't need to go to Toronto. Whatever they have, we have right here." By October, however, curiosity mounted and the priests attended the Toronto church's first "Catch the Fire" conference. On his return, Ames confessed, "Brothers and sisters, I know what I said—and I have to repent. I now say, whatever Toronto has, we want (personal interview by the author, audiotape of Sunday Service at St. Luke's Church, Bath, Ohio, November 6, 1994).

Ames shared more about the renewal and the way it began to immediately influence St. Luke's on a Sunday morning in early November (audiotape of Sunday Service at St. Luke's Church, Bath, Ohio, November 6, 1994):

> If you were here last week, I don't need to tell you that the Lord broke out in a fresh way—even renewing the renewal! The exciting kinds of things [we heard] from the sharings of Les and Bonnie Barker from Ontario and from the increasing number of people who have gone to Toronto to visit the Vineyard. (We

had more people go this weekend.) You may wish to see this in its original place, even though it is clearly being exported and imparted and moved out as the Lord wants it.

It's an outbreak of God's love—that is what it is. It is as if God's spout is open and people are getting a fresh sense of God's love in their lives—people who have never felt things before.

Sometimes it takes a number of tries. It's like parched ground. You turn on the water and it runs off, but after a while the ground begins to absorb the water. So I just encourage you to keep after that if you didn't receive.

[Ames began to talk about the revival that broke out in the youth group meeting the previous Wednesday after some had been to the Vineyard.] Some had been out on the floor for a couple of hours, and we had to call parents and tell them we would see that they got home. There were a couple of them here until 12:30—just being prayed for and out in the Spirit.

Ames took a risk in embracing the Toronto Blessing within a successful existing congregation, and the risk seemed to pay off. The building campaign and the transition to the new church building on Pentecost Sunday 1997 were successful beyond expectations. The congregation grew to fit the new facilities, increasing around 30 percent to around seven hundred people in attendance each Sunday.[6] When Ames was asked in an interview to summarize what effect the Toronto Blessing had on his congregation, he responded:

It has revitalized the old and given us new perspectives. It has increased our awareness of our early Christian roots. It has also increased intercessory prayer. The intercessors have become more contemplative. We will see if this spirit of contemplation moves into the Body. Intercession does undergird our mission work, our conferences, and our increased outward focus. (Personal interview with Roger Ames by the author, Akron, Ohio, May 4, 2000)

St. Luke's, linking with five other churches to the north of Akron, became one of the charter members of HarvestNet, and Ames became one of the regular instructors at HarvestNet Institute. Located on a major highway to downtown Cleveland, St. Luke's has proven to be a good location for intercity church renewal conferences, training, and meetings. Some resources that were once directed toward renewal in the Episcopal denomination have been diverted away from the denomination toward the cooperative ministries in the regional community.

Metro Church South

Although Metro Church South has a somewhat different history and church structure than does St. Luke's, the two congregations often work together to promote HarvestNet activities. Founded by Steve Witt during the height of the Toronto Blessings, Metro Church South has a membership at the time of this writing of around four hundred (including children). Witt left the church he had helped to start in a western Cleveland suburb to plant a church in eastern Canada in 1986 and soon became a regional leader of the Canadian Association of Vineyard Churches (AVC). Although he had established two other churches (including one in the same area of Cleveland as his present church) prior to visiting the then Toronto Airport Vineyard (TAV) in 1994, Witt describes this newest church plant as having a different quality from his earlier ventures, in part because of the intense experience he had in Toronto.

Witt jokingly described the fruit of his first visit to TACF in April 1994, as a "baptism into the spirit of 'I don't care.'" He elaborated by sharing more about this experience:

> I was stone drunk and hit with waves of laughter. I was leaning against the wall, laughing and laughing. The laughter was so deep in my stomach that I was aching. I used muscles in my face that were not used to exercise. The next morning my face was swollen from the laughter. I left Toronto feeling invincible. I was able to leave my concerns about security, numbers, public response, etc. I felt as if I had been baptized into God. One cannot be a God-pleaser and a man pleaser. There was a washing off of all my cares and concerns—they were simply washed off. (Personal interview with Steve Witt by the author, Cleveland, Ohio, April 20, 2000)

As with the majority of TACF survey respondents of whom 90 percent reported being more in love with Jesus than ever before, the visit to Toronto touched in Witt a moment of "first love"—the love he compares to the discussion in Revelation about the Church of Ephesus. As Witt commented, "The only thing that really matters is the Lord. That experience simplifies the reason as to why we are here. Only God matters. We can forget everything else."

It was in this spirit of abandon that Witt and his family left the Canadian Vineyard they had started for Cleveland in the summer of 1996. When they arrived in Cleveland, the area had little experience with renewal (save for one church in the western suburbs and COTK on the east side of the city).[7]

Witt was eager to bring renewal to the greater Cleveland area through the establishment of a local church (rather than a renewal center). As a start-up, Witt felt impressed to go on Christian radio, calling for people "who loved the Lord but were dissatisfied with church" to join him. As a successful church planter, Witt "knew" that such an advertisement would probably bring malcontents who were unlikely to stay put in any church, but he felt a divine direction to make this call. (Surprisingly, most of the ninety-two people who answered this call and met with him on September 13, 1996 are still with him.) In contrast to his earlier church plants, Witt was now more interested in seeing intense worship in his church than ministries and programs that he once thought were so essential for a successful church launch. As Witt describes it: "This is the first church I've planted out of renewal. The focus was on worship. There were no other ministries (no youth groups, Sunday school, etc.) for the first year. Our main reason for coming together was to worship" (personal interview with Witt by the author, Cleveland, Ohio, April 20, 2000). Worship remains a prime reason for Metro, but other ministries and programs are now in place to disciple and serve the mostly young families in his congregation. Although Witt continues to have respect for the AVC, Metro Church South reflects TACF's approach to renewal and is a member of PIH.

Witt has a high regard for prophecy and is especially adept at recognizing the synchronicity that enters his life—common incidents that he regards as "not mere coincidences but prophetic parables that open people's hearts and prepare them for God's love." He shared one such prophetic parable that changed his ministerial direction in an account he wrote for *Spread the Fire* (Witt 2000). In the 1990s (with the blessing of his new church), Witt became one of the major international itinerant speakers for the Toronto Blessing. He describes an encounter with Marc Dupont that spoke to the shift that was about to take place in his ministry:

> One day I was shopping with my close friend, Marc Dupont. He noticed me looking at a belt and said, "I'd like to buy you that belt." I responded politely that I already had a belt, but Marc insisted. A few minutes later, I walked out with a $36 belt! Then he spoke a prophetic word to me. He told me that the belt was a symbol of a "binding" that the Lord was bringing into my ministry. I would be spending more time at home. (Witt 2000, 18)

Witt did not think much about the prophecy until the next day when the buckle of the new belt broke apart in his hand. Later that day while talking to Dupont on the phone, Witt related what happened. Dupont continued with his prophetic word, noting that the broken belt was a sign of the "end of the old and my dependency on it." On reflecting on the events, Witt responded to the "prophetic parable" as follows: "I wondered if this could be God speaking to me. Within a year and a half, my international travel ministry had come to a halt. God had "bound" me to the local church we're planting. Then I remembered Marc's word to me"(Witt 2000, 17).

Such prophetic events are woven into the pivotal role that Witt plays on the board of HarvestNet. Witt's being "bound" to the local church (and being "broken" from his brief career as an itinerant evangelist) has also allowed him a more pivotal role in implementing the goals of HarvestNet. (It is not without significance that the director of the Healing Rooms is a member of Witt's church as were Jim and Carolyn Wies, the new pastors of the Akron City Vineyard whose narrative is soon to be told.) Witt's focus in outreach is what he terms "presence evangelism"—to take the divine presence so real to those in the renewal to the streets of the city. Just as Wimber democratized healing (and indirectly helped to give rise to the healing rooms developing throughout the country), Witt wishes to see prophecy increasingly practiced by ordinary Christians who can minister in their places of play, study, and work.

Akron's City Vineyard Church

Like the Toronto Blessing itself, Mark Perry's story begins with his affiliation in the AVC. While still a school teacher in California, Perry began to feel the call to plant a church—a call that was confirmed when the Vineyard where he began to serve on staff selected him to copastor a new church plant in nearby Five Cities, California. Perry assumed full pastoral responsibilities within a year and saw the church grow to 250 members within three and a half years. Perry then "felt called" to leave this growing church to begin another Vineyard in Akron, Ohio. Perry's "Welcome to the Vineyard" letter introduces himself and the church he planted with the following description:

In May of 1996, we moved our family to Akron, Ohio from the Central Coast of California, where we were pastors of a growing Vineyard church. Through His guidance, we believe God directed us to move to Akron to start this church.

Since we've arrived, we have enjoyed the warmth of good people who have welcomed us and have helped us to build a really great church here in Akron. What
started as a single family now involves dozens of families and individuals who
have caught the vision. Our vision at Vineyard City Church is a family of happy,
effective Christians loving our city into relationship with Jesus.

Mark Perry remembers well his first visit to TACF in April 1994, a visit that
came shortly after he planted his first church. It began on the Tuesday after Easter
with one of the leaders talking about repentance—and Perry wept. The next day
he felt the Lord was telling him to drink freely, and he experienced the joy that
comes with being "drunk in the Spirit." Then on Thursday he was hit with "holy
laughter," one of the most common experiences during these early days of the
revival. On Friday, Perry "shook, crunched, and trembled," an experience during
which he felt he was "given power." Plans to relocate to Akron, Ohio, were made
during the height of the Toronto Blessing, and he made five other pilgrimages to
this renewal site with each bringing a well-remembered significance (personal
interview with Mark Perry by the author, Akron, Ohio, April 2000).

Perry's narrative is filled with prophecy and divine serendipity that has guided
his ministry.[8] Prompted by a series of signs and prophecies, he and his family left
their native California for Akron, Ohio, in June 1996. One prophecy given them
just before they left Five Cities stated that at first Akron would be a "desert-like
experience," but "in three years you will be vindicated." This early desert experience was exacerbated by the difficulties of testing out ways to put flesh on his
vision for the new church. Perry was convinced that those in the renewal community "needed to give away to the whole community what had been given to
them," but it was difficult to implement in a new area of the country that was
quite different geographically, culturally, and socially from Southern California.

In December 1999 Perry received an e-mail message from a prophetess in his
old Five Cities Vineyard who reported to him: "The test is over. You almost
didn't make it, but the next season will be fun. You will receive clear direction of
the spring." I first formally interviewed Perry at the end of April 2000 (Akron,
Ohio), just after the spring rains seemed to have fallen on the new congregation.[9] It then had a membership of just over 100 people, a number that
increased to 150 within the next year, and the church seemed on solid ground.[10]
The second interview was conducted in May 2002 in Akron, Ohio, as he and his
family were preparing to leave Akron to plant another church in California.

By the fall of 2001, Perry was beginning to sense that he had begun the first lap for Akron City Vineyard, but someone else would be leading it for the sec ond lap. He intuited a call to "hook up" with Steve Witt of Metro Church South, asking him to pray with him and help to mentor him. Witt was there to assist Perry in his decision to return to California and in his choice of a successor. In the meantime, confirmation that the move was to take place came during the last trip that Perry made to TACF in January 2002, when he asked for "someone to pray for him who was prophetic." Trish Bootsama, a newer member of TACF's pastoral staff and a prophetess, reported that she saw an eagle traveling a long distance to change nests. Perry felt this was a confirmation of the call he sensed to move back to California. As he expressed it, "I feel I could stay. God is giving me a choice. It's not that one is right and the other is wrong. As I continue to grow in the Lord, I feel God is saying, 'Do what you want to do'" (personal interview by the author, May 2002, Akron, Ohio).

Perry believed that God was facilitating the changing of leadership at Akron City Vineyard in giving him the sense that Jim Wies, a minister who had moved to the greater Cleveland area from Florida only two years earlier and who was a member of Witt's church, would be the new pastor. Perry had asked Witt to pray for guidance about a new pastor and then asked Witt if he sensed any divine guidance. Witt replied, "The Wieses."

Both Jim and Carolyn Wies are ordained ministers through Christian International—Network of Prophetic Ministries.[11] Prior to moving to Cleveland, they pastored Cornerstone Church in DeFuniak Springs, Florida. Jim Wies (1999) shared how their "personal prophetic pilgrimage" confirmed their decision to leave Florida and reestablish themselves in the greater Cleveland area:

> We began to realize quickly, however, that God had a plan He had been putting together for years. One of our strong clues was that we, ourselves, had received a prophetic word 10 years before about a fork in the road that God would bring us to, and at that fork, the Lord would give us a house to live in that would be adequate for us, and specifically that it would have a courtyard, and that this house would be a sign for us that we were right in the middle of God's will.
>
> As is our custom, in our desire to "steward" prophetic words that have been spoken to us, we type out and preserve prophetic utterances for periodic review. So throughout the years, in several moves within Florida, I had always kept my eye open for the "house with the courtyard," though it never materialized. However,

when it became evident to us that we were to move to Cleveland, one of the ladies in our Florida church had a dream in which she saw a stone archway leading into a courtyard in the house we were to live in. Since she was unaware of the 10-year-old prophecy, we took it to heart.

Armed with a directive from God to relocate to Cleveland, we took a four-day window of time during a ministry trip in July to find a house to rent. We had exhausted all our other leads when on the last day, we went to our last listing. There, just as had been prophesied, and exactly matching the dream, was the house with the courtyard. We now reside in Seven Hills, Ohio, which is directly in the geographical center of the entire Cleveland Metropolis.

The Wies's church in Florida entered "into a season of spiritual impact" directly as a result of the Toronto Blessing. Wies reported in a personal e-mail message to me on September 11, 2002: "From the time that renewal hit our church in the summer of 1994, we saw a doubling in size of the congregation and our own ministry catapulted into a trans-local ministry with travel into many places in the USA and Canada." When the revival broke out at BAOG in Pensacola, Florida, the Wieses "also became very involved with that." In the summer of 2000, they relocated to the Cleveland area to partner with Steve Witt. As Jim Wies noted in Weekly Article #141, September 4, 2000 (e-mail message to author, September 11, 2002): "What God is up to, however, is really much bigger than our own personal prophetic pilgrimage." Jim Wies believes he and his wife have been called to northeastern Ohio as part of a larger prophetic promise, one repeated recently during the "Intimacy Conference" held at St. Luke's Church in April 2002:

And then I heard God say that He has sworn an oath—a covenantal decree—that He WILL rain upon Northeast Ohio. There has been a progressive work pertaining to this area just as was with Abraham, who received a conditional prophetic promise and responded, then received another prophetic promise and responded, sometimes not too perfectly, but numerous times until there came a point at which God swore a covenantal oath, that in blessing He would surely bless Abraham.

And so has the Lord decreed, pertaining to this region that what He has promised He also has destined and decreed by an oath; that He WILL rain upon this region. He will do it! And thus the smoke and incense continues to be stirred; and the atmospheric mixture is being changed, and the rain clouds are forming, and the rain will come.

A NEW REFORMATION?

Although the story of northeastern Ohio's city church can be told through prophetic lenses with the focus on divine leadings that put players into place, the visible result of the divine intervention is believed to be a new form of church. This church is to see a completed restoration of the so-called fivefold ministries, including the prophetic and the apostolic. For those who embrace this model endorsed and developed by writers such as Bill Hamon (1997), Jim Wies (1999) and C. Peter Wagner (1999); men like John Arnott (TACF) and Ché Ahn (HRC); as well as some who are discussed in this chapter are evidence of the restoration of apostolic leaders. Hamon (1997, xxv–vi) states:

> The Church has been in a continual state of restoration since the "Period of the Great Reformation" began some five hundred years ago. . . . Christ's Church has two restorational movements that are restoring two major ministries back into the Church. Jesus gave the Prophet and the Apostle ascension gifts of Christ to be a vital part of His Church until His Second Coming. Nevertheless, church theologians who did not have an understanding of God's full purpose for Apostles and Prophets took them out of the present Church. They dispensationally depleted [sic] them from being active in the Church.

While the prophets function in "revelatory gifts" and "supernatural revelation," apostles are men (and occasionally women, like Heidi Baker who is discussed in the next chapter) who are characterized by "gifts of power and signs" and "supernatural wisdom" to build a divinely ordered church (Wies 1999, 70). Sometimes the prophetic and the apostolic can be found in husband-wife teams (as with Pam and Rick Wright of HIM and Carolyn and Jim Wies), where the wife is the prophetess who "sees," and the husband the prophet who "builds."

What is apparent at the time of this writing is that despite attempts to develop a new paradigm church, what has emerged thus far looks very old. Gender inequality in this male-dominated movement is more reminiscent of the 1950s than the twenty-first century. Denominational cooperation is limited to a particular brand of evangelicalism, with little inroads made into mainstream Protestantism and Catholicism. Most churches are suburban, white, and conservative Protestant with agendas that reflect that peculiar sociodemographic trait. Despite the abundance of prophecies, few reflect the concerns for peace and justice found in the Old Testament prophets.

Having made this observation, however, it is only fair to note that the city church in the greater Cleveland area is still in its formative stages, and its prophecies are still unfolding. Although its becoming a model for a new kind of twenty-first-century church seems highly unlikely, the rise of global Pentecostalism from the short revival on Azusa Street (1906–1909) in Los Angeles would have seemed impossible.[12] Proponents (and prophets) point to the changes that can be seen in Cleveland's skyline as a prophetic symbol of the changes "beginning in the heavenlies" that will alter Christianity in Cleveland. Only with the passage of time can a verdict be rendered.

NOTES

1. TACF, as we have seen, did experience what most would call a renewal or revival, and its effects were felt around the world. It did not, however, influence the city of Toronto in any noticeable way. Many Toronto residents never heard of TACF, and others who did have never stepped foot on its premises. The prophecies of Marc Dupont and others were given new life when the Toronto Blessing was transported to Ohio during the first year of the revival.

2. At the time of this writing it appears that these "two works" might be the development of an International House of Prayer (IHOP) and Healing Rooms in the greater Cleveland area. Both will be briefly discussed later in this chapter.

3. The practice of church planting, which usually begins with a core group sent out from an existing church or through a small study group begun by a would-be pastor, facilitates the emergence of a congregation that shares a common vision. Although some denominational churches are involved in HarvestNet, the present intent is to launch churches imbued with city-church "values and vision" rather than any particular denominational label. Steve Neptune, one the three original visionaries, now leads Gateway Church (in an east suburb of Cleveland), a congregation founded in April of 2002. This interdenominational venture has Neptune drawing on other HarvestNet congregations for founding members and other needed resources to start up this new church. Gateway Church serves as a pilot project for the Pioneer Ministry Path, in which a regional church network has worked with another network (Apostolic Team Ministries) to launch a new church.

4. HarvestNet presently includes four African American congregations: Cleveland's Mt. Sinai Baptist Church, (pastored by C. J. Matthews); House of Glory (pastored by Tossie Wiley), Kingdom of Life Center (pastored by Gary Pleasant), and House of the Lord in Akron, Ohio (pastored by Joey Johnson). It remains to be seen whether these pastors will be able to help diversify a growing organization that is primarily suburban and white.

5. Jim White's account about his call to establish healing rooms could be used to tell another story filled with interrelated serendipitous incidents and unsolicited prophecies that might appear surreal. The prophecy given to him in early 2001 that "thousands will soon come to receive healing from healing rooms," had him soon searching the Internet to learn something about healing rooms (a term with which he was unfamiliar). He found a website on the Spokane healing rooms and (thinking that the founder of the original healing rooms was still alive) sent an e-mail message to John G. Lake! Before he could get an answer from Cal Pierce (who reestablished the healing rooms in Spokane), White had an "open vision" in which he was passed a torch that contained the words "healing rooms" and received unsolicited information about a recently deceased renewal evangelist, John Rowe, who had believed he had been called to establish healing rooms in the greater Cleveland area. John Rowe's widow, Terry, and others (both with and without HarvestNet connections) believe that the torch for healing rooms has indeed been passed to Jim White.

6. The trajectory of the Toronto-like revival at St. Luke's mirrors the one discussed for North America in chapter 6. During late 1994 through 1996, signs of a revitalized Charismatic movement permeated the congregation as it increased to its present size. By 1997 there were indications that the first wave of the revival had receded, as the day to day working of the church "returned to normal." Conferences, attended by only a sampling of the congregation, still provide revival-like services several times a year.

7. It was in the spring of 1995 that Tom Hare, then pastor of COTK, felt the Lord was telling him to "invite Steve Witt" as a renewal speaker, even though he had only a nodding relationship with him. When Witt came to COTK, Hare's wife prophesied that Witt would be "returning to Cleveland." Prior to establishing his church in Cleveland, Witt had also heard from another Canadian minister associated with TACF revival that he was going to be "called back to Cleveland."

8. Perry's call to Ohio began with a California prophetess seeing him in the "Midwest." During the spring 1995 renewal meetings, he began to sense the Holy Spirit saying "you are done here" and had a vision of himself passing the baton to another person. He then saw a U-Haul travel trailer with "Akron, Ohio," on it and sensed the Spirit saying, "Have you thought of Akron?" In Toronto, he encountered two lay leaders from St. Luke's Episcopal Church that further nurtured the call to Akron. After his first visit to Akron, he saw a questionnaire that I had distributed, with the instructions to return the completed instrument to the University of Akron. (Perry then called me, asking me what I knew about churches in Akron. He then told me that he felt God was calling him to plant a church in Akron.) These were just a few of the incidents that Perry believed directed him to Akron and then confirmed his decision.

9. Perry first got a vision of planting a new church in 1993 while still in California. It was to be a church that would be relationship based, with weekly services to celebrate relationships, and its multiethnic and cross-class membership would minister to other churches in the city.

10. Around this time Vineyard City Church sent a small group of some of its most able to plant a new church in Colfax, Washington. Perry also thought of leaving Akron, but sensed he was to stay put in the Akron area for the time being.

11. The AVC does not ordain women and would not permit a woman to pastor a church. If the Akron City Church remains with the AVC, Carolyn and Jim would not be considered copastors. The teamwork will continue with Carolyn exercising the role of prophetess and Jim assuming the mantle of apostle according to the model suggested by Peter Wagner's New Apostolic Reformation Church and further developed by Wies (1999).

12. John Arnott (2001b, 8) expanded this line of thought in an article he wrote for *Spread the Fire* on revival: "Only thirteen thousand attended the Azusa Street Revival during its 3½ years, and most of them were Christian leaders from the US and all over the world. They came and were revived and empowered by the baptism and the gifts of the Holy Spirit, but there was no mass evangelism that took place, at least not then. Because they didn't have a sufficient tally of souls saved, the Azusa Street Revival is often left out of the list of historical revivals. However, it has turned out to be the greatest revival of all time. Throughout the last 100 years, the Pentecostal/Charismatic revival now has over 5 million adherents and has resulted in the salvation of millions of lost souls. Not bad growth for less than 100 years. Sounds like a Holy Spirit authored revival to me!"

Mysticism in Service: Taking the Renewal to the Streets

I am saying that I have predestined you to carry my glory to the ends of the earth. Who will go? Who will go? Who will carry His Presence to the ends of the earth? Who will die and let Jesus live in them? *A new creation in Him!* You have been called for the praise of His glory—to carry his presence unto the ends of the earth—into the darkest darkness, into the far corners of the inner slums, into the nations that have been closed by Islam. You have been called to carry His Presence into the darkness, into the gas stations, into the hospitals, into the schools. You have been predestined as sons and daughters to carry the glory of the King.

—Heidi Baker

America may be a birthplace of P/C revivals, but these intermittent times of refreshing are generally short-lived. Once the laughter, drunkenness, and party atmosphere of the Toronto Blessing lost its freshness, some who experienced this "first wave" began seeking something "more." A minority found the presence and power in communities of the poor, both in North America and abroad. Some of the original voices who spoke in the Toronto Blessing, although they retained close ties with Toronto Airport Christian Fellowship (TACF), began to address in various ways the mystery of pain and suffering. The prophet Marc Dupont, the religious historian/theologian Guy Chevreau, and the minister who launched the revival, Randy Clark, were among those who demonstrated some discomfort with limiting their ministry to the overwhelmingly white, middle-class, middle-age pilgrims who could afford the extended trip to revival sites in North America.[1] Joining others in ministry to the poor, both in other countries and on the North American continent, allowed their teachings to begin to address issues that were largely overlooked in the early party days of the renewal.

A concern about a limited and somewhat distorted view of Christianity besetting the renewal can be gleaned from the results of the 1997 follow-up survey of pilgrims who had visited TACF prior to 1995 (the date of the first survey). Although the vast majority of the respondents had attended at least one renewal conference during the interlude (86 percent), were involved in renewal at a local site (82 percent), and believed "the best was yet to come" (82 percent), approximately half saw problems with a potentially Pollyannaish presentation of Christianity. Only 46 percent were satisfied with the balance in renewal theology "between a theology of blessing and a theology of suffering." Four out of ten respondents (42 percent) were uncomfortable with the end-times eschatology that was being taught by some in the movement. Approximately one-third (35 percent) expressed some concern about the "prophetic thrust of the renewal." Although the overwhelming majority believed that they had been touched by the renewal and that their experiences were genuine (94 percent), they were divided as to whether the renewal had in any way influenced the larger church (with 51 percent saying that it had). The dissenters were most likely to be pastors and to come from mainline traditions (rather than Pentecostals or members of independent charismatic churches).

An unbalanced American interpretation of the Christian message, especially when fueled with fresh revival experiences, has often led to caricatures about the "happy clappy" Christian who has embraced a culture of narcissism. A closer look at the recent revivals will demonstrate that, like their Pentecostal fore parents, leaders have sought to redress extremes. In a prelude to one of his sermons given at a recent "Signs and Wonders" conference in Georgia, Randy Clark offered the following prophetic message:

> For much of U.S. Christianity, the focus is on mountain top experiences. We want to have the glory of the Mount of Transfiguration, and we want to move into the victory of the Mount of the Ascension. But biblical Christianity doesn't focus on two mountains, but three. It's that third mountain that we spend too much of our time trying to avoid—and that's the one in between: the Mount of Calvary. It is the mount of the cross; it is the place of death. (Clark, 2002)

Clark goes on to suggest that the only way one can "die to self" or to "take on sacrifice" is to be empowered by the Holy Spirit: "After we are empowered by His Spirit, it is to die—so that we can live."

MYSTICISM, EMPOWERMENT, AND SERVICE

A relationship between experiences of divine love, empowerment, and service to others can be seen through the lenses of the follow-up survey findings. A significant number of 1997 respondents reported a decided increase in service and outreach to others as a result of their experience of the renewal. For most this increase took the form of reaching out to family and friends (64 percent), acquaintances (57 percent), and to their local church (55 percent). For others it included an increased giving to missionary activities (44 percent) and almsgiving to the poor (35 percent). A significant minority became personally involved in outreach to the poor and homeless (24 percent) or other works of mercy (20 percent). As the first step toward testing whether there was a relationship between these indicators of service and spiritual empowerment, the items reporting an increase in outreach to others were combined to form a "service index."

The next step in this analysis to assess the relationship between service and empowerment was to create an "empowerment index" by combining the seven items that were used to measure an experience of an increase in spiritual gifting through the renewal. Of the respondents to the 1997 questionnaire, 62 percent reported being more prophetic, 47 percent received more words of knowledge, 48 percent became involved in prophetic intercession, and 41 percent were experiencing more prophetic dreams. Approximately one in three respondents (34 percent) reported being used to pray for the physical healing of others, 49 percent in the emotional healing of others, and 27 percent in deliverance ministries.

There was a statistically significant relationship between outreach/service and spiritual empowerment ($r = .32$). In other words, those who reported higher scores on spiritual empowerment were significantly more likely to be involved in outreach and service. It is noteworthy that those who reported higher scores on empowerment were also more likely to report a wider range of the controversial physical manifestations (discussed in chapter 3) and also more likely to report higher scores on both spiritual healing and inner healing (discussed in chapter 4). In other words, experiencing the perceived presence of God in a dramatic way and experiencing a deeper sense of God's love, which may be accompanied by the "flashing light" of somatic reactions, are positively related an increase in empowerment (measured by forms of healing and prophetic ministry). In sum, it appears that mystical experiences of God are often empowering, causing the recipient to be "clothed with power from on high." This empowerment can then be a catalyst for outreach and service to others (see Poloma 1998 for additional statistics).

Heidi Baker, a missionary to Mozambique whose fresh voice can often be heard during this phase of the revival (and whose personal story will be told in this chapter as an example of empowered service), recently spoke the following admonition to those attending a "Signs and Wonders" conference sponsored by Nehemiah Ministries in Kinnesaw, Georgia (see also preceding epigraph).[2] Her words serve as an example of the kind of preaching that supports the analysis and interpretation of the survey data just presented in tying together service and empowerment:

> I know that what I am after is what you are after. And I know that we cannot do mission, we cannot do ministry, we cannot do what God has called us to do unless we have His manifest presence. We have never done a good job—we have not reached the world for Christ Jesus. So when people say—when they look at people on the floor, when they look at people crying and slobbering, and shaking and falling—when they say "aw, please!" (they do not understand). What they are not understanding is that unless God takes a hold of the human being and unless God takes a hold of that little tiny heart and makes it huge, they will never—never, ever—be able to carry His glory. So what God is doing in these meetings is not frivolous—it is not frivolous people, listen to me! It is not frivolous to see people stuck to the floor—it is not frivolous to see people crying— it is not frivolous to see people shaking and quaking and feeling the power of God. I want you to know that unless God touches you, you will not go in his power and you will not see what he wants you to see. (Baker 2002)

P/C CHRISTIAN REVIVALS AND MISSION

The P/C approach to Christianity is reportedly "the most rapidly growing missionary movement in the world"—a fact that may help to explain its growth from zero to nearly a half billion people in less than one hundred years. From its earliest days when followers who had been "baptized in the Holy Ghost" and "spoke in tongues" set out for places unknown trusting in divine providence for provisions, P/C Christians have taught that empowerment and missionary activities went hand in hand.[3] While it might be argued that some Pentecostals, given their end-times eschatology, were far more interested in saving souls before the final curtain than wrestling with mundane problems of life in the mission field, most missionaries have recognized the need to provide services in the host countries. One good description of the threefold program of mission, evangelism, and social concern has emphasized its holistic nature:

> Although Pentecostal mission focuses on evangelization, it is not to the exclusion of social concern and never has been. Holistic mission has been part of Pentecostal mission work. In fact, Pentecostals have worked with the poor for social renewal in unobtrusive ways and have initiated major social reform programs and institutions. (Karkkainen 2002, 883)

What these missionaries do take to the target culture is an alternate worldview with its miracles and mystery that travels well, especially to two-thirds of the nations where most of the dramatic growth in the P/C movement has occurred.[4]

As the American P/C movement crossed the tracks in the second half of the twentieth century finding a solid niche in middle-class suburbia, some began to see the need to share the gospel and material resources with victims of poverty in this country. Whether working in the slums of America or abroad, a revitalized P/C approach to such endeavors readily reflects the often-cited Scripture passage: "'Not by might, nor by power, but by my spirit,' says the Lord." Once again prophetic lenses shared through the narrative of insiders can provide a unique vantage point for understanding P/C evangelism. Two stories of two ministries will be briefly recounted here—one domestic and one international—demonstrating the role that outreach to the poor can have for the revitalization of Pentecostalism's alternate worldview.

BLOOD-N-FIRE: REVIVAL ON THE STREETS OF ATLANTA

The Blood-N-Fire (BNF)[5] narrative begins within John Wimber's Association of Vineyard Churches (AVC) and the mandate to "take the stuff to the streets"—the "stuff" being the "signs and wonders" that has ebbed and flowed within the P/C movement since its inception. This torch was taken up in Atlanta and carried by David VanCronkhite,[6] "an entrepreneurial businessman

with a six-figure income" who began taking food to the poor in the inner city
under the auspices of the Atlanta Vineyard in May of 1991:

> Led by Johnny Crist of the VCF Atlanta and loaded with sixteen bags of gro-
> ceries, David recalls that they "took off from white, very middle class Atlanta
> and headed south to find the poor. We drove for an hour and a half—we didn't
> even know where to go to look. Most of us had never ventured anywhere into
> that part of America." They had no idea where they were when they pulled into
> the parking lot of Capitol Homes, which at that time was in the top five of the
> most drug infested, violent areas of Atlanta. "We just felt like God divinely put
> us there in the midst of drug deals." They gave away the sixteen bags of groceries
> "in about sixteen seconds" and were "scared to death." David recalls getting in
> the van and heading back to the safety of suburbia, thinking he'd never go back.
> (Bogart 1997, 23)

This initial distribution of groceries was only the humble beginning of the
ministry that would develop over the next years—one to which VanCronkhite
and his wife, Janice, would give their lives. What was needed to move beyond
the initial reaction of being "scared to death" was an empowering encounter
with God. That experience came to VanCronkhite through the ministry of
Jackie Pullinger-To, a speaker at a Vineyard-sponsored conference in Anaheim, California, that would change their lives.[7] VanCronkhite (2002, 32) describes his encounter with "that woman" (as he affectionately refers to
Pullinger-To) as follows:

> She quickly began what was one of the hardest messages I had ever heard
> preached. It was a fiery, passionate message about the poor and compassion for
> the poor. But frankly, it left me angry. Angry at her for telling me the truth about
> who I was in regards to the poor and where the Church was in regards to the
> poor. I didn't think I much liked this woman! When she finished, she called a
> time of ministry where she invited all to come forward, repent and receive im-
> partation for this thing she called "compassion for the poor." I recall thousands
> of men and women going forward (there were over 10,000 in attendance). Jan-
> ice and I were in the back of the auditorium and I was not going forward for any-
> thing. See, I was still angry at "that woman" over her message and for telling me
> I didn't have compassion for the poor (which I of course didn't have). But a mir-
> acle happened that day. Something caused Janice and me to finally get up toward
> the end of that prayer of impartation and meekly ask God to give us what "that
> woman" was talking about, this thing called "compassion for the poor."

VanCronkhite (2002, 32) reported that he "didn't feel any different" while being prayed with, but over the next weeks and months he found himself "falling in love with the poor, the harassed, the oppressed. I found myself looking for ways to help men and women I had never even noticed before. I found myself weeping over people I had never cared about before, never even noticed. I knew then what had happened. God had changed a heart."

VanCronkhite was doing well in the corporate world when he began his street ministry. He was enjoying "a healthy six-figure salary as head of Integrated Health Systems Inc, a hospital information systems company based in California." His wife, Janice, "was once a professional tennis player, hobnobbing with tennis students like Clint Eastwood and Gene Hackman and tennis stars like Jimmy Connors" (Daigle 2002, B2). As VanCronkhite was trying to "sort out" his life, weighing the mix between corporate success and ministry to the poor, he said he heard the Father speak to him: "David, I will bless you in the business world, but I'll bless you even more if you go to the poor" (Van Cronkhite 2002, 8).

During the earliest years of the ministry, VanCronkhite and a group of twenty people would "march through the housing project, preach, teach, barbecue chicken and play their music," but they had no place to meet. They were a street ministry without a building. During one of these marches as he was standing in front of a huge abandoned warehouse, he sensed God saying, "That's yours. Go get it." VanCronkhite got permission to meet in an area outside the building during, and over, an eighteen-month period where he watched the proposed sale of the 3.7-acre complex fall through on three occasions. The representative for the building's trust called him unexpectedly one morning, saying to VanCronkhite: "This is the third time we've had it sold and it's fallen through closing. Would you come back and buy it?" Although the building was valued at $2,800,000 and the asking price dropped to $1,200,000, VanCronkhite countered at $450,000. The offer was accepted. VanCronkhite continues his story:

> We're on the fortieth floor of a downtown office building at this big table with sixteen different owners and lawyers. The lead guy said, "Okay, now let me get this right. We're going to sell this building worth $2,800,000 to them for $450,000, right?" Everybody nodded their heads. Then he turned to me and asked, "Now, guys, how big is your church?" Well, we don't have one yet, I replied. "How much money do you have?" We don't have any money. "Well, where are you going to get it?" We don't know. The lead lawyer slammed his fist

on the table and said, "This is the stupidest thing I have ever seen." (Bogart 1997)

The owners offered to finance the building, with the first payment of $50,000 due two years later. With only $60 in their account on the due date, it appeared that the church was about to lose the building. Seemingly as part of a divinely mandated script, a man from another church walked into the warehouse with a check for $50,000 to meet the payment.[8]

God not only changed David and Janice VanCronkhite's hearts, directed them into full-time ministry, and provided a building for the ministry, he also provided a name for the church: Blood-N-Fire. VanCronkhite found out only later that "Blood and Fire" was the motto that appears on the flag of the Salvation Army. He knew little about the Army—even when a prophet told him that he and Janice had "the William and Katherine Booth anointing." It was only after researching the church that VanCronkhite learned of the similarity between his ministry of his vision and the Booths' Salvation Army. "We know we are to impact our society with 'social reform,'" writes VanCronkhite (2002, 21), "in much the same way that William and Katherine Booth did when they established the first 'Blood N Fire' in London some 150 years ago—the Salvation Army."

In March 1998 as VanCronkhite (2002, 40) was doing street ministry with a group from his church, he again heard the voice of God that caused a turning point in his ministry:

And He then said this, "David (He always calls me David), if you will pray and sing songs to Me where the prisoners can hear, I will set the prisoners free. I will break off the chains. I will do the signs and wonders." Then I heard this, "Signs and wonders are nothing for Me. I will set the 'prisoners' in the city free. But where will they go?"

The question—*where will they go?*—haunted him as he broke with some ordinary operations to allow the ministry to take a new shape. The next year became pivotal with BNF being "put on hold" as VanCronkhite sought an answer to the divine query. At one point, in a move that seemed daring to some and reckless to others, he cancelled Sunday morning services and (as might be predicted) BNF lost many of its suburban members and their accompanying financial contributions. This radical move was made to sort out those who were willing to enter "into relationship with the poor" out of which a structure and programs could emerge that would emphasize interpersonal relationships rather than impersonal strategies and programs. Those who worked with VanCronkhite over the next few years did develop a new structure (at the basis of which is a familial commitment within a small group of followers) to provide an answer to the divine question that had challenged him (Daigle 2002; VanCronkhite 2003).

VanCronkhite (2002, 14-15) described his journey as:

Falling in love with the poor became a consuming desire. Getting a heart for the oppressed and the youth was and is unbelievably difficult. The ministry I found was easy. All I had to do was show up and the Holy Spirit always changed lives, signs and wonders would take place, people's lives were changed. Jesus would suddenly become real. But it always ended with me ready to "go home" and let the lost, the poor, and the new "believers" figure out the next step.

In the process my heart's purposes changed. I was beginning to understand a little—very little—about relationships and the Father heart of God—His desire to build relationally—to establish "community"—to bring the lost, the poor, the youth—bring them into a community of supernatural believers. Now rebuilding and planting churches took a step back. My passion was to see if it were possible to build genuine community that would include the rich and poor, black and white, brown, yellow and red, and young and old—relational community.

Well, if going to the poor was difficult, it was nothing compared to this relational issue of becoming sons and daughters in the Kingdom of God and beginning the process of working it out. Relationship, I found out, is something we are desperate for, all of us, but we are equally afraid of it. The walls are high!

When BNF resumed its Sunday services in the spring of 2002, it had developed a communal and relational base with a renewed vision: "Atlanta is to raise up leaders from among the broken Atlanta poor who will be used by God to advance the Kingdom of God in the City of Atlanta." A striking physical change could be seen in the warehouse as a kind of sacramental testimony to the changes that had taken place within the BNF church. The Sanctuary, once used primarily for worship, became a sanctuary in an interrelated way. Still the site for the restored Sunday morning worship, with band instruments and musicians to lead the time of vibrant celebration and some pews to accommodate the worshipers, it now has beds and tables that fill the edges of the large room as a reminder that the Sanctuary has another purpose. It has become a temporary home with a familial structure to model relationships for transients whose family ties have been weakened or severed.

Hundreds of the poor, broken, and addicted enter BNF through the doors of its Sanctuary each night. Some will move on to a BNF training center to experience its process for "rebuilding broken lives," a few of whom will remain as members of BNF after the restoration is completed. Scores of young suburbanites are also working shoulder to shoulder with the VanCronkhites as BNF seeks to move beyond the warehouse to become a presence in adjacent communities. Through a gift from a local business establishment, BNF has a mobile kitchen, part of "a renewed effort to take our ministry 'to the streets.' " Its ministry extends outside of Atlanta as churches in other communities have affiliated with BNF and as BNF members establish churches in other cities. In a recent *Blood-N-Fire Newsletter* (September 2002) VanCronkhite writes: "Nearly twelve years ago now, we were just four guys from the suburbs trying to find the poor of Atlanta to give away sixteen bags of groceries. Today Blood-N-Fire is in 10 cities and 3 nations, with mission teams preparing to move into ten new cities in seven new nations. . . . There's excitement at Blood-N-Fire like we've not seen for the last three years! During that time, we were temporarily 'on hold' while we got our House in order and dealt with some major foundational issues. We did just that."

This is assuredly not the end of the BNF story. By the time this book appears in print, there are sure to be other divine leadings, confirmations, miracles, and changes in strategy and structure.[9] What has not changed over the years is the sense of mission and the need for the "supernatural" to make the vision a reality. In the midst of the three-year period described by VanCronkhite (2002, 14) as being "on hold," the founder wrote the following:

Then our hearts were captivated by new pieces of the vision stirred by prophetic words. We started with a simple understanding of "rebuilding cities by planting churches of the poor in the inner cities" which came from a proclamation of "seeing stadiums filled with youth and poor, lines, miles long, with people trying to get in to hear nameless and faceless men and women of God proclaiming the Good News with unbelievable healings taking place . . . Atlanta being transformed." I still believe it's going to happen, ten years later. It will happen because "God is not man that he should lie or a son of man that He should change His mind." (Num. 23:19)

MISSIONARIES VISIT TACF: HEIDI AND ROLLAND BAKER'S STORY

Like the VanCronkhites, the Bakers had also had an encounter with Jackie Pullinger-To. While the VanCronkhites experienced her at a conference sponsored by the Anaheim Vineyard in Southern California, the Bakers worked with her ministry in Hong Kong. Until encountering Pullinger-To's ministry, the Bakers made use of their background in creative media and the performing arts for evangelism in the Philippines, Taiwan, Indonesia, and Hong Kong. After working with Pullinger-To, the Bakers "had a strong feeling that the Lord wanted to change the direction of their ministry." Their hearts were increasingly broken for the poor and unwanted. They wondered about their crusade converts and wanted to concentrate more on the specific daily needs of those to whom they ministered" (Iris Ministries, December 24, 2002, www.irismin.org).

In 1992 Heidi and Rolland Baker left Asia to do their Ph.D.'s in systematic theology at King's College, University of London. At the same time they planted a church among the homeless, drug addicts, and alcoholics who lived on the streets of central London. It was only after they researched many different countries that they chose Mozambique, one of the poorest nations in the world, for their new home.[10] As soon as the civil war ended in this African country, the Bakers left London to begin missionary work in Africa.[11] Rolland Baker briefly shared the story at a TACF Pastors' Conference in 1998 (January 14) about how their ministry in Mozambique began:

> We looked for kids. We found an orphanage the government didn't want, churches didn't want, South Africa didn't want—absolutely no one wanted these children. They were sick, they were dying, they were full of disease, they were starving, they were mean! Nothing good had ever happened to them in their entire life. I just stood there—we didn't have support. We are interdenominational—there is only Heidi and me. But I said, "We'll take it—we'll take it— I can't help it. There is nothing more exciting that anyone can see than to watch God do something who have never seen—ever, ever, ever seen—anything good happen to them and to see God do His very best for them."

The orphanage would be run as a joint venture with Mozambique's Department of Education.

But Mozambique was different from, and more desolate than, the other places that the Bakers had ministered. Few family members or friends could understand why they had chosen this poor nation as their mission field, and both Bakers soon found themselves overwhelmed by the great needs of the people and their lack of resources to help meet these needs. Rolland Baker, who became acquainted with revival stories as a small child sitting on his missionary grandfather's lap, was eager to experience for himself what was happening at TACF. In October of 1995, he came to Toronto for the second "Catch the Fire" conference, and like vast numbers of pilgrims who came before and after, he found his life revolutionized by a fresh experience of divine love. As Rolland Baker writes (Baker and Baker 2000, 52–53):

> The goodness of God leads to repentance, and I was so impacted by the Lord's grace that I wept for joy and I wept in relief. I was excited; I was thrilled. And I was staggered by the purity and power of the grace of God being poured out like a mighty waterfall—so clean, so refreshing and so awesome that nothing could resist it. Receiving God's love was like being lost down in the mist at the base of Niagara Falls, completely awed by the thundering noise, deep currents and brilliant white all around.

Heidi Baker's first visit to TACF was not until the summer of 1996. She had become physically ill and emotionally exhausted from the demands of missionary life in Mozambique and checked herself out of the hospital to make the trip. She (Baker and Baker 2000, 53–55) described the desperation that beset her in seeing "dying children in the dumps and streets" every day as God led her to minister to children, many of whom were orphans:

> We had gone to Mozambique with nothing, and we had never tried to raise support or send out appeals. I felt the Lord leading me to pick up hurting, outcast and dying children on the streets of Maputo and, after a few months, I had gathered several hundred of them. It was a challenge to feed the children each day. Corrupt bureaucrats in Mozambique's Department of Education were hassling me daily. Although I was filled with joy to finally be ministering in the poorest nation on Earth, the daily struggles of existence seemed to squeeze all the energy out of me. I was deep-down bone tired (Baker and Baker 2000, 55).

Heidi Baker's experience at TACF provided physical healing, refreshment and a vision that has sustained her during difficult times that followed:

> During the very first meeting, although I was unable to sing because I couldn't breathe very well, I was overwhelmed by the worship and the presence of God that permeated the place. At one point in the service, I knew that I was totally and

instantly healed. I began to breathe normally and to sing and dance. I was filled with incredible joy. When they asked for testimonies, I went forward I told them what God had done, and then members of the prayer team began to pray for me. As they did, God completely blasted me! I was on the floor for hours.

I saw a vision of Jesus. I saw His face. I saw His burning eyes of love piercing through my soul. I saw His broken, bruised body. There were thousands of children surrounding Jesus. I began to weep and I cried out, "no, no, there are too many!"

The Lord replied, "Look into my eyes." My heart melted as I looked into His face. He handed me a piece of His broken, bruised body and said, "Give it to them to eat." His body became bread in my hands. I gave it to all of the children and everyone ate. Jesus said, "I died so that there would always be enough."

Again he said, "Look into my eyes," and He handed me a cup of blood and water that flowed from His side. I knew it was a cup of bitterness and joy. At first I drank it; then I gave it to the children to drink and they all drank their fill. Once more he said, "I died so that there would always be enough (Baker and Baker 2000, 58).

Several weeks after their return to Mozambique, the Bakers were issued a forty-eight-hour eviction notice. Marxist factions of the government decided that they could not hold worship services on government property, and they had nowhere to go with the 320 children they had begun to think of as their own children. Over a hundred children left the orphanage to find "Papa" and "Mama" in the little quarters in which they had settled in a nearby town. It was there that a tangible "miracle" happened that would supplement the vision as the Bakers' ministry expanded. Heidi Baker (Baker and Baker 2000, 56) shared her story:

After several days of children drifting in, there were over 100 children living everywhere in our little office with one toilet. Because we had lost everything, including our pots and pans, we hadn't eaten in days. A friend from the embassy called to say she was bringing over chili and rice for our family. When she arrived, I told her we had a really big family. She said, "no, no, I made this for your family of four!" I opened the door and showed her all the children and said, "Jesus told me there is always enough!"

She was upset and wanted to go home and make more food. But I had a bit of cornmeal and her pot of chili and rice. I told all the children to sit down and pulled out the plastic bowls and began filling them up. Every single child ate. Then Rolland and I and Crystalyn and Elisha ate too. God multiplied the food. There is always enough if we seek his face.

Because of their involvement in TACF, they lost the sponsorship of at least one major contributor to their missionary work (who had promised $1 million to build a children's center) only to gain the support of revivalists around the world through TACF. Not only did contributions from the TACF pilgrims provide sponsorship of programs to support Iris Ministries, but return visits to TACF continued to personally restore and revitalize the Bakers. "We had come to that meeting having lost everything and wanting to quit missionary work," reported Heidi Baker (Baker and Baker 2000, 57). "Instead, we were tremendously empowered for service."

Heidi Baker describes herself as "a type A, driven person" for whom "the concept of resting and soaking in God was not at all appealing" (Baker 2001, 17–19). Her experiences at TACF provided a different model for prayer and ministry. Heidi explains:

> During one week at TACF everything changed. John Arnott was preaching about the weight of the glory and the anointing. Suddenly I felt heavy and ended up stuck to the floor in the morning service, unable to move. It was as if I was being cradled in the loving arms of the Father. He soothed away all the years of exhaustion as I rested close to His heart. I could hear His voice clearly, and felt affirmed in His intense love and acceptance of me."

Heidi Baker described another experience and a new vision she received during the pastors' conference in January 1998.[12] While Randy Clark, the minister who launched the Toronto Blessing, preached on "dying to self and the holy fire of God," Heidi jumped from her seat, ran forward, and knelt beneath the stage. Heidi Baker (Baker and Baker 2000, 59) later would write:

> The fire of God hit me, and I felt like I was literally going to burn up and die. I began to cry out, "I'm dying; I'm dying!" I heard the Lord say, "Good, I want you dead!" Not knowing who I was, Randy grabbed my hand and told me there was an apostolic anointing on my life. He declared that I would see the blind healed and many miraculous healings. He asked me, "Do you want the nation? God's giving you a nation." I cried out, "Yes!" and for hours the power of God flowed through my body like an electric current.
>
> Then I heard the Lord say, "You'll have hundreds of churches!" I began slapping the floor and laughing. It was the funniest thing I had ever heard! It had

taken us 18 years to plant four churches. How could there ever be hundreds? But I knew I had heard the Lord.

Times were not easy in Mozambique as the country suffered hurricanes and severe flooding in 2000. Yet the Bakers' ministry flourished. By Christmas 2000 they had helped to plant over five hundred churches, "had a thousand pastors serving in churches all across Mozambique and into South Africa and Malawi," and were caring for over one thousand children (Baker and Baker 2000).[13] The pastors of these churches, following the model the Bakers had provided, began themselves to take in orphans and abandoned children. The flooding resumed in 2001, and Rolland Baker reported (February 2001) from Maputo (Iris Ministries, www.irismin.org):

> God isn't done with his drastic dealings with Mozambique. Almost ceaseless rain for the last month up and down the country has resulted in the overflowing of major river systems again this year. Last year's incredible flooding, the worst in memory anywhere in the world, affected one million people. Already the current flooding is "affecting" 390,000, and the weather forecast is for more of the same.

The Bakers became personally involved "with thousands and thousands of suffering victims" in their own churches. Many of these churches were planted in the bush within the previous two years where relief supplies were slow to come when they came at all.

> Iris Ministries is facing an awesome cry for help all over Mozambique. Rain is severe even in the south at our Maputo center. Our own house is soaking with leaks. Our one hundred twenty pastors in our current Bible school session are in constant intercession for their people and country. The Holy Spirit is falling on our worship meetings. And at the same time hunger and disease are spreading out of control. Fifty of our own children are in the hospital and many more are overflowing our clinic getting emergency treatment.

The situation continued to worsen, and an outbreak of cholera hit the Bakers' center near the capital city of Maputo. Within days they had taken seventy children, pastors, and workers to a special hospital (actually a big tent where the patients were quarantined). The health officials in Maputo were terrified of a citywide epidemic that was believed to have started through contaminated food brought to a wedding at the Bakers' church. The director of health reportedly "put her finger in Heidi's face and told her, 'You will be responsible for killing half of Maputo!'" (Iris Ministries, March 1, 2001, R. Baker, www.irismin.org). Only Heidi was allowed to visit and to tend the sick in the hospital where "she would go in and spend hours and hours with our kids, holding them, soaking them in prayer, declaring they would live and not die. They vomited on her, covered her with filth, and slowly grew weaker. Many were on the edge of death, their eyes sunken and rolling back." A critical situation seemed to be resolved "miraculously," Rolland Baker reports:

> Three days ago our entire future in Mozambique was in question. No one had any more answers. Our weakness was complete. Then some of our children began coming home from the hospital, even as others were being taken there. And then there were no more new cases. Extraordinary. And then yesterday everyone was home! Just like that, the cholera is gone. And Heidi is fine.
>
> The doctors and nurses at the hospital are in the state of shock and wonder. The director of Health again put a finger in Heidi's face. "You! This is God! The only reason you got through was God! You and dozens of these children should be dead!" Eight of the medical staff there want to work with us now. "This is miraculous! You know God! We've never seen God do anything more like this. We've never seen such love! We don't want to work here anymore. We want to work with you!" And so they will. (Iris Ministries, March 1, 2001, R. Baker, www.irismin.org)

In August 2002 the newsletter (Iris Ministries, www.irismin.org) reported that the last months have seen a nonstop series of meetings all over Mozambique and Malawi. Partners in Harvest/Iris Ministries has "well over 4,000 churches spread into ten countries." The ministry has raised up homes to care for orphaned and abandoned children as well as a Bible school to train pastors. Rolland Baker notes: "The spiritual hunger, physical needs and demand for ministry we encounter are indescribable. Daily and weekly we receive desperate calls for yet more bush conferences in hundreds of locations we have not been able to visit ourselves." These conferences spawn new churches and new pastors who create an infrastructure not only for spiritual enrichment but, most importantly, for getting food and medicine into the bush.

What is it that has brought the phenomenal growth to Iris Ministries? Rolland Baker writes in April 2002 (Iris Ministries, March 1, 2001, R. Baker, www.irismin.org):

We are often asked what brings about church growth here. Is it our Bible teaching, Bible school structure, bush conferences, strategy, what? Many things may be involved, but our own pastors tell us that it is miracles that bring the people. They go where Jesus heals them, loves them and does things for them. We might say those things shouldn't be necessary, but our people are very simple. They don't want to go where they can't feel or appreciate the presence of Jesus, even if the place is a beautiful, traditional church. They don't want to exchange their powerful witch doctors for a powerless church. They want a living God involved with their lives who can be trusted in everything, and who has more power than any opposition.

A SOCIOLOGICAL CAVEAT

Revival as briefly illustrated by the Bakers' ministry in Mozambique is rapidly changing millions of lives and contributing to the growth of Christianity in so-called two-thirds nations. One may question the claims of multiplication of food, the blind regaining sight, and even the dead returning to life, but one cannot question the phenomenal growth in mission and outreach by the Bakers and Iris Ministries, an exemplar of countless other revival-oriented ministries that can be found dotting the globe.

What has been described here is reminiscent of Rodney Stark's (1996) sociohistorical account of the rise of early Christianity. While not seeking to refute the assertion that the rapid growth of Christianity in the second half of the third century was "miraculous" (miracles "could have happened" he said), Stark sought "to understand human action in human terms" (p. 4). According to this self-proclaimed "village atheist," "The basis for successful conversionist movements is growth through social networks"—a premise that he creatively explored in the rise of early Christianity (Stark 1996, 20). The propelling factor in energizing the networks was an ideology very new for the pagans of Greco–Roman times: "The idea that God loves those who love him" (Stark 1996, 213). Although found in ancient Judaism, Christianity took this image of a merciful God who loves human beings and commands them to love one another, but stripped it of its ethnocentrism. This "idea" was not merely an epiphenomenona, but it had consequences that changed the social fabric of the existing world. According to Stark (1996, 211) "Central doctrines of Christianity prompted and sustained attractive, liberating, and effective social relations and organizations."

The importance of love in Christian ideology and the emergence of relational networks as described by Stark can be found in both Blood-N-Fire and Iris Ministries. Whether through drugs and disease in Atlanta or war and the AIDS epidemic in Mozombique, natural familial relations have often been severed leaving behind misery and chaos. Stark's (1996, 161) contention that "Christianity served as a revitalization movement that arose in response to the misery, chaos, fear and brutality of life in the urban Greco-Roman world" could be altered to describe the chaos in many contemporary sites. And as did ancient Christianity in its time, revitalized Christians continue to quietly revitalize the contemporary world. Today as in antiquity, Christianity can provide "new norms and new kinds of social relationships able to cope with many urgent urban problems," "charity as well as hope," "an immediate basis for attachments," "a new and expanded sense of family," and a "new basis for social solidarity" (p. 161).[14]

If the doctrine of loving God by loving one's neighbor was the "ultimate factor in the rise of Christianity" as Stark (1996, 211) suggests, it still does not explain why those who share the same ideology can differ greatly in their expressions of it. It would appear that what has been described as "empowerment" in this chapter plays a critical role in living out a doctrine that many believers profess only with their lips. While doctrine plays a role in the revitalization process, this research on the P/C movement suggests that doctrine alone does not empower. Personal experiences of the Holy Spirit are the unexamined power behind the doctrine.[15]

What has been demonstrated throughout the chapters is a cast of actors in the American P/C movement who are empowered people, living out their conviction that God walks and talks with them. Many report specific incidences that they believe represented a call to build the Kingdom of God on earth and increased their empowerment to prophesy, to heal, and to work miracles. These religious experiences are often not only personal transformations but can also provide the energy for changes within the social order.

Stark's analysis of the growth of early Christianity, particularly his discussion of epidemics, networks and conversions, is helpful for understanding the present-day growth of Christianity. Natural and humanly produced crises in the late Greco–Roman Empire, as in the present troubled world, provide "crucial opportunities for the growth of Christianity and downfall of paganism" (and the cerebral faith of many intellectuals). As Stark (1996, 194) noted about paganism in the ancient world:

> Paganism, after all, was an active, vital part of the rise of Hellenic and Roman empires and therefore *must* have had the capacity to fulfill basic religious im-

pulses—at least for centuries. But the fact remains that paganism did pass into history. And if some truly devastating blows were required to bring down this "enormous thing," the terrifying crises produced two disastrous epidemics that may have been among the more damaging. If I am right, then in a sense paganism did indeed "topple over dead" or at least acquire its fatal illness during these epidemics, falling victim to its relative inability to confront these crises socially or spiritually—an inability suddenly revealed by the example of its upstart challenger.

As Stark goes on to suggest, early Christianity grew not so much because of the miracle working in the marketplaces (the self-described "village atheist" is willing to acknowledge such miracles may have occurred), but because of Christian love, Christian compassion, and Christian networks. Yet there is more. When one takes a closer look at the heroes and heroines who are revitalizing Christianity with love, compassion, and networks, one finds people who claim to have been empowered. The love, compassion, and networks are the seeming fruits of perceived mystical encounters with God.

Stark credits Christianity with providing the world with "a coherent culture entirely stripped of ethnicity"—one based on a doctrine proclaiming that loving one's neighbor was essential for knowing and loving the God who loved all humans—and that it flourished in response to social disorganization. Old ethnicities were submerged "as new, more universalistic, and indeed cosmopolitan, norms and customs emerged." In a world that continues to be filled with both natural and humanly devised crises, a form of revivalized and empowered Christianity continues to make gains not unlike those described by Stark.

The narratives that have made up the second part of this book are multilayered ones in which social structure and individual action are separate yet interdependent. I, working as a sociological ethnographer, have sought to be a bridge—to overcome the dichotomy between positivism (which would have gutted the meaning from the revival) and humanism (which would have rendered the accounts simply as stories of human interest). At the same time, I have been an involved participant and observer, with the strengths and weaknesses that involvement brings. The concluding chapter seeks to reflexively address my role as a researcher of the Toronto Blessing within the context of a reflexive account of the course of the revival from 1994 to the present.

NOTES

1. For an account of Guy Chevreau's (2000) encounter with a community who takes the revival to the streets in Spain, see *We Dance Because We Cannot Fly. Stories of Redemption from Heroin to Hope.*

2. Michael Ellis, founder of Nehemiah Ministries, went to TACF in November 1994 where he experienced the Toronto Blessing. "I came home filled with excitement and a new zeal for the Lord. I would go on to travel for one year with Randy Clark, founder of the Toronto Blessing all over the world, ministering healing, deliverance and salvation." Ellis founded Nehemiah Ministries in 2002 "to bring inner healing and deliverance to as many as possible and to raise up others to do the same." (Letter accompanying brochure inviting people to the "'Signs and Wonders" conference, 2002.)

3. It is worth noting that while missionary activity once meant Americans going to other countries to evangelize, during this revival the going and coming has been in both directions. It can be argued that the Argentine revival as well as the ministry of the former South African evangelist, Rodney Howard-Browne were both major catalysts for TACF revival. There appears to be a dialectical relationship between missionary work and revival in the global context.

4. Whereas many early missionaries doctrinally focused on the coming of the reign of God with the immanent return of Jesus, that eschatology plays but a minor chord today. More present-day missionaries seek to usher the Kingdom of God into the present-day world through the "signs and wonders" made possible through the Holy Spirit.

5. I first visited Blood-N-Fire (BNF) in July 1998, returning the end of August for a "Spirit Summit" and again in September for a "Catch the Fire" conference. This visit coincided with a peaking of the renewal in Toronto. I was refreshed by the spiritual power combined with loving outreach that I observed at BNF. During this first visit I compared in my field notes what I observed in Atlanta with the "stadium Christianity" and "spiritual Pac Man" mentality that seemed to be on the upswing in renewal circles: "The 'renewal' is gasping for breath in North America while its leaders are trying to come up with new 'spiritual technologies'. I am not at all convinced that we have moved into the ultimate prophetic and apostolic eras, nor that we are about to bring down the principalities and powers allegedly hovering over our cities. BNF offered insight on how 'revival fire' could be used in ways that would satisfy even the most staunch critics of revival."

6. Daigle (2002, B1) opened his news account of BNF with the following description of VanCronkhite: "Dressed in faded bluejeans, black corduroy jacket and a gray, untucked Harley-Davidson T-shirt, 56-year old David VanCronkhite doesn't look like a man who once wore Armani suits and tasted of the American dream."

7. For an account of Pullinger-To's story, (described as "how one woman's faith resulted in the conversion of hundreds of drug addicts, prostitutes, and hardened criminals in Hong Kong's infamous Walled City") see Pullinger (1980).

8. The unusual financing and eventual paying off the building has in itself become "a sign and a wonder." When I was having lunch with VanCronkhite in Atlanta in the spring of 2001, he commented that he needed $300,000 within the next three weeks for the final payment on the warehouse. If it did not come in, they would lose the building. When I asked where he was going to get the money, he replied, "I don't know—I don't have it. This is God's ministry, and if He doesn't bring the money in, it's all over." The money came in on time without any fund-raiser or mass appeal, in part a gift from the business community of Atlanta and an anonymous donor who contributed $100,000. As VanCronkhite shared in a newsletter sent out in August 2001, "In 1993 God said, 'that is your building, go get it' and he has provided in every way ever since."

9. Although the founding of BNF predates the Toronto Blessing, a shared focus on the Father's love and the empowerment by the Spirit taps into the same Christian well. In a recent personal interview with Janice VanCronkhite (wife of the founder of BNF), I learned of a minirevival that occurred at BNF at approximately the same time as the beginning of TACF revival. According to the narrative, a small group from the Toronto Airport Vineyard (TAV) who were returning to Toronto from the Argentine revival visited BNF on January 20, 1994. During a prayer service they experienced a strong presence of God together with unusual physical manifestations that become the hallmark of the 1990s revival. When a representative from the TAV group telephoned the Toronto church to share what had occurred in Atlanta, they were countered with reports of similar experiences. (Personal interview with J. VanCronkhite by the author, Atlanta, Georgia, May 2003.)

There was no formal contact between the two churches until David VanCronkhite and a small team from BNF visited TACF in February 2003. On April 28, 2003, John and Carol Arnott came to Atlanta with ten other TACF leaders to visit BNF for a week. Both churches expressed a "sense" of these meetings being a "divine appointment" as they ministered to and prayed with each other. Whether this encounter marks the beginning of an explicit focus at TACF of "taking the renewal to the streets" remains to be seen.

10. Mozambique, according to a recent report from Rolland Baker, has a life expectancy of under forty years, 180, 000 AIDS orphans, and the government spends only $2 per person per year on public health. Civil unrest, massive flooding, droughts, and more flooding as well as government corruption has left the nation in even worse straits than when the Bakers first arrived in 1995.

11. While they were in London, the Bakers had heard about the "Father's Blessing" in Toronto, but their church of street people had no way of visiting Toronto. Heidi Baker (Baker and Baker

2000, 50) shared how they had prayed for God to move (with)in their church and how revival broke out in a Sunday morning service in 1994: "I prayed that the Lord would pour out His blessing on us just as He was doing in Toronto. The whole church began to cry out to God, falling all over the place. One crippled young man began leaping in the air. A city lawyer began rolling on the floor, laughing with incredible joy. Others were weeping in repentance. Lives were transformed and our church was never the same!"

12. I was present at that conference and was eager to meet and talk with Heidi Baker. I had been teaching at Vanguard University in Southern California where Heidi had earned her undergraduate degree and where I had met a young woman who worked with the Bakers in England. Heidi was in a state of "divine inebriation" through the duration of the conference and was unable to do anything by herself, including interview with this sociologist!

13. The Iris Ministries website (www.irismin.org) at the time of this writing in February 2003 reports expanding "to over 5,000 churches all over Mozambique and into neighboring countries."

14. Paganism was no match for emerging Christianity in dealing with the epidemics, plagues, and disease that descended on the ancient Greco–Roman world. According to Stark (1996:74–75): "When disasters struck, the Christians were better able to cope, and this resulted in *substantially higher rates of survival.* This meant that in the aftermath of each epidemic, Christians made up a larger percentage of the population even without new converts. Moreover, their noticeably better survival rate would have seemed a 'miracle' to Christians and pagans alike, and this ought to have influenced conversion."

15. I do not wish to assert that only P/C Christians can experience the Spirit, but that P/C ideology and identity *emphasizes* a doctrine and experience of the Spirit that tends to play a minor chord (when played at all) in more routinized denominations.

Narrative and Reflexive Ethnography: A Concluding Account

We know this social reality because we are, or can become through our actions, a part of it. Clearly in so doing we both attain insight into this social reality and alter it through our presence. This essential reflexivity is a part of all research, but probably more characteristic of ethnographic research than any other form. . . . Thus, a critical self-consciousness must be developed and incorporated into the research from the initial stage of selecting research topics through the interactions with others in the field to the final analytical and compositional process. Such critical self-awareness is not simply about the individual ethnographer's social identities and personal perspectives; it also needs to encompass disciplinary perspectives and broader cultural background. At the same time, this critical reflexivity is not an end in itself—the research is not about the ethnographer; rather it is a means—in fact, the only means—of coming to know, however imperfectly, other aspects of social reality.

—*Davies 1999, 213*

Multiple narratives from countless voices have been used to produce this metanarrative of the so-called Toronto Blessing and its role in revitalizing American Pentecostalism. The accounts of participants have been selected with an ear on capturing the meaning they themselves have given to this on-going revival. True to Taves's "mediating position" described in chapter 1, I make no pretense at having sorted out "truth" from "fantasy" or, in the words of critics, "true revival" from its "counterfeit" forms. I sought a polyphony of voices to produce an account that could describe Pentecostal/Charismatic (P/C) revival for scholars both inside and outside of the P/C movement. The narratives of the participants have been complemented (especially in the first part of this book) by theories (narratives?) from diverse fields of study, including anthropology, sociology, psychology, neurology, and musicology to enable the reader to "make sense" of the revival of the 1990s and its aftermath.

Throughout the eight-plus years of being involved as both a researcher and a participant in this recent wave of revivals, I have taken the stance of Georg Simmel's stranger who is both on the inside and simultaneously an "outsider" to revival happenings. During this time I sought a wide array of informants, perspectives, research sites, and media reports to answer questions about P/C religious revivals that previously had not been addressed. As in all ethnographies "there are a variety of voices in the text: some of them the voices of informants, others the different voices of the ethnographer, who may speak for example as interlocutor, social actor or analyst." (Davies 1999, 221).

As Davies has astutely noted, not only does this ethnography employ select voices of those leading and participating in the revival and scholarly works that have importance for the understanding of its dynamics, but it also employs different chords found within my own voice. My narrative can shift unwittingly from a fully involved and enthused participant to one that subtly distances myself to reflect on other perspectives. At times my voice as a detached social scientist blends with that of an activist seeking to redress an injustice or to question whether the emperor has clothes. My voice reporting the stories and statistics of others can shift to one that self-discloses a personal narrative.

In sum my voice is one that reflects both my charismatic Christianity and my training as a sociologist to weave together a coherent tale. Like other charismatic Christian scientists studied by anthropologist Karla Poewe, I have tried to "put together what was parallel and separate so that science and religion came to sit on the same foundation" (Poewe 1994, 254). As Poewe has observed, the sense of the numinous has been gutted from the scientific perspective (even from the social science of religion), and it is a sense of the numinous that the charismatic scholars she studied sought to put back into accounts of reality. One of Poewe's scientists expressed it well in saying:

> To experience a *holy* God is the most important thing about charismatic Christianity, that and its internationalism. A holy God is not one who lacks color, lives in the dust of empiricism, or in the sterile sentence of a biblical scholar. Experiencing God is an actual experience—it's an experience I see in color, I hear in sound, and I feel in touch." (Poewe 1994, 250)

The variety of voices (especially those that I claim as my own) seeking to express personal experiences and then to create meaning out of the revival became more evident as I reread the hundreds of pages of field notes one last time in preparation for this concluding chapter. What follows is an exercise in personal reflexivity intertwined with observations from pilgrims and leaders on North America's alleged "longest revival."

THE VOICE OF A PILGRIM

My first visit to Toronto in late November 1994 is best described as a personal pilgrimage rather than a quest for a research project. Although I had heard about the events in Toronto earlier in the summer (and even visited Toronto on a holiday), I made no effort to seek out the rumored "renewal" (as it was then known). It was a session with a professional counselor that became the spark for what I believe was a "divine invitation" to visit the revival site at the Toronto Airport Vineyard (TAV). The therapist asked a seemingly simple question about whether I could say without reservation that I loved myself—a question that I regarded as irrelevant to my personal problem. After providing what I thought was a healthy response to defend my reluctance to engage in "navel gazing," the therapist retorted, "You seem to be a person of prayer. Why don't you pray about this question? I am sure you will come up with something."

As I sought divine direction the following week, I was challenged by what I was intuitively "hearing." The voice within seemed to be saying, "You are very hard on yourself—and you are hard on other people. It is important that you learn to love yourself if you are to do a better job in loving others. The reason you don't know how to love yourself is because you have no idea how much I love you." Then the voice became silent leaving me to wait for the confirmation and invitation.

Later in that week I paid a visit to St. Luke's Episcopal Church in Akron, a charismatic congregation that I would visit from time to time. During the service the officiating priests, who I quickly learned had just returned from the first "Catch the Fire" conference at TAV, had set aside the lectionary readings for the day and focused on Eph. 3:14–19 NIV that reads:

> For this reason I kneel before the Father, from whom his whole family in heaven and on earth derives its name. I pray that out of his glorious riches he . . . may dwell in your hearts through faith. And I pray that you, being rooted and established in love, may have power, together with all the saints, to grasp how wide and

long and high and deep is the love of Christ, and to know this love that surpasses knowledge—that you may be filled to the measure of all the fullness of God.

The text, they said, recapitulated the message of the revival—a message of knowing the "heights and depths" of the love of God. I stood there in dismay, as if I were hearing this familiar biblical passage for the first time!

While some might attribute this encounter to coincidence and others to Jungean synchronicity, I felt it was a divine invitation to visit the revival site to learn more about God's love. Within a couple of weeks, I was able to clear my calendar for a four-day trip to Toronto. My role during the November 1994 visit was that of a pilgrim (although one who took field notes and did some informal interviewing). I was unable to return for a second visit until mid-February 1995. During this two-month interlude I watched as a local revival took off at St. Luke's Episcopal Church where I became a member. Still maintaining the stance of a pilgrim, I returned to TAV where once again I heard a fresh message of God's love and desire for human intimacy.

Byron and Jan Mote from the Dallas area (see narrative in the prelude) were the primary speakers. I was particularly moved by a revelatory prayer word given by Byron as I stood in line with hundreds of other unknown pilgrims: "Lord, may her heart inform her head." By this time I was beginning to think about doing research on the revival, wondering how I would be able to retain the heart of a pilgrim and the head of a trained researcher simultaneously. (When I approached Byron the next day in the cafeteria and reminded him of his prayer, he replied, "So you are the one. I have never prayed that prayer with anyone before.") It was during this visit that I introduced myself to one of the renewal pastors, Val Dodd, and asked him to serve as a liaison for meeting John Arnott during my next visit. The call to do research seemed to intensify.

VOICE OF A PILGRIM RESEARCHER

I made my third trip to the revival at the end of March 1995 where I met with Arnott, pastor of TAV, for the first time. Although I had seen Arnott on the church platform during my November visit, I did not recognize him among the nameless and faceless people who often went without introductions during the services. (Arnott was out of town during the February visit.) On March 30 I broached the possibility of doing a survey of TAV visitors with Arnott. After listening to my credentials and my thoughts, he responded,

"What can we do to help you?" I soon began to prepare a questionnaire, to which Arnott gave his approval during another visit in early May. Slowly, while still retaining the stance of a pilgrim, I became what John Arnott termed the "fruit inspector" for the Blessing.

My earlier research on the P/C movement and later on the Assemblies of God had used a Weberian perspective during which I looked at the tendency of charisma to routinize within the movement. Using the same frame of Thomas O'Dea's application of Weberian theory to the "institutional dilemmas," I assessed the Blessing as being in its "charismatic moment" in the first paper I presented on Toronto at Orlando '95, Congress on the Holy Spirit and World Evangelism in July (Poloma 1995a). The revival was excitingly fresh, and I concluded the presentation with the following statement:

> Charisma, despite its problems, is still welcome at TAV as well as at other renewal sites that have developed around the world. The practices discussed in this paper have made TAV and TAV-like settings a suitable home for this "gift of grace." Whether the wind keeps blowing, however, is beyond the power of the TAV leaders. True charisma remains a fragile and illusive gift that cannot be manufactured. Once given, however, it can be either nurtured or stifled by institutional norms and structures. How long Toronto Airport Vineyard and other benefactors of the Toronto Blessing are able to stay the forces of institutionalization remains to be seen. (pp. 36–37)

The paper was required reading for those on TAV's pastoral staff.

By the time I revised the article for publication in the *Journal for the Scientific Study of Religion* in 1996, TAV had been dismissed from the Association of Vineyard Churches (AVC) and the Blessing seemed to be entering a new stage. The published paper noted (largely through footnotes) some of the changes I was observing, and the conclusion was revised. I added the following:

> At the same time, the Toronto Blessing has moved through the early stages recognized for the natural history of a social movement, quickly progressing from incipiency, coalescence, and now taking organizational form (Blumer 1974; Mauss 1975; Tilly 1978). As has been demonstrated time and again, the charisma that animates a social movement tends to decrease with successful institutionalization. The inevitable tensions between charisma and institutionalization are usually resolved through social mechanisms to the detriment of the

early charismatic flow. Whether the newly emerging institutional form is in fact
an unprecedented "flexible wineskin to hold the new wine," as its leaders claim,
or whether it, in fact, signals the demise of the Toronto Blessing, as suggested by
O'Dea's theory, remains to be seen. (Poloma 1997, p. 269)

I visited TAV a total of nine times during 1995, averaging four days for each
visit. In addition, I regularly attended St. Luke's Church and paid periodic visits to Church of the King (COTK) in an east suburb of Cleveland where the
revival happenings were as intense as those I observed in Toronto. There was
also a revival going on at an independent church very near my home in Akron
led by an itinerant minister from Arkansas, John Rowe. Rowe's style often reminded me of a stand-up comedian who seemed to focus on his ongoing experiences, a stance with which I became increasingly uncomfortable.[1] The
service looked very much like those at TAV, and many who attended the services were testifying to being moved experientially in ways very similar to the
Toronto reports. I visited Gloryland Chapel of Praise in Stow, Ohio, about a
dozen times over the two years of Rowe's ministry at this small church.[2]

I also visited a revival in Melbourne, Florida, that began when Randy Clark
first ministered at The Tabernacle in January 1995. Despite all the talk about
the Melbourne revival, by the time I arrived in late July (six months after its
well-publicized beginnings), the revival had crested. It apparently took more
than media coverage, visiting evangelists, a local interdenominational network of pastors, and a well-developed organization to keep the fire falling.

By the end of 1995 I recognized that I was watching the river of revival
quickly pass through the life stages delineated by scholars of social movements,
from inchoate social action and religious agitation to some degree of legitima-
tion, routinization, and beaucratization. It was also apparent that although the
revival fires were passed on to many local churches, few outside Toronto would
be able to sustain ongoing revival meetings beyond a few months.

As an ethnographer of the movement, I usually tried to stand back to observe, although I continued to allow myself to experience renewal refreshing
as it came my way, especially through prayer and prophecy. I also began to
permit myself to be used as a conduit for passing the Blessing on to others. I
joined the prayer teams at St. Luke's and then at the Toronto Airport Christian Fellowship (TACF), accepted some speaking engagements at colleges and
universities to present my 1995 survey results, and even served as a speaker for

a few renewal meetings and conferences. Having taken early retirement and accepted emeritus status from the University of Akron and not being con-strained by the stipulations of a research grant, I was free to test the revival waters for roles that went beyond pure research. I followed the Spirit as I per-ceived the Spirit leading and at times became an active voice for the revival.

As Davies notes in the quotation used to open this chapter, however, an ex-ercise in "critical reflexivity" is not simply about the researcher. Critical reflex-ivity is more importantly an important medium for understanding how social reality is created and recreated in the articles and monographs reporting research findings. Paradoxically, the researcher is not only an observer but can be involved as a player in the drama through which this social reality unfolds.

ACTIVE PARTICIPATION IN A TIME OF TRANSITION

TAV had successfully made the move from its small rented facilities to a much larger center to accommodate the influx of pilgrims by early 1995. It was not long, however, before clouds of dissention that had been gathering within the AVC around the Toronto Blessing grew darker and more ominous. The charges were often nebulous (lacking "Vineyard values" or a failure to "man-age" the renewal) or seemingly trite (arranging for catchers to assist those who "fell" to the ground during prayer). The straw that broke the proverbial camel's back was a chapter Arnott wrote for a book published in late 1995 that included a chapter on the controversial animal sounds. Although John Wim-ber had written an endorsement for the manuscript, admittedly he had not read it. Overwhelmed by his own illness and the terminal illness of his eldest son, Wimber seemed not to be in a frame of mind for dialogue or due process in handling difficulties that accompanied a controversial revival.

It was during a site visit to TAV in late November 1995 (with preliminary survey results still coming in) that Arnott asked me to write a letter to Wimber about the "fruits" of the Blessing. My first thoughts were not about how it might affect the data or my reputation, but a concern that a breach between AVC and TAV would negatively influence the future of the revival. On Novem-ber 27 I sent a four-page statement to Wimber that included the assessment of four major issues that I gleaned from critical comments Wimber had written about TAV: a failure to mirror the "Vineyard model," TAV's alleged overem-phasis on questionable religious experiences, the danger of developing a theol-ogy of manifestations, and the charge that TAV was promoting itself as a model for "doing church." I accompanied this statement with a letter introducing my-self, my research, and some preliminary findings from the 1995 survey.

The letter and its accompanying statement had little or no impact on the outcome of the controversy. Wimber arrived at TAV a week later to pronounce that he had not come to "discuss" but to "announce" that the ties between TAV and AVC were severed. Although nationally known P/C leaders attempted to repair the breach, Wimber reportedly refused to converse with them.[3] I arrived for a site visit just after the AVC team had departed from Toronto. I could sense—and personally share—the shock and the pain felt by many at TAV. When I returned home several days later, I decided to mail my letter to Wim-ber (including the preliminary survey findings) and some of my most recent observations at TAV on the New Wine list serve. Part of the letter (December 18, 1995) read:

> I had the privilege of spending the last five days at the Toronto Airport Vine-yard. I felt heaviness upon my arrival on Wednesday after having just learned of the breakdown of discussions between TAV and AVC. I left on Sunday afternoon with a sense of deep peace after listening to John Arnott's sermon and then talk-ing with him after the service.
>
> As many of you know, TAV's mission statement (found on a banner in the back of the auditorium) is simple but profound: "That we may walk in God's love and then give it away." As John A. shared with his people yesterday, "We are about to write our final exam on that theme. And I am going to pass. Fortu-nately, all 'passing' *this* exam requires is making a decision. I made a decision to love."
>
> John continued, "We have been wronged and misunderstood. On the other hand, we have done the same to others in different situations. Only one thing works—forgiveness. I want mercy to triumph over justice!" Then he went on to say, "If you want to escape justice, move into mercy. . . . Mercy and justice meet at the cross."

There are times when truth and friendship are more important than silence in the name of scientific neutrality, even for seasoned researchers.[4]

Despite the care taken not to denigrate the AVC, there was no question that January 1996, two years after the Blessing first began, marked a time of transition and new beginnings. The Toronto Airport Vineyard now became the Toronto Airport Christian Fellowship (Beverley 1996). Being freed from the AVC constraints opened the doors for new voices and agendas to find a hearing from the renewal platform. While the basic message of the TACF renewal always seemed to play somewhere in the background, the revival showed signs of floundering.[5]

I paid fewer visits to TACF in 1996 (January, May, October, and December) than I had in 1995. I was able, however, to visit other renewal sites throughout the nation and to focus more on local revivals. Given an extended stay in Southern California, I had the opportunity to begin systematic observations of Harvest Rock Church (HRC) in Pasadena (see chapter 7), a church birthed out of the Toronto Blessing. In 1997 I made only two visits to TACF, with more of my research efforts being devoted to local revivals, including HRC and the revivals in northeastern Ohio (including St. Luke's Episcopal Church and Metro Church South—see chapter 8).

REVIVALS, REVIVALS, REVIVALS

With the rise of the revival at Brownsville Assembly of God (BAOG) in Pensacola, Florida, on Father's Day, 1995, TACF had a major competitor. Touted by some as the "real revival" because of the number of alleged conversions that occurred during each of the nightly services, this new site provided for a revival in dress that was different from that of TACF.[6] In March 1996 the Smithton Revival, sparked by Pastor Steve Gray's experience at the BAOG meetings, broke out in a small town of some five hundred people in rural Missouri, bringing yet another major player and model to the revival forum.[7]

In visiting these and other revival sites, I experienced firsthand the different voices that could be heard in different streams of the renewal—ones that could not help but influence TACF. My own affinity was toward the laid-back voices and positive message often given by nameless and faceless preachers about the love and mercy of God that characterized the earliest revival days. It was hard for me personally to enter into the revival drama when confronted with evangelists whose preaching seemed to manipulate the audience with hellfire and damnation, ushers who were overbearing and controlling in enforcing preset rules, or intrusive "pray-ers" who were loud and "in your face" (with all that can bring!). I personally was and remain much more comfortable with Arnott's pastoral and equipping style that often had him moving to the side of the performance than the evangelical model with its well-recognized leaders playing the major roles in the revival drama.[8]

In all this, the sociologist that I am knew that revivals (including TACF's) were socially constructed—and I clearly had my preferences. As I wrote in my field notes during this period:

It is interesting for me to reflect on how history is being made by those computer technicians who had the savvy to use e-mail to link early renewal junkies together. The Internet provided a forum for daily proclamations about new revival sites and experiences. Smithton's self-promotion through advertisements in *Charisma* magazine is also an interesting departure from TACF and BAOG. There are plenty of places where the revival flows quietly for a least a short while, aside from those who are using/have used marketing tools to self-promote. Some of the places that the Risses (Richard and Kathryn) mentioned in their history of the revival may not be significant a few years from now. I have already seen some that were blips on the screen, making the screen only because someone knew how to effectively market something which occurred at that site.

Many whom I knew personally began backing away from the renewal, saying that it had run its course. Magazine articles and Internet postings seemed to be raising similar concerns. The headline for an August 1998 article in *Charisma* magazine read "When the Fire Fizzles," and its author writes:

It has become common practice lately for pastors to "import" revival from such places as Toronto and Pensacola, Florida. The hope is to reignite bored congregations and flagging enthusiasm for ministry. We seem to be asking: How do I and my congregation get fired-up again? We might better ask: How do we press on to spiritual maturity when the fire fizzles? (Hazard 1998, 82)

A few months later, *IRN News*, a popular electronic source of revival information, attempted to refute claims that the "renewal is going nowhere" with a message from Tony Black:

It's sad to see even a small minority of folk citicising what God is doing today. Comments range from it being too noisy in Church, and often about people falling over (known as "slain in the Spirit") or about groaning noises (of intercession). The most common complaint, surprisingly, seems to be based around its being too "inward looking and going nowhere." We need to refute that :o). If you have belonged to IRN for long, you may have seen—and will continue to see—a progression. From times of refreshing to times of serving. "Freely you have received, therefore freely give." Nothing to give? Then God says to you the same thing He's been saying to the Renewal Churches—"don't GO before you do—and especially not without the Power of my Presence!!" That's what it's all about—equipping FOR service. Like the camel (a picture I like)—it takes a huge drink, then bears its burden of goodies to a destination, then comes back for another drink. (main@revivalnet.net; October 5, 1998)

Black sent another message through the Internet waves in January 1999, relaying a vision and urging people to "Come Back to the River." It began with:

I received a vision of many people clambering out of a river, partially dressed and looking very tired. The impression I got was that the river had slowed and they thought it must be time to get out—and get busy. But I felt a deep sense of sadness, as they had not gone far enough. I also sensed that they were in real danger. (main@revivalnet.net; October 5, 1998)

In the vision Black also saw the mocking critics who had never been in the river on a road "going nowhere." Finally, he was shown people who had rounded the bend in the river and "died" but came back to life as they lay in the warmth of the sun. He concludes:

If the people had stayed in the river just a bit longer it would have carried them right to the spot where they needed to be—i.e. a full process of going with the flow, into death, then resurrection and then, importantly, a Sabbath rest. Instead some were leaving the river and taking things back into their own control. (main@revivalnet.net; October 5, 1998)

The message imparted through the vision was one that was heard many times over the years from different voices and in diverse revival situations, with God calling the reader "back to the river" for what was yet to come (main@revivalnet.net; October 5, 1998).

Melinda Fish, editor of *Spread the Fire*, undoubtedly speaks for many who deny the revival had ended. In an editorial that deals with the question of how long the renewal will last, Fish (2001, 2) writes:

I believe that God has chosen "the River" as a metaphor for this revival because rivers never end; they just keep flowing. Navigating a river sometimes means floating through a season where not much new seems to be happening, but then reaching a confluence [*sic*] and the River is still the River, but it's flowed into another even wider body of water. What you have been flowing in suddenly brings you into a new dimension without leaving the old behind.

After seeing the Toronto outpouring continue for eight years, I'm now convinced that the notion that a revival should be temporary is a traditional myth in the Church, and it's the number one revival quencher. I used to be infected with this belief that God would invade our lives with a burst of supernatural power once every ten years or so. The rest of the time we would be condemned to an unending cycle of religious boredom, "doing church" without the power of His presence. I call it "cyclical cessationism."

DANCING BETWEEN INVOLVEMENT AND DETACHMENT

Powdermaker (1966, 19) has suggested that participant observation requires both involvement and detachment achieved by "stepping in and out of society." As the years of revival moved along, my sense of being a child with her nose pressed against a window as she watched others enjoying the party seemed to intensify!

After being heavily involved in the Blessing during 1995, I found myself stepping back as it moved into a period (1996–2000) Hilborn (2001, 281) has labeled "decline and transmutation." Despite ongoing reports of new revival hot spots, exciting and stimulating new conferences, new revival leaders, and reports of phenomenal miracles from overseas, the Toronto Blessing seemed to be floundering as it sought to redefine itself in a post-Vineyard milieu. As I stepped back from the insider voices, I recognized that the revival in North America had a limited market—and the market was saturated with new competitors. None of the revival voices seemed to be able to speak effectively to mainline churches as the Charismatic movement had done in the 1970s, and most classical Pentecostals appeared wary of revival—even when it occurred in churches of their own denominations. The market seemed to be primarily composed of and led by those involved in independent charismatic/third-wave streams of the larger P/C movement.

Even TACF's own publication began to raise questions about the future of the renewal/revival. In mid-1996 an issue of *Spread the Fire* had as its theme "Are We in Renewal or Revival?" (August 1996). Seemingly recognizing that the renewal had failed to meet some expectations, various contributors were attempting to provide meaning and promises for the future. "Using the term 'renewal,'" wrote then editor Daina Doucet, "resulted in unfortunate consequences because it has meant that people have attempted to shape what God is doing into their own conception of what should happen during revival rather than simply allowing God to do what He has always done in times past during outpourings of the Spirit" (Doucet 1996, 4). Church historian Richard Riss (1996, 19) addressed the issue of "revival or renewal" with a similar caution: "By calling the current out-pouring only 'renewal' and looking for something better called 'revival,' we de-value what God is doing now, preferring our own expectations."

Despite the seeming confusion and chaos of the earliest months of the Blessing, a clear message could be heard—a simple message of God's love. This clear message was in danger of being eclipsed by voices from other sectors of the renewal, some of which reflected well what the Harvard theologian Harvey Cox (1995, 281) has dubbed "body snatchers and spiritual warriors" in his description of American Pentecostalism. In part a search for liturgical forms, in part a response to criticism of its simple theology, and in part a search for "fresh fire," spiritual warring, breaking strongholds of the devil, and imaginary swords had the bride of earlier renewal imagery now wearing combat boots. (See also the discussion of the "waves of revival" found in chapter 6.)

I was aware of my personal dissatisfaction and disappointment with what the British have dubbed "happy-clappy Christianity" now with a superim-posed warlike dimension but was also acutely aware that what I was seeing, hearing, and experiencing was partial and one-dimensional. To confuse mat-ters further, there were times when in the midst of renewal boredom, the Spirit seemed to come from nowhere to inexplicably refresh me! Reflecting on my personal vacillation as a barometer to predict the revival's course or gaug-ing its intensity with personal emotions and preferences was not acceptable ethnography. It seemed that another more "objective" source of information was needed.

I approached Arnott about doing a follow-up survey of 1995 respondents in 1997 to measure once again the pulse of the movement, and he agreed to sponsor the survey. The results spoke to my concerns but also demonstrated a common conviction that more blessings were on their way. The following is a summary of some of the relevant findings that would support the sense of ambiguity that I was experiencing:

A majority of those who answered the follow-up survey are still "swimming in the river," to use a popular renewal metaphor, but there does not seem to be a unified vision about where the river is taking them. Fifty-six percent (56%) of the respondents disagreed with the statement that the "power (of the renewal) seems weaker than it once was" (with 44 percent either agreeing or having no opinion). Respondents were nearly evenly divided as to whether the renewal had "impacted the larger church" in their country, with 51 percent responding affirmatively and 49 percent having either no opinion or giving a negative response. They are also nearly evenly divided about the role the critics have played to alter the course of the revival. Forty-five percent (45%) expressed the opinion that "the critics have played a significant role in preventing the spread of the renewal," while 55 percent disagreed or had no opinion. At the same time, few respondents (9%) agreed that the season of the renewal "appears to be over." The vast majority (82%) professed an unreserved hope that the best was yet to come. (Poloma 1998a, 43–70)

Despite the basically optimistic report produced by the 1997 follow-up, differences of opinion were clearly reflected in the data. Furthermore, I knew I was dealing with only those respondents who were willing to respond to the second questionnaire. Beyond the survey, it appeared that the Blessing was a kind of revolving door for many pilgrims. A sea of new faces replaced the familiar faces of old pilgrims both at TACF and at local conferences by the end of the millennium.

AFTERGLOW OR ANOTHER WAVE?

Charisma magazine titled its (December) 1998 article "Toronto's Afterglow," reflecting a common perspective that the embers were still burning but the intense revival fires may have died down. The article acknowledged that despite the setbacks experienced by TACF due to its forced separation from the Vineyard, TACF's nightly renewal meetings were still being held, "mostly for out-of-town visitors." The author concludes by saying: "Almost five years and more than 1,500 renewal services later, there are still millions of people within driving distance of Toronto who haven't been touched by the Blessing. They need to know that this wild, undignified revival isn't over yet. In fact, the party is just getting started (Grady 1998, 123)."

Many who continued to swim in the revival waters, however, would assert that the party never stopped. In addition to the local revivals that continued to spring up (and usually quickly die down) across North America, BAOG (1995) and Smithton (1996) joined TACF special pilgrimage sites that persisted into the new millennium. At times a new evangelist would appear from seemingly nowhere to ignite the fire again. One of the best known of the evangelists to emerge during this stage of the renewal was Tommy Tenney, an itinerant preacher who longed to see what old fashioned Pentecostals called the glory in his services. Tenney catapulted to fame when the glory fell as he was serving as a guest speaker in Houston's Christian Tabernacle on October 20, 1996:

> Guest speaker Tommy Tenney and pastor Richard Heard were standing on the stage when a loud cracking sound jolted the audience. At the same instant the church's acrylic pulpit split in half and fell on the carpet with a thud.
>
> It was a moment of holy terror. Heard fell back several feet, and people in the audience rushed to the altar or lay prostrate in the aisles when they realized that nobody had touched the pulpit. It was as if an invisible lightning bold had come from heaven. The atmosphere became electric as people wept and worshipped. Tenney says the experience ruined him forever. (Grady 2000, 54)

Almost overnight Tenney became a coveted revival conference speaker and a household name in revival circles.[9] Tenney's challenge to become a devout "God seeker" seemed to be a fresh call for deeper and more intense experiences of God that resonated with those in the revival river.

The year 1996 also brought a pilgrim to TACF seeking a deeper experience of God who was destined to add a neglected dimension to the revival and to raise the expectations of followers as the revival moved toward the millennium. As discussed in the previous chapter, seeing the change that an extended visit to TACF in late 1995 made in the life of her husband, Rolland, Heidi Baker embarked on her pilgrimage to Toronto in August 1996. Her expectations for a powerful encounter with the divine were met. As *Charisma* magazine reported: "As she lay under the power of God, Heidi says that she saw Jesus' face and broken body and looked into His eyes which she described as 'fiery eyes of love.' It was an experience that created an awareness in her of her own need for brokenness" (Flinchbaugh 2000, 78).

During the next year and a half, Heidi and Rolland Baker experienced one crisis after another after their return to the mission field in Mozambique (see chapter 9). In January 1998 they came once again to TACF (her second and his third visit) during which Heidi Baker experienced what she called "the fire of God" while Randy Clark, the minister who was used to launch the Blessing in 1994, was preaching. *Charisma* reports: "Clark prophesied that there would be an apostolic anointing over Heidi, declaring she would see the dead raised, the blind healed, miracles performed and many churches started in Mozambique.

Clark then prophesied that God was going to give her the nation of Mozambique" (Flinchbaugh 2000, 82). Heidi, who was "under the power of the Spirit" for almost all of her time during the 1998 visit, was on her way to becoming a fresh voice in the revival.[10]

Problems continued when the Bakers returned to Mozambique, including Heidi Baker's being diagnosed with multiple sclerosis (from which she has since been reportedly healed). Clark's prophecy began to unfold, however, as the Bakers saw hundreds and then thousands of churches planted under their ministry in that poor African country. Revival seems to be going on unabated in their ministry, and it is now the Bakers who are ushering in a fresh message of God's love, power, and faithfulness for the larger movement.[11]

The Toronto Blessing made the headlines again in 2000 with the so-called Golden Revival that spread through many P/C churches at the turn of the millennium (see chapter 6). Most churches that were still "in the river" seemed to be reporting being touched by the gold phenomenon in one fashion or another. It was during that time that the pastor of a small local church in Barberton (just outside of Akron) made his first trip to Toronto. On Mike Guarnieri's return from TACF, he immediately saw a rash of gold fillings reported by those who came to his church. It was the beginning of an ongoing revival at Grace Fellowship Assembly of God. In a recent phone conversation (February 17, 2003) with Guarnieri, he reminded me how his church had been prepared prophetically before he went to TACF with the prophecy that there was "a new way of doing church" that they had not yet experienced. Now known as the Father's House, the church appears to still be in its charismatic moment as it prepares to move into larger facilities and continues to host revival meetings. Although admitting that his church may have come into the revival on the "last crest of the wave," Guarnieri informed me that the church continues two and a half years after his visit to TACF to see the physical manifestations characteristic of this revival and also a decided upturn in physical healings. (Even the gold flakes recently appeared during a Sunday morning service.) An important key to maintaining a revival, Guarnieri believes, is a willingness of the pastor "to lay down control and reputation" and to permit God to have his way.

Whether revival or afterglow, unusual phenomena persist in Toronto and continue to influence many local churches. TACF still holds nightly renewal meetings (except for Monday nights) and to host revival conferences both at TACF and at other locations. It has an itinerant team that goes out to spark new revival fires and to fan the flames of dying embers in local churches around the globe, as well as a daily television program to spread the renewal. Its conferences at TACF continue to draw first-time visitors at a fairly steady rate of two return visitors to one newcomer.

Reflections written while I attended the The Father Loves You conference at TACF on May 10, 2002, serve as a preface to the revised a monograph I wrote to disseminate the statistics of the two surveys.[12] They include the following autobiographical statement (Poloma 2003):

> Over seven years have passed since I first visited the little church in a nondescript strip mall where the revival in Toronto was birthed. It has been nearly as long since I collected the first wave of survey data in 1995, and five years since I collected the follow-up data and wrote the report on the two survey waves. . . . Although 2002 marks three years since my last visit to TACF, I have remained in close contact with many of the tributaries of the revival river, especially in the Cleveland/Akron/Canton area of Northeastern Ohio. I have been and continue to be personally refreshed by my participation in Shiloh Church in North Canton, Ohio, where the Blessing has been richly manifested for nearly six years. My research, reading and personal experiences have led me to various other tributaries and streams of the river of revival, including Pasadena's Harvest Rock Church, Brownsville Assembly of God in Pensacola, and the Smithton Outpouring. Some of the streams continue to flow with a mighty force, others seem to have changed direction, and still others seem to have dried up. I have seen some tributaries merge with the larger river and new ones spring from the refreshing waters of revival. *Despite such changes, the message of God's love at TACF remains constant.* (Poloma 2003)

SUMMARY AND CONCLUSION

"Investigators do not have direct access to another's experience. We deal with ambiguous representations of it—talk, text, interaction, and interpretation. It is not possible to be neutral and objective, to merely represent (as opposed to interpret) the world" (Riessman 1993, 8). Despite my best attempts to employ what Taves terms a "mediating position," I am well aware of the controversies that can arise for one in traveling this road. First, it is impossible to present a neutral and objective account of a revival. I have chosen to present the events of the revival as straightforward as possible rather than to shroud them with obtuse theories that would remove the reader even further from the experiences being described. I recognize that what I have presented is one portrait of an involved ethnographer. Because I have submitted my analysis to others involved in the revival—especially those whose extended narratives I shared in the second part of the book—I feel confident, however, that what I have written is far more than a personal account.

Speaking as an involved ethnographer was my choice of voice from among any number of other theoretical and methodological voices I might have taken. As an involved ethnographer, I am aware of how incomplete any single book on this worldwide revival is bound to be. For one the focus is on North America, particularly on how a Canadian revival influenced the P/C movement in sections of the United States. Another story needs to be told to demonstrate its impact on global Christianity. If Philip Jenkins is correct in his assessment of *The Next Christendom,* what has been happening in North America is but a pale reflection of the revivals underway in Africa, Asia, and Latin America. The worldview discussed in these pages is much of the reason why the P/C movement is the fastest growing sector of global Christianity.

Finally, there were many other narratives from other voices reflecting outbreaks of revival and development of ministries in areas that have not been discussed here. I am reminded of the Apostle John (21:25) when he wrote at the end of his gospel: "Jesus did many other things as well. If every one of them were written down, I suppose that even the whole world would not have room for books that would be written." According to the P/C worldview, the Spirit of Jesus is still actively working, and no single book—no single account—could adequately capture all that is transpiring. The Kingdom of God, while *within* and *among* the followers of Jesus, is also still *unfolding.* The Toronto Blessing is but one wave in a sequence of revival waves that have periodically swept over Christianity. Whether the promised new waves come through Toronto or develop elsewhere, revival history seems to suggest that they will come—for Pentecostalism and its derivatives are in constant need of revitalization for a retention of its distinctive identity.

NOTES

1. Rowe also seemed somewhat uncomfortable with my presence, something I had not experienced at any of the other research sites over my years in the field. As I often do, I was taking notes during the meeting while Rowe was seemingly "drunk in the Spirit." At one point he stopped and asked what I was doing. I replied that I was taking notes, and he laughed saying "What are you writing? No one can make sense out of what I am saying in these meetings." He then decided it was time to pray for me so that I, too, might receive the Spirit. The congregation watched as Rowe came over and laid hands on me. I adopted my "receiving" mode, eyes closed, and hands outstretched, although I felt nothing spiritually. After a short time, Rowe began proclaiming that I was "receiving" and then "she has received." I went back to my observation and note taking while Rowe went back to his revival theatrics, permitting both of us to save face.

2. In July 1995, the *Akron Beacon Journal* published an article from the *Dallas Morning News* on revival under the heading "Spiritual Happy Hour" (Soto 1995). Printed beneath the heading was a box with information about Gloryland Chapel of Praise's "Holy Laughter" services with John Rowe. It was after he moved to northeastern Ohio from Arkansas in 1996 that Rowe reported being given the mandate to open healing rooms in the greater Cleveland area. He died of colon cancer before that vision became a reality, but Rowe remains a name in the history of the Healing Rooms of Greater Cleveland. Jim White (see chapter 8) never met Rowe but he and others believe that White has inherited Rowe's vision and mantle for healing rooms.

3. I first learned of the ouster, as did many, through an e-mail message sent by revival historian Richard Riss (on his initiative) to those on his revival list serve (December 6, 1995). The subject line read "TAV Expelled from AVC." Attached was a message Riss had sent to Arnott shortly before the infamous meeting with Wimber in which he notes that such separations are often the usual course in revival history.

4. On February 13, 1996, while on a teaching assignment in Southern California, I met with John Wimber (at his response to an invitation I made in the November letter) and two of his staff (Todd Hunter and Robert Fulton) to discuss the action TAV took against the Toronto Church. It was apparent that Wimber lacked firsthand experience with the Toronto revival. He seemed tired and relieved that the old TAV and AVC split was behind him.

5. At least one of my inside informants during an interview on December 17, 1995, speculated that the schism would not make much difference to the revival. He noted in an interview that although no one seemed to know exactly why, the nightly meetings seem to have lost much of their character even before the rift occurred. Although conferences were often filled to capacity, the nightly meetings dropped in size to a couple hundred people. Some are questioning, he reported, whether the anointing had lifted.

6. The differences in style between TACF and Brownsville Assembly of God (BAOG) are discussed at length in Poloma (1998). Although BAOG was packaged in a southern Pentecostal rather than third-wave Vineyard dress, the experiential essence of the two revivals seemed remarkably similar. This is not surprising given common Argentine ties and the fact that major players in the BAOG revival were "touched" directly at TACF or indirectly through TACF-sparked ministries in the United Kingdom.

7. In March 2001 the Smithton church moved to Kansas City where it is now known as the World Revival Church of Kansas City.

8. I have chosen to focus on the revival at TACF for my analysis, but it is worth noting some of the major differences I observed in the three best-known sites. *TACF,* as can be seen especially in chapter 4 dealing with healing, can be described as *clinical.* There is a disposition toward renewal and incorporating "mainline" Christianity with its therapeutic religious culture. Its message and style is laid-back, emphasizing God's love and mercy over judgment. *BAOG,* in comparison, was firmly planted in the Classical Pentecostal "southern revivalist" tradition with an emphasis on the singular individual conversion experience and a strong eschatological impulse. As noted by one anonymous Internet partner, "Many Assemblies of God members come for what might be considered a 'pilgrimage.' Overall, they come to watch others experience salvation. Many enjoy watching "those sinners come to Jesus." The *Smithton Outpouring*'s administration (now World Revival Church of Kansas City), structure, and focus seem firmly in the hands of the Pastor Steve Gray and his charismatic wife, Kathy. Its style is said to reflect the three major influences of the pastor, namely Wesleyan, Charismatic, and Pentecostal. Gray grew up in the Nazarene and United Methodist Churches, was saved during the Charismatic renewal, and ministered within AG churches. The ministry's most recent focus is on bringing "a revival of healing to the nations."

9. I first experienced Tenney's ministry at HRC in 1997 when he came to Pasadena reportedly in response to a perceived divine call. Tenney, who was already receiving more speaking engagements than he could fill, found himself free the weekend of HRC's annual "Catch the Fire" conference. Although he said he would have preferred to use the weekend to relax with his family, he believed God was telling him to go to Pasadena. As it would be, the prophet Paul Cain (see chapter 6), one of the major speakers to the conference, was unable to come, and Tenney was on site to take his place.

10. The reciprocal role that the revival in Mozambique is believed to play in a revitalization of the American revival was addressed in a prophetic message delivered by Marc Dupont and reproduced in *Spread the Fire*:

> The Lord says that just as the fire of Toronto went to the ends of the earth, and it went to Mozambique, so the fire of Mozambique is coming back to Toronto and it's going back again to the ends of the earth. . . .

The Lord says that He has chosen this little, insignificant church on the end of the run-way to start this revival to pour out His spirit, and that He has chosen the least, poorest and most desperate nation to pour out His spirit. There is a link and a bridge between the two. . . . God chooses the obscure, humble, out-of-the-way places and out-of-the-way people. . . . Now it's coming back again. (Dupont 2002, 21–23)

11. On November 14, 2001, Heidi Baker, reportedly under a divine mandate, came to minister for one evening at Grace Fellowship (The Father's House) in Barberton, Ohio. Pastor Mike Guarnieri described her as "one of the most anointed people we have ever encountered, and a true apostle to Africa." As she was the time I saw her at TACF, Heidi was "under the power of the Spirit," unable to give a coherent sermon. She sat on the floor praying and urging people not to look at her: "I have nothing to give; it is Him that you must seek."

12. "Fruits of the Father's Blessing: A Sociological Report" (2003) distributed by the resource center at TACF (www.tacf.org).

References

REFERENCES

Ahn, Ché. 1998. *Into the Fire*. Ventura, CA: Gospel Light.

———. 2000. "An Unexpected Fire." In *Experience the Blessing*. Edited by John Arnott, 214–23. Ventura, CA.: Renew.

Ahn, Ché, and Lou Engle. 2001. *The Call Revolution*. Colorado Springs, CO: Wagner Publications.

Albrecht, Daniel. 1999. *Rites in the Spirit. A Ritual Approach to Pentecostal/Charismatic Spirituality*. Sheffield, U.K.: Sheffield Academic Press.

Anderson, A. H., and W. J. Hollenweger. 1999. *Pentecostals after a Century: Global Perspectives on a Movement in Transition*. Sheffield, U.K.: Sheffield Academic Press.

Armstrong, Karen. 2000. *The Battle for God*. New York: Ballantine Books.

Arnott, John. 1995. *The Father's Blessing*. Orlando, FL: Creation House.

———. 1997. *The Importance of Forgiveness*. Kent, U.K.: Sovereign World.

———. 1998. "The Toronto Blessing: What Is It?" *Spread the Fire* (January) 4–5.

———. 1999. "When It All Began." *Spread the Fire* (February): 5–9.

———. 2000. "Overcoming Prophetic Pitfalls." *Charisma* 2: 4–7.

———. 2001a. "He Holds the Future." *Spread the Fire* 6: 3–5.

———. 2001b. "Living in Revival." *Spread the Fire* 5: 6–9.

———. 2003a. "The Leaven of the Kingdom." *Spread the Fire* 1: 5–7.

———. 2003b. "Soaking in His Presence." *Spread the Fire* 3: 5–7.

Austin, James. 1998. *Zen and the Brain: An Understanding of Meditation and Consciousness.* Cambridge, MA: MIT Press.

Bader, Chris. 1999. "When Prophecy Passes Unnoticed: New Perspectives on Failed Prophecy." *Journal for the Scientific Study of Religion* 38, no. 1: 110–31.

Baker, Bob. 1994. "Times of Refreshing." *Light the Fire Again. Live Worship.* Vineyard Music Group. Anaheim, CA. Compact disc.

Baker, Heidi. 2001. "Soaking in His Presence, Ministering to the Poor." *Spread the Fire.* 3: 17–19.

———. 2002. "Signs and Wonders" conference presented by Nehemiah Ministries, Kennesaw, Georgia, August 2, 2002.

Baker, Rolland, and Heidi Baker. 2000. "There Is Always Enough!" In *Experience the Blessing: Testimonies from Toronto.* Edited by John Arnott, 47–61. Ventura, CA: Renew (A Division of Gospel Light).

Barnes, D. J. 2002. "Brownesville Revival." In *The New International Dictionary of Pentecostal and Charismatic Movements.* Edited by Stanley M. Burgess, 445–47. Grand Rapids, MI: Zondervan.

Barrett, David. 1988. "The Twentieth-Century Pentecostal/Charismatic Renewal in the Holy Spirit, with Its Goal of World Evangelization." *International Bulletin of Missionary Research* 12, no. 3: 119–29.

Begley, Sharon. 2001. "God and the Brain. How We're Wired for Spirituality." *Newsweek* (May 7): 52–58.

Benson, Herbert. 1984. *Beyond the Relaxation Response.* New York: Times Books.

———. 1996. *Timeless Healing.* New York: Scribner.

Berger, Peter. 1970. *A Rumor of Angels.* Garden City, NJ: Anchor.

Beverley, James A. 1995. *Holy Laughter and the Toronto Blessing: An Investigative Report.* Grand Rapids, MI: Zondervan Publishing House.

———. 1996. "Vineyard Severs Ties with 'Toronto Blessing' Church." *Christianity Today* (January 8): 66.

———. 1997. *Revival Wars: A Critique of Counterfeit Revival.* Canada: Evangelical Research Ministries.

Bickle, Mike. 1996. "Here Comes the 'Big One.'" *Spread the Fire* (December): 9.

———. 1997. *Prophetic History of MVC.* Audiotape. Metro Christian Fellowship of Kansas City. PO Box 229. Grandview, MO.

———. 2000. *The Bride's Anthem.* Praying the Bible Series. PTB06. Compact disc.

Bickle, Mike, and Jim W. Goll. 1997. "Four Levels of Prophetic Ministry." In *Prophetic Maturation Ministry to the Nations.* Edited by J. W. Goll, 31–34. Antioch, TN.

Blumer, Herbert. 1974. "Social Movements." In *The Sociology of Dissent.* Edited by R. Serge Denisoff, 65–121. New York: Harcourt, Brace, Jovanovich.

Blumhofer, Edith L. 1993. *Restoring the Faith: The Assemblies of God, Pentecostalism, and American Culture.* Urbana: University of Illinois Press.

Bogart, Jon. 1997. "Blood n Fire." *Voice of the Vineyard.* Fall: 20–25.

Briggs, David. 2002. "At Intersection of Religion, Health." *The Canton Repository* (Reprinted from *The Cleveland Plain Dealer*), May 19.

Brookes, Adrian. 2002. "Howard-Brone Tells Australians It's No Time for 'Sunday Morning' Faith." *Charisma* (February): 19–20.

Bruce, Billy. 1999. "God, Give Us the City." *Charisma* (November): 69–75.

Bruner, Edward M. 1986. "Experience and Its Expression." In *The Anthropology of Experience.* Edited by Victor W. Turner and Edward M. Bruner, 3–32. Chicago: University of Illinois Press.

The Call Revolution. www.thecallrevolution.com [accessed April 2, 2003].

Campbell, Don. 1991. *Music Physician for Times to Come: An Anthology.* Wheaton, IL: Quest Books.

Campbell, Joseph. 1987. *The Masks of God: Primitive Mythology.* New York: Penguin Books.

Cartledge, Mark J. 2001. "Charismatic Women and Prophetic Activity." *The Spirit and Church* 3, no. 1: 97–111.

Chamberlain, Theodore J., and Christopher A. Hall. 2000. *Realized Religion.* Philadelphia, PA: The Templeton Foundation.

Chevreau, Guy. 1994. *Catch the Fire.* London: Marshall Pickering.

———. 2000. *We Dance Because We Cannot Fly. Stories of Redemption from Heroin to Hope.* London: Marshall Pickering.

Clark, Randy. 2001. "In the Beginning: The First Days of the Toronto Outpouring." *Spread the Fire* 1: 23–25.

———. 2002. "Signs and Wonders" conference presented by Nehemiah Ministries; Kennesaw, Georgia, August 2, 2002.

Cohn, Norman R. 1962. "Medieval Millenarianism: Its Bearing on the Comparative Study of Millenarian Movements." In *Millennial Dreams in Action: Essays in Comparative Study.* Edited by S. I. Thrupp. The Hague: Mouton.

Cooke, Graham. 1994. *Developing Your Prophetic Gifting.* Kent, U.K.: Sovereign Word.

Cox, Harvey. 1995. *Fire from Heaven.* Reading, MA: Addison-Wesley Publishing.

Crowe, Barbara J. 1991. "Music—The Ultimate Physician." In *Music Physician for Times to Come*, 111–20. Wheaton, IL: Quest Books.

Csikszentmihalyi, Mihaly. 1990. *Flow: The Psychology of Optimal Experience.* New York: Harper & Row.

Csordas, Thomas J. 1988. "Elements of Charismatic Persuasion and Healing." *Medical Anthropology Quarterly* 2: 121–42.

———. 1994. *The Sacred Self: A Cultural Phenomenology of Charismatic Healing.* Berkeley: University of California Press.

Cutting Edge Ministries. www.the-cutting-edge.org, 1999 [accessed April 2, 2003].

Daigle, Richard. 2002. "Saving Souls—12 by 12." *Atlanta Journal-Constitution* (November 30): B1–2.

Davies, Charlotte Aull. 1999. *Reflexive Ethnography.* New York: Routledge.

DeArteaga, William. 1992. *Quenching the Spirit: Examining Centuries of Opposition to the Moving of the Holy Spirit.* Lake Mary, FL: Creation House.

Deere, Jack. 1993. *Forward to Passion for Jesus by Mike Bickle.* Orlando, FL: Creation House.

Deikman, Arthur. 1982. *The Observing Self: Mysticism and Psychotherapy.* Boston: Beacon Press.

Dein, Simon. 2001. "What Really Happens When Prophecy Fails: The Case of Lubavitch." *Sociology of Religion* 62 (Fall): 383–401.

DeLoriea, Renee. 1997. *Portal in Pensacola.* Shippensburg, PA: Revival Press.

Dempster, Murray W. 1999. "Issues Facing Pentecostalism in a Postmodern World." In *The Globalization of Pentecostalism.* Edited by M. W. Dempster, B. D. Klaus, and D. Peterson, 261–67. Carlisle, CA.: Paternoster Publishing (Regnum).

Denzin, Norman, K. 1984. *On Understanding Emotion.* San Francisco: Jossey-Bass.

———. 1992. "Emotion as Lived Experience." In *The Cutting Edge: Advanced Interactionist Theory.* Edited by John Johnson, Harvey A. Farberman, and Gary Alan Fine, 303–19. Greenwich, CT: JAI Press.

DiSabatino, David. 1999. *The Jesus People Movement.* Westport, CT: Greenwood Press.

Doerksen, Brian. 1994. "Light the Fire Again." *Light the Fire Again. Live Worship.* Vineyard Music Group. Anaheim, CA. Compact disc.

Do It Again Lord. 1993. "Arms of Love." Toronto Airport Worship Team. Vineyard Christian Fellowship. Toronto Airport. Ontario, Canada. Compact disc.

Doucet, Daina. 1996. "Revival Now." *Spread the Fire* (August): 4–7.

Dupont, Mark. 1995. "Renewal Is Especially for the Western Churches." *Spread the Fire* (May/June): 22.

———. 1996. "The Next Wave." *Spread the Fire* (December): 4–8.

———. 1997. *The Church of the 3rd Millennium.* Shippensburg, PA: Revival Press.

———. 2000. "Real Prophecy Brings Faith, Not Fear." *Charisma* 2: 8–10.

———. 2002. "The Coming Release of the Glory of God." Prophesy through Marc Dupont, December 15, 2001 in Toronto. *Spread the Fire* 3: 21–23.

Durrand, Tom Craig, and Anson Shupe. 1983. *Metaphors of Social Control in a Pentecostal Sect.* New York: Edwin Mellen Press.

Ellwood, Robert S. 1999. *Mysticism and Religion.* New York: Seven Bridges Press.

Engle, Lou (with Catherine Paine). 1998. *Digging the Wells of Revival.* Shippensburg, PA: Revival Press.

Fernandez, James W. 1986. "The Argument of Images and the Experience of Returning to the Whole." In *The Anthropology of Experience.* Edited by Victor W. Turner and Edward M. Bruner, 159–87. Chicago: University of Illinois Press.

Festinger, L. H., H. W. Riecken, and S. Schacter. 1956. *When Prophecy Fails*. New York: Harper & Row.

Festival Generation. 1999. "I Could Sing of Your Love Forever." Worship Together, A Division of EMI Christian Music Group. Brentwood, TN. Compact disc.

Fish, Melinda. 1996. *The River Is Here*. Grand Rapids, MI: Chosen Books.

———. 1999. "The Oil and the Wine." *Spread the Fire* 4: 2.

———. 2000. "Fishes Find the River." In *Experience the Blessing*. Edited by John Arnott, 109–19. Ventura, CA: Renew (A Division of Gospel Light).

———. 2001. "How Long Will This Last." *Spread the Fire* 5: 2.

Flinchbaugh, C. Hope. 2000. "Floods of Love in Mozambique." *Charisma* (June): 72–84.

Frangipane, Francis. 2002. Cited in "HarvestNet Institute—Modeling a Cutting Edge Concept!" Harvest Times, PO Box 606094, Cleveland, OH: 1, 5.

Freeman, Walter. 2000. "The Neurological Role of Music in Social Bonding." In *The Origins of Music*. Edited by N. L. Wallin, B. Merker, and S. Brown, 411–24. Cambridge: The MIT Press.

Garzon, F. L., and L. Burkett, 2002. "Healing of Memories: Models, Research, Future Directions." *Journal of Psychology and Christianity* 21, no. 2: 42–49.

Geissmann, Thomas. 2000. "Gibson Songs and Human Music from an Evolutionary Perspective." In *The Origins of Music*. Edited by N. L.Wallin, B. Merker, and S. Brown, 103–24. Cambridge: The MIT Press.

Glik, D. C. 1990a. "Participation in Spiritual Healing, Religiosity, and Mental Health." *Sociological Inquiry* 60, no. 2: 157–76.

———. 1990b. "The Redefinition of the Situation: The Social Construction of Spiritual Healing Experiences." *Sociology of Health and Illness* 12, no. 2: 151–68.

Glock, Charles Y., and Rodney Stark. 1965. *Religion and Society in Tension*. Chicago: Rand McNally.

Goldingay, John. 2001. "Old Testament Prophecy Today." *The Spirit and the Church* 3, no. 1: 27–46.

Goll, Jim W. 2001. "Dial 911: A Prophetic Perspective on Recent Days." *Spread the Fire* 6: 23–24.

Gonzales, Mark. n.d. *Psalm Eighteen: The Warriors Psalm.* Berea, OH: Metro Church South.

Grady, J. Lee. 1998. "Toronto's Afterglow." *Charisma* (December): 70–78, 123.

———. 1999. "Silly Rumors, Crazy Fears." *Charisma* (December): 6.

———. 2000. "Who Is This 'God Chaser'?" *Charisma* (March): 54–55.

Green, J. C., J. L. Guth, C. E. Smidt, and L. A. Kellstedt. 1997. *Religion and Culture Wars.* Lanham, MD: Rowman and Littlefield Publishers.

Griffith, R. Marie. 1997. *God's Daughters. Evangelical Women and the Power of Submission.* Berkeley: The University of California Press.

Hamon, Bill. 1997. *Apostles, Prophets and the Coming Moves of God.* Santa Rosa Beach, FL: Christian International.

HarvestNet Institute. www.harvestnet.net, April 3, 2003 [accessed April 3, 2003].

Harvest Rock Church. www.harvestrockchurch.org [accessed April 2, 2003].

Hazard, David. 1998. "When the Fire Fizzles." *Charisma* (August): 82.

Helland, Roger. 1996. *Let the River Flow.* London: Marshall Pickering.

Hilborn, David. 2001. "Toronto." In *Perspective: Papers on the New Charismatic Wave of the Mid-1990s.* Carlisle in Cumbria, U.K.: Paternoster Press.

Hill, P. C., K. I. Pargament, J. P. Swyers, R. L. Gorsuch, M. E. McCullough, R. W. Hood, and R. F. Baumeister. 1998. "Definitions of Religion and Spirituality." In *Scientific Research on Spirituality and Health: A Consensus Report.* Edited by D. B. Larson, J. P. Swyers, and M. E. McCullough, 14–30. Washington, D.C.: National Institute for Healthcare Research.

Hill, P. C., K. I. Pargament, R. W. Hood, Jr., M. E. McCullough, J. P. Swyers, D. B. Larson, and B. J. Zinnbauer. 2000. "Conceptualizing Religion and Spirituality: Points of Commonality, Points of Departure." *Journal for the Theory of Social Behavior* 30: 51–77.

Hollenback, Jess Byron. 1996. *Mysticism: Experience, Response and Empowerment.* University Park: The Pennsylvania State University Press.

Hollenweger, W. J. 1997. *Pentecostalism: Origins and Developments Worldwide.* Peabody, MA: Hendrickson Publishers.

Hood, Ralph W., Jr., ed. 1995. *Handbook of Religious Experience*. Birmingham, AL: Religious Education Press.

Hood, Ralph W., Jr., R. J. Morris, and D. Harvey. 1993. "Religiosity, Prayer, and Their Relationship to Mystical Experience." Paper presented at the annual meeting of the Religious Research Association, November, Raleigh, North Carolina.

Hood, Ralph W., Jr., N. Ghorbani, P. J. Watson, A. F. Ghramaleki, M. N. Bing, H. K. Davison, R. J. Morris, and W. P. Williamson. 2001. "Dimensions of the Mysticism Scale: Confirming the Three-Factor Structure in the United States and Iran." *Journal for the Scientific Study of Religion* 40 no. 4: 691–705.

Hunt, Stephen, Malcolm Hamilton, and Tony Walter. *Charismatic Christianity. Sociological Perspectives*. New York: St. Martin's.

Hyatt, Eddie. 2002a. *2000 Years of Christianity*. Orlando, FL: Charisma House.

———. 2002b. "When Prophetic Ministry Goes Awry." *Spread the Fire* 3: 25–27.

Idler, E. 1995. "Religion, Health, and Nonphysical Senses of Self." *Social Forces* 74: 683–704.

Iris Ministries. www.irismin.org, [accessed April 3, 2003]. (This website applies to all the Iris Ministries citations. Once the site is opened, click Archives for the individual reports.)

Irish, Charles. M. 1993. *Back to the Upper Room*. Nashville, TN: Thomas Nelson Publishers.

Jackson, John Paul. 1999. From a talk given at the October 1999 "Catch the Fire" conference at St. Luke's Episcopal Church; Fairlawn, Ohio.

Jackson, William 1999. *The Quest for the Radical Middle: A History of the Vineyard*. Capetown, South Africa: Vineyard International Ministries.

Jacobs, Cindy. 1995. *The Voice of God: How God Speaks Personally and Corporately to His Children Today*. Ventura CA: Regal Books.

———. 2000. "A Reverence for the Prophetic." In *Hosting the Holy Spirit*. Edited by Che' Ahn, 108–21. Ventura, CA: Renew.

James, William. [1902] 1961. *Varieties of Religious Experience*. New York: Collier Books.

Janzen, Connie, and Melinda Fish. 1999. "What about the Gold Teeth?" *Spread the Fire* 3: 4.

Jenkins, Colette M. 2001. "Golden Blessings." *The Beacon Journal* (Akron, OH) (August 4): 10–11.

Jenkins, Philip. 2002. *The Next Christendom: The Coming of Global Christianity.* New York: Oxford University Press.

Johns, J. D. 1999. "Yielding to the Spirit: The Dynamics of a Pentecostal Model of Praxis." In *The Globalization of Pentecostalism.* Edited by M. W. Dempster, B. D. Klaus, and D. Peterson, 70–84. Carlisle, CA: Paternoster Publishing (Regnum).

Johnson, Cathryn. 1992. "The Emergence of the Emotional Self: A Developmental Theory." *Symbolic Interaction* 15, no. 2: 183–202.

Joyner, Rick. 1993. *The World Aflame.* Charlotte, NC: MorningStar Publications.

———. 1996. *The Final Quest.* Charlotte, NC: MorningStar Publications.

Kakar, Sudhir. 1982. *Shamans, Mystics and Doctors: A Psychological Inquiry into India and Its Healing Traditions.* Boston: Beacon Press.

Karkkainen, V. M. 2002. "Missiology: Pentecostal and Charismatic." In *The New International Dictionary of Pentecostal and Charismatic Movements.* Edited by Stanley M. Burgess and Eduard M. Van Der Maas, 877–85. Grand Rapids, MI: Zondervan.

Kilpatrick, Joel. 1999. "Breaking through America's Bamboo Curtain." *Charisma* (June): 47–52.

Kingsley, David. 1996. *Health, Healing and Religion: A Cross-Cultural Approach.* New York: Prentice Hall.

Koenig, H. B. 1998a. *Handbook of Religion and Mental Health.* San Diego. Academic Press.

———. 1998b. *The Healing Power of Faith: Science Explores Medicine's Last Frontier.* New York: Simon and Schuster.

Ladd, Kevin, and Bernard Spilka. 2002. "Inward, Outward, and Upward: Cognitive Aspects of Prayer." *Journal for the Scientific Study of Religion* 41: 475–84.

Land, Steven. 1993. *Pentecostal Spirituality: A Passion for the Kingdom.* Sheffield, U.K.: Sheffield Academic Press.

Lane, Deforia. 1994. *Music as Medicine*. Grand Rapids, MI: Zondervan Publishing House.

Larson, D. B., J. P. Swyers, and M. E. McCullough (1998). *Scientific Research on Spirituality and Health: A Consensus Report*. (A report based on the Scientific Progress in Spirituality Conferences.) The Templeton Foundation.

Levine, Peter A. 1997. *Waking the Tiger: Healing Trauma*. Berkeley, CA: North Atlantic Books.

Lewis, David. 1989. *Healing: Fiction, Fantasy or Fact*. London: Hodder & Stoughton.

Light the Fire Again. 1994. "No One Like You." *Touching the Father's Heart. Vineyard Music Group*. Anaheim, CA. Compact disc.

Lindvall, Terry. 1996. *Surprised by Laughter*. Nashville, TN: Thomas Nelson Publishers.

Lyon, David. 2000. *Jesus in Disneyland: Religion in Postmodern Times*. Cambridge, U.K.: Polity Press.

Ma, J. C. 2002. "Animism and Pentecostalism: A Case Study." In *The New International Dictionary of Pentecostal and Charismatic Movements*. Edited by Stanley M. Burgess and Eduard M. Van Der Mass, 315–18. Grand Rapids, MI: Zondervan.

MacNutt, F. 1977. *Healing*. New York: Bantam Books.

Marcus, Warren. 1997. *Go Inside the Toronto Blessing*, a Christian film produced, directed, and narrated by Warren Marcus. Lanvin Company. Videocassette.

Maslow, Abraham H. 1970. *Religions, Values, and Peak-Experiences*. New York: Viking Press.

Matter, Joseph Allen. 1975. *Love, Altruism, and World Crisis*. Totowa, NJ: Littlefield, Adams, and Co.

Mauss, Armand. 1975. *Social Problems as Social Movements*. Philadelphia, PA: Lippincott.

May, Rollo. 1991. *The Cry for Myth*. New York: Delta.

McClenon, James. 1994. "Shamanic Healing, Human Evolution and the Origins of Religion." *Journal for the Scientific Study of Religion* 36, no. 3: 345–54.

McDermott, Scott. 2000. "Running Life's Race." In *Experience the Blessing*. Edited by John Arnott, 13–22. Ventura, CA: Renew (A Division of Gospel Light).

McGuire, Meredith. 1982. *Pentecostal Catholics. Power, Charisma and Order in a Religious Movement.* Philadelpha, PA: Temple University Press.

——. 1988. *Ritual Healing in Suburban America.* New Jersey: Rutgers University Press.

Metro Church South. n.d. Cleveland: City of God's Dreams. Berea, OH.

Miller, Donald. E. 1997. *Reinventing American Protestantism.* Berkeley, CA: University of California Press.

Minor, David. 1996. "Blessing & Judgment with Increased Anointing." *Spread the Fire* (December): 10–11.

Newberg, Andrew, Eugene d'Aquili, and Vince Rause. 2000. *Why God Won't Go Away: Brain Science and the Biology of Belief.* New York: Ballantine Books.

Nichols, Michael P., and Melvin Zax. 1977. *Catharsis in Psychotherapy.* New York: Garner Press.

Nortje'-Meyer, S. J. (Lilly). 2001. "Is there any indication of female phophesies in Matthew's Gospel?" *The Spirit and Church* 3, no. 1: 129–45.

Orcutt, Ted L., and Jan R. Prell. 1994. *Integrative Paradigms of Psychotherapy.* Boston: Allyn and Bacon.

Pargament, Kenneth I. 1997. *The Psychology of Religion and Coping: Theory Research and Practice.* New York: The Guilford Press.

Park, Andy. 1995. "The River is Here." *Winds of Worship 4. Live from Brighton England.* Vineyard Music Group. Anaheim, CA. Compact Disc.

——. (n.d.). "The Mysterious Power of Music." www.vmg.com/resources [accessed May 14, 2003].

Partners in Harvest. www.partners-in-harvest.org, 2002 [accessed April 2, 2003].

Pattison, E. M., N. A. Lapins, and H. A. Doerr. 1973. "Faith Healing: A Study of Personality and Function." *The Journal of Nervous and Mental Disease* 157, no. 6: 397–409.

Pierce, Robert A., Michael P. Nichols, and Joyce R. Dubrin. 1983. *Emotional Experience in Psychotherapy.* New York: Gardner Press.

Poewe, Karla. 1994. "Rethinking the Relationship of Anthropology to Science and Religion." In *Charismatic Christianity as a Global Culture.* Edited by K. Poewe, 234–58. Columbia: University of South Carolina Press.

Poloma, Margaret M. 1982. *The Charismatic Movement: Is There a New Pentecost?* Boston, MA: Twayne Publishers.

———. 1989. *The Assemblies of God at the Crossroads.* Knoxville: The University of Tennessee Press.

———. 1995a. "On the Toronto Blessing." Paper presented at Orlando '95, Congress on the Holy Spirit and World Evangelism, July 1995.

———. 1995b. "The Sociological Context of Religious Experience." In *Handbook of Religious Experience.* Edited by R. W. Hood, 161–82. Birmingham, AL: Religious Education Press.

———. 1996. *The Toronto Report.* Wiltshire, U.K.: Terra Nova Publications.

———. 1997. "The 'Toronto Blessing': Charisma, Institutionalization, and Revival." *Journal for the Scientific Study of Religion* 36: 257–71.

———. 1998a. "Inspecting the Fruit of the 'Toronto Blessing': A Sociological Assessment." *Pneuma: The Journal for the Society for Pentecostal Studies* 20: 43–70.

———. 1998b. "The Spirit Movement in North America at the Millennium: From Azusa Street to Toronto and Beyond." *Journal of Pentecostal Theology* 12: 83–107.

———. 1999. "The 'Toronto Blessing' in Postmodern Society." In *The Globalization of Pentecostalism.* Edited by M. Dempster, B. Klaus, and D. Peterson, 362–85. Irvine, CA: Regnum Books International.

———. 2000. "Pilgrim's Progress: Reflections on a Journey." In *Experiencing the Blessing.* Edited by John Arnott, 202–13. Ventura, CA: Renew.

———. 2002. "The Toronto Blessing." In *New International Dictionary of Pentecostal and Charismatic Movements.* Edited by Stanley M. Burgess and Eduard M. Van Der Maas. Grand Rapids, MI: Zondervan.

———. 2003. "Fruits of the Father's Blessing: A Sociological Report," Available through TACF's Resource Centre. www.tacf.org [accessed May 24, 2003].

———. n.d. "Charisma and Structure in the Assemblies of God: Revisiting O'Dea's Five Dilemmas." *In Organizing Religious Work Project.* Edited by David Roozen. William B. Eerdmans Publishing. In press.

Poloma, Margaret M., and George H. Gallup, Jr. 1991. *Varieties of Prayer: A Survey Report.* Philadelphia, PA: Trinity Press International.

Poloma, Margaret M., and Lynette F. Hoelter. 1998. "The 'Toronto Blessing': A Holistic Model of Healing." *Journal for the Scientific Study of Religion* 37: 258–73.

Poloma, Margaret M., and B. Pendleton, 1989. "Exploring Types of Prayer and Quality of Life: A Research Note." *Review of Religious Research* 31: 46–53.

———. 1991. "The Effects of Prayer and Prayer Experiences on Measures of General Well-Being." *Journal of Psychology and Theology* 19: 71–83.

Powdermaker, H. 1966. *Stranger and Friend: The Way of an Anthropologist*. New York: Norton.

Pullinger, Jackie. 1980. *Chasing the Dragon*. Ann Arbor, MI: Servant Books.

Quebedeaux, Richard. 1983. *The New Charismatics II*. San Francisco: Harper & Row.

Quinn, Naomi. 1991. "The Cultural Basis of Metaphor." In *Beyond Metaphor: The Theory of Tropes in Anthropology*. Edited by James W. Fernandez, 56–93. Stanford, CA: Stanford University Press.

Redman, Matt, and Martin Smith. 1999. "The Heart of Worship," *Festival Generation*. Worship Together, a Division of EMI Christian Music Group, Brentwood, TN. Compact Disc.

Reynolds, Larry T. 1990. *Interactionism, Exposition, and Critique*. Dix Hills, NY: General Hall.

Richter, Philip. 1996. "Charismatic Mysticism: A Sociological Analysis of the 'Toronto Blessing.'" In *The Nature of Religious Language: A Colloquium*. Edited by Stanley E. Porter, 100–130. U.K.: Sheffield Academic Press.

Riessman, Catherine Kohler. 1993. *Narrative Analysis*. Newbury Park, CA: Sage Publications.

Riss, Richard. 1987. *Latter Rain*. Ontario, Canada: Honeycomb Visual Productions.

———. 1996. "Are We in Renewal or Revival?" *Spread the Fire* (August): 19.

———. 1999. "Some Gold Explanations." *Awakening List* (May 6): awakening@listserver.com.

———. 2002. "Howard-Browne, Rodney M." In *The New International Dictionary of Pentecostal and Charismatic Movements*. Edited by Stanley M. Burgess, 774. Grand Rapids, MI: Zondervan.

Riss, Richard and Kathryn. 1997. *Images of Revival*. Shippensburg, PA: Revival Press.

Robeck, Cecil M. 1988. "Gift of Prophecy." In *Dictionary of Pentecostal and Charismatic Movements*. Edited by Stanley M. Burgess and Gary B. McGee, 728–40. Grand Rapids, MI. Zondervan.

Roberts, Dave. 1994. *The "Toronto" Blessing*. Eastbourne, U.K.: Kingsway Publications.

Ruis, David, 1992. *True Love*. Grace Music Kansas City, MO. Compact Disc.

———. 1994. "Sweet Wind," *Winds of Worship 3*. Live from Toronto Canada. Vineyard Music Group. Anaheim, CA. Compact Disc.

Ryle, James. 1993. *Hippo in the Garden. A Non-Religious Approach to Having a Conversation with God*. Orlando, FL: Creation House.

———. 1995. *A Dream Come True. A Biblical Look at How God Speaks through Dreams and Visions*. Orlando, FL: Creation House.

Sadler, William A., Jr. 1970. "The Scientific Study of Religion and Personality." In *Personality and Religion*. Edited by William A. Sadler, Jr., 1–31. New York: Harper and Row.

St. Romain, Philip. 1994. *Kundalini Energy and Christian Spirituality*. New York: Crossroad.

Sandford, John L., and Paula Sandford. 1977. *The Elijah Task*. Plainfield, NJ: Logos International.

———. 1982. *The Transformation of the Inner Man*. Tulsa, OK: Victory House.

———. 1985. *Healing the Wounded Spirit*. Tulsa, OK: Victory House.

Sanford, Agnes. 1950. *The Healing Light*. St. Paul, MN: Macalester Park Publishing.

———. 1958. *Behold Your God*. St. Paul, MN: Macalester Park Publishing.

Sapp, Roger. 2002. "Secrets of Healing Ministry." Spread the Fire 2: 25–27.

Sargant, William Walters. 1957. *Battle for the Mind*. London: Heineman.

Schechner, Richard. 1986. "Victor Turner's Last Adventure." Preface to Victor Turner's *The Anthropology of Performance*. New York: PAJ Publication.

Scheff, T. J. 1979. *Catharsis in Healing, Ritual and Drama*. Berkeley: University of California Press.

Schutz, Alfred. 1964. "Making Music Together." In *Collected Papers II: Studies in Social Theory.* Edited by A. Broderson The Hague: Nijhoff.

Seamands, David. 1981. *Healing for Damaged Emotions.* Wheaton, IL: Victor Books.

———. 1985. *Healing of Memories.* Wheaton, IL: Victor Books.

———. 1988. *Healing Grace.* Wheaton, IL: Victor Books.

Shake Off the Dust. 1999. "Only One Love." 1999. Recorded live. Winnipeg Centre Vineyard. Winnipeg, CA. Compact disc.

Sheppard, Gerald T. 2001. "Prophecy from Ancient Israel to Pentecostals at the End of the Modern Age." *The Spirit and Church* 3, no. 1: 47–70.

Shiflett, Dave. 2000. "Gold Rush in Glory Land." *Wall Street Journal,* March 31.

Sinnott, Jeremy. 1995. *Thursday Pastors Meeting: Worship.* Audiotape. Toronto Airport Christian Fellowship.

———. 1999. *Intimate Bride.* Rejoice Publishing & Productions. Brampton, Ontario, Canada. Compact disc.

———. 2000. *Passionate Bride.* Rejoice Publishing & Productions. Brampton, Ontario, Canada. Compact disc.

———. 2001. *Warrior Bride.* Rejoice Publishing & Productions. Brampton, Ontario, Canada. Compact disc.

Skarda, Christine. 1989. "Alfred Schutz's Phenomenology of Music." In *Understanding the Musical Experience.* Edited by J. Joseph Smith, 43–100. New York: Gordon and Breach.

Slater, Will, Todd W. Hall, and Keith J. Edwards. 2001. "Measuring Religion and Spirituality: Where Are We and Where Are We Going?" *Journal of Psychology and Theology* 29, no. 1: 4–21.

Sorokin, Pitirim A. 1954. *The Ways and Power of Love.* Boston: The Beacon Press.

Soto, Monica. 1995. "Spiritual Happy Hour." *Akron Beacon Journal,* July 29, A9–10.

Spickard, James V. 1991. "Experiencing Religious Rituals." *Sociological Analysis* 52: 191–204.

———. 1993. "A Sociology of Religious Experience." In *A Future for Religion? New Paradigms for Social Analysis.* Edited by W. H. Swatos. Beverly Hills, CA: Sage.

Stace, Walter T. 1960. *Mysticism and Philosophy*. London: Macmillan and Company.

Stambaugh, Joan. 1989. "Expressive Autonomy in Music: A Critique." In *Understanding the Musical Experience*. Edited by J. Joseph Smith, 167–78. New York: Gordon and Breach.

Stark, Rodney. 1965. "A Taxonomy of Religious Experience." *Journal for the Scientific Study of Religion* 5: 97–116.

———. 1991. "Normal Revelations: A Rational Model of 'Mystical' Experiences." In *Religion and the Social Order*. Vol. 1. Edited by D. G. Bromley, 225–38. Greenwich, CT: Jai Press.

———. 1996. "Why Religious Movements Succeed or Fail: A Revised General Model." *Journal of Contemporary Religion* 11, no. 2: 133–46.

———. 1999. "A Theory of Revelations." *Journal for the Scientific Study of Religion* 38, no. 2: 287–308.

Synan, Vinson. 1984. *In the Latter Days*. Ann Arbor, MI: Servant Books.

———. 1987. *The Twentieth-Century Pentecostal Explosion*. Altamonte Springs, FL: Creation House.

———. 1997. *The Holiness-Pentecostal Tradition. Charismatic Movements in the Twentieth Century*. Grand Rapids, MI: William B. Eerdmans Publishing.

TACF. www.tacf.org, 2003 [accessed April 4, 2003].

Tan, S. Y. 1992. *The Holy Spirit and Counseling Ministries: The Christian Journal of Psychology and Counseling* 7: 8–11.

———. 1996. "Religion in Clinical Practice: Implicit and Explicit Integration." In *Religion and the Clinical Practice of Psychology*. Edited by E. Shafranske, 365–87. Washington, DC: APA.

Taves, Ann. 1999. *Fits, Trances and Visions*. Princeton, NJ: Princeton University Press.

Tilly, Charles. 1978. *From Mobilization to Revolution*. Reading, MA: Addison-Wesley.

Troeltsch, Ernst. 1931. *The Social Teaching of the Christian Churches*. Vol. 2. Translated by Olive Wyon. New York: Macmillan.

Turner, Victor. 1969. *The Ritual Process: Structure and Anti-Structure*. Ithaca, NY: Cornell University Press.

———. 1986a. *The Anthropology of Performance*. New York: PAJ Publications.

———. 1986b. "Dewey, Dithey, and Drama: An Essay in the Anthropology of Experience." In *The Anthropology of Experience*. Edited by V. W. Turner and E. M. Bruner, 33–44. Chicago, IL: University of Illinois Press.

———. 1993. "Body, Brain, and Culture." In *Brain, Culture and the Human Spirit*. Edited by J. B. Ashbrook, 77–108. New York: University Press of America.

VanCronkhite, David. 2002. *I Want a Story. A Collection of Letters from the First Ten Years of Blood n Fire*. Blood-N-Fire, PO Box 38194, Atlanta, GA.

———. 2003. *Blood-N-Fire Twelve: Intense Commitment to Relational Community*. Atlanta, GA: Blood-N-Fire Ministries.

Wacker, Grant. 2001. *Heaven Below: Early Pentecostals and American Culture*. Cambridge: Harvard University Press.

Wagner, C. P. [1988] 2002. "Third Wave." In *The New International Dictionary of Pentecostal and Charismatic Movements*. Edited by Stanley M. Burgess and Eduard M. Van Der Maas, 11–41. Grand Rapids, MI: Zondervan Publishing House.

———. 1999. *Churchquake*. Ventura, CA: Regal Books.

Wallin, Nils L., Bjorn Merker, and Steven Brown, eds. 2000. *The Origins of Music*. Cambridge, MA: The MIT Press.

What a God! 1997. "You Are the Love of My Life." Produced by Believers Church. Tulsa, OK. Compact disc.

White, John. 1988. *When the Spirit Comes with Power*. Downer's Grove, IL: InterVarsity Press.

Wies, Jim. 1999. *The House of His Choosing. . . : A Solid Foundation for the 21st Century Church*. Shippensburg, PA: Destiny Image Publishers.

Wilson, W. J. 2002. "Pentecostal Perspectives on Eschatology." In *The New International Dictionary of Pentecostal Charismatic Movements*. Edited by Stanley M. Burgess, 601–05. Grand Rapids, MI: Zondervan.

Wimber, John, and Kevin Springer. 1987. *Power Healing*. San Francisco: HarperSanFrancisco.

Winds of Worship 4. 1994. "My Jesus I Love Thee." *Live from Brighton England*. Vineyard Music Group. Anaheim, CA. Compact disc.

Winkelman, Michael. 2000. *Shamanism: The Neural Ecology of Consciousness and Healing.* Westport, CT: Bergin & Garvey.

Witt, Steve. 2000. "Prophetic Parables or Signs and Wonders?" *Spread the Fire* 2: 17–18.

Wulff, David. M. 1991. *Psychology of Religion: Classic and Contemporary Views.* New York: Wiley.

Yamane, David. 2000. "Narrative and Religious Experience." *Sociology of Religion* 61, no. 2 (Summer): 171–90.

Zygmunt, Joseph F. 1972. "When Prophecies Fail: A Theoretical Perspective on the Comparative Evidence." *American Behavioral Scientist* 16, no. 2: 245–68.

Index

access to ultimate reality, in mysticism, 28–29

active prayer, 117–18

affect, in mystical experiences, 30–31

affective response, in spiritual encounter, 119–20

African Americans: and HarvestNet, 212n4; and Pentecostal/Charismatic religion, 21

Ahn, Ché, 174–81, 190n4–5, 191n11; and The Call, 186–87; and Harvest International Ministries, 184–86; and Partners in Harvest, 183–84

Akron City Vineyard Church, 207–10

Albrecht, Daniel, 21, 56n1

Alcala, Augustine, 149, 169n7

altar call, 5–6

altered states of consciousness (ASC), music and, 43–44

Ames, Roger, 10–11, 203–4

Anaheim Vineyard Christian Fellowship, 178

animal sounds, 67, 70–72; and prophecy, 133n3

apostolic ministry, 211; Ahn and, 185–86, 191n11

Argentina, 60, 148, 153, 234n3

Armstrong, Karen, 34n6

Arnott, Carol, 60, 136n18, 153, 171n17

Arnott, John, 4, 11, 60–61; and animal sounds, 70–71; and bodily manifestations, 63–64; on efficacy, 214n12; on forgiveness, 92–93; and Harvest Rock Church, 178; and healing, 112n16; on love, 120; on mysticism, 27–32; and Partners in Harvest, 182–83; on prophecy, 147, 152–54, 170n13; on second wave, 163; on September 11, 166; on spiritual drunkenness, 73; and survey, 240–41, 249

arts, liturgical, 201

Association of Vineyard Churches (AVC), 33n1; and Akron, 207–10; and bodily manifestations, 60, 70; break with TACF, 18, 243–45; characteristics of, 15, 148–49; and Harvest Rock Church, 180; and

About the Author

Margaret M. Poloma, earned a Ph.D. in sociology from Case Western Reserve University (1970). Immediately following the award of the degree, she began teaching at the University of Akron, being employed there until retiring from full-time service in 1995. Margaret maintains an office and residency as Professor Emeritus at the University of Akron (Ohio) in the department of sociology. She has been recently awarded a grant from the Institute for Research on Unlimited Love to study Blood-N-Fire, a neo-Pentecostal "church of the poor" in Atlanta.

For the past twenty years Margaret has been engaged in sociological research dealing with religious experience with a particular focus on the Pentecostal/Charismatic (neo-Pentecostal) movement. She is the author of *The Charismatic Movement: Is There a New Pentecost?* and *The Assemblies of God at the Crossroads: Charisma and Institutionalization,* as well at scores of articles, papers and monographs dealing with the movement.

Her observations and findings on the role of spiritual healing in the lives of Pentecostal/Charismatic Christians raised questions about the religious/spiritual experiences of those outside the movement. She became especially interested in the relationship between spirituality and health for the larger population of Americans. It was the 1985 Akron Area Survey that provided a data base for her to explore the link between religion and subjective perceptions of well-being, resulting in the book co-authored with Brian B. Pendleton, Exploring Neglected Dimensions of Religion in Quality of Life Research. A specific focus was the role that different types of prayer and prayer experiences play in health and well-being. This topic became the subject of her work with pollster George H. Gallup, Jr. and a national study to explore the topic of prayer (Varieties of Prayer: A Survey Report).

In the mid-1990s she began systematic research on a Pentecostal/ Charismatic revival that was sweeping across North America. Over a dozen preliminary articles, papers, and monographs have been written on this revival that served to herald the present sociological narrative of *Main Street Mystics: The Toronto Blessing and Reviving American Pentecostalism.*